Advance Praise for
Hidden in Plain Sight

"A must-read to understand the mindset of human traffickers and their victims."
—*Susan Ingram, Founder, Walk Her Home, and Congressional Victims' Rights Award Recipient 2017*

"*Hidden in Plain Sight* is a vital resource, not only for anti–human trafficking advocates, but for anyone who cares about humanity. Dr. Mehlman-Orozco's interviews with the traffickers are shocking, but they provide insight that can be used when trying to combat this horrific crime. Our organization will be implementing this book into our Advanced Law Enforcement Investigation Course. The material is presented in such a compelling and understandable way that this book will certainly be a powerful contribution to understanding the fastest growing crime in the world."
—*Sandra Sparks, Executive Director, ERASE Child Trafficking*

"By carefully documenting the realities of human trafficking and the failures of prevention and enforcement, this eye-opening book is the antidote to every hyped scare story and pointless policy 'solution.' Knowledge is more than power — it is our obligation if we truly want to help the most vulnerable victims of sexual and labor slavery."
—*Mark Obbie, criminal justice journalist; Soros Justice Media Fellow; and former executive editor of* The American Lawyer *magazine*

"*Hidden in Plain Sight* reveals the diverse and disturbing manifestations of human trafficking in the United States. Using accessible language and clear illustrations, Mehlman-Orozco illuminates the complexity and tragic dimensions of human trafficking. Based on her own research, this work helps us see a phenomenon that many traffickers prefer we do not notice. The work should be eye-opening to its readers."
—*Louise Shelley, Omer L. and Nancy Hirst Chair and Director, Terrorism, Transnational Crime and Corruption Center (TraCCC), Schar School of Policy and Government, George Mason University, and author of* Human Trafficking: A Global Perspective

"A clear and easily digestible primer on human trafficking. Calling upon insights from traffickers, victims, and customers, Kim Mehlman-Orozco details the diverse exploitive models and highlights a hopeful pathway to stop traffickers by vigorously enforcing the law."
—*John Cotton Richmond, Former Federal Human Trafficking Prosecutor and Founding Director of the Human Trafficking Institute, McLean, Virginia*

"Kimberly Mehlman-Orozco has written an absorbing—and sometimes horrifying—account of a crime that most Americans consider remote from their daily lives, but reaches into every family and neighborhood. It's a wake-up call to action."
—*Stephen Handelman, Editor,* The Crime Report

"This book provides important empirical evidence of the many harms caused by labor and sex trafficking and the limited ability of the police to do much about it."
—*Alex S. Vitale, Professor of Sociology, Brooklyn College*

"Kimberly Mehlman-Orozco's book absolutely delivers on its promise to provide an honest, revealing glimpse behind the hidden world of modern slavery in the USA. Within the first five pages, I was hooked—I couldn't put it down. While many books on this topic tend to be filled with clichés and unsubstantiated nuances, Mehlman-Orozco offers detailed stories and evidence-based descriptions that help to offer clarity and an understanding of this often-misunderstood topic. Even after addressing this issue for over 27 years, I walked away with many new insights that significantly changed some of my existing views. For those who are seeking a book that truly captures the essence of this important issue, along with a thoughtful and compelling analysis, this is a must-read."
—Matt S. Friedman, CEO, The Mekong Club

"Hidden in Plain Sight is a compelling account of human trafficking, analyzed from a social scientist's perspective with a journalist's tenacity and attention to detail. Mehlman-Orozco's narrative vividly documents and describes the various actors and their interactions at the core of the problem of human trafficking today; what really stands out is the author's first-hand experiences coming face-to-face with traffickers, victims, and those who struggle, often unsuccessfully or counterproductively, to find solutions to these problems."
—Ric Curtis, Professor of Anthropology, John Jay College of Criminal Justice,
City University of New York

"At a time with growing interest in—and growing misunderstanding of—the human trafficking industries in the United States, Hidden in Plain Sight is a necessary and clarifying resource. Through dozens of interviews with incarcerated pimps, Kim Mehlman-Orozco debunks myths surrounding the commercial sex trade and shines light on one of the most coercive criminal industries of our time. She also exposes the reality that the United States is a major player in the global trafficking industry. From U.S. military base camps abroad, to the chocolate we buy for Halloween and the clothes on our backs, human trafficking touches nearly every area of our lives and every corner of our national industries—whether we notice it or not. Kim's book gives us new eyes to see it."
—Blythe Hill, CEO, Dressember Foundation

"A brutally honest, well-researched, and comprehensive look into the horrors of modern-day slavery and trafficking in human beings which has become embedded into the fabric of today's society."
—Laura D. Jones, President, Soroptimist International/SIA/SAR/Mid-Atlantic Online

"This courageous, personal, and meticulously documented behind-the-scenes account of human trafficking is a must-read for everyone. Human trafficking is in your backyard—you just need to know where to look and how to see it, and Kimberly Mehlman-Orozco gives you that knowledge."
—Susan Camardese, RDH, MS, President, Mid-Atlantic Prevent Abuse and Neglect through
Dental Awareness (P.A.N.D.A.)

Hidden in Plain Sight

Hidden in Plain Sight

America's Slaves of the New Millennium

Kimberly Mehlman-Orozco, PhD

 PRAEGER™

An Imprint of ABC-CLIO, LLC

Santa Barbara, California • Denver, Colorado

Library of Congress Cataloging-in-Publication Data

Names: Mehlman-Orozco, Kimberly, author.
Title: Hidden in plain sight : America's slaves of the new millennium / Kimberly Mehlman-Orozco, PhD.
Description: Santa Barbara, California : Praeger, an imprint of ABC-CLIO, LLC, 2017. | Includes bibliographical references and index.
Identifiers: LCCN 2017029215 (print) | LCCN 2017030908 (ebook) | ISBN 9781440854040 (e-book) | ISBN 9781440854033 (print : acid-free paper)
Subjects: LCSH: Human trafficking—United States. | Slavery—United States. | Forced labor—United States. | Foreign workers—Crimes against—United States. | Immigrants—Crimes against—United States. | United States—Social conditions—1980– | United States—Ethnic relations.
Classification: LCC HQ281 (ebook) | LCC HQ281 .M435 2017 (print) | DDC 306.3/620972—dc23
LC record available at https://lccn.loc.gov/2017029215

ISBN: 978-1-4408-5403-3 (print)
      978-1-4408-5404-0 (e-book)

21 20 19 18 17   2 3 4 5

This book is also available as an e-book.

Praeger
An Imprint of ABC-CLIO, LLC

ABC-CLIO, LLC
130 Cremona Drive, P.O. Box 1911
Santa Barbara, California 93116-1911
www.abc-clio.com

This book is printed on acid-free paper ∞

Manufactured in the United States of America

Contents

Prologue   ix

Preface   xv

Part One   Sex Trafficking   1

Chapter 1   Runaways, from the Frying Pan into the Fire   5

Chapter 2   Happy Beginnings, Sad Endings   17

Chapter 3   Disposable Wives   33

Chapter 4   Child Sex Tourism   43

Chapter 5   Adult Sex Tourism   51

Chapter 6   Human Trafficker Deployment   63

Chapter 7   Trafficked to La Mara   71

Chapter 8   Now Recruiting for an Exciting Summer Abroad   93

Chapter 9   Mentality of a Monger   103

Part Two   Labor Trafficking   113

Chapter 10   Legal and Still Exploited   115

Chapter 11   Domestic Servants, Diplomatic Slaves   123

Chapter 12   Knocking at Your Door   129

Chapter 13   Dark Side of Chocolate from the Côte d'Ivoire   135

Chapter 14   Slaved in India, Retailed in America   143

Chapter 15   Cheap Luxury   149

Chapter 16   Stealing Our Jobs?   155

Part Three   **Overcoming Barriers to the Abolition
                   of Modern Slavery**   **161**

Chapter 17   Hidden in Plain Sight   163

Chapter 18   Disposable Kids   171

Chapter 19   Whac-a-Mole Crusade Online   177

Chapter 20   Blaming the Hotel   185

Chapter 21   Crimmigration and Labor Trafficking   191

Chapter 22   Out of the Shadows   195

Acknowledgments   205

Appendix A: Sex Work and Sex Trafficking Argot   209

*Appendix B: Sample Human Trafficking Expert Witness
               Testimony Outline*   217

Appendix C: Gathering Data from Human Trafficking Survivors   219

Appendix D: Sample Sex Tourist Timeline—Dirk   223

Appendix E: Additional Quotes from Mongers   225

*Appendix F: Sample Tool to Identify Youth at High Risk
               of Being Trafficked*   229

Index   235

Prologue

Montclair, Virginia, is a quintessential bedroom community, surrounding a man-made lake and golf course, 32 miles outside of Washington, DC. When my children, husband, and I first moved here, my oldest daughter literally turned to me with a smile and said, "Mom, this kind of place only exists in the movies."

As soon as we had settled into our four-bedroom, three-bathroom house, we immediately felt like we were home. Our neighbors were so incredibly kind and went above and beyond to welcome us to the neighborhood. One neighbor actually showed up at our door with a vase full of flowers, a tin with fresh-baked cookies, and a card. Up until then, my children had never experienced the joy of living in a tight-knit, middle class community. I felt proud to be able to provide them with a childhood in a place like this.

Right before giving birth to my fourth child, and second son, I joined our community Facebook page—the "Montclair Moms." When I returned home from the hospital, one of the group's founders organized a meal train for my family, so I didn't have to cook and could rest with my newborn. The women in my community brought us dinner for nearly two weeks. The online group provided even more of an opportunity for me to become closer with our neighbors, share recipes, and coordinate play dates. Soon after I joined, the membership ballooned to over 500 Montclairion women, including doctors, military veterans, lawyers, federal government employees, and lots of stay-at-home moms.

Everyone seemed to be so incredibly giving: sharing time, resources, food, and information. Each mother contributed something to our community and would always try to pay the good deeds forward, in order to help others.

In addition to cooking for other new moms and sharing recipes, I quickly became known as the resident criminologist of the group.

Shortly after moving into our home, I successfully defended my doctoral dissertation and graduated with a PhD in criminology, law and society from George Mason University. The Montclair Moms would often ask my advice on how to protect their kids from victimization.

For example, in August 2013, I posted a link to the Virginia Sex Offender Registry so that moms in my community could double check and make sure their child wouldn't be visiting a convicted sex offender's home for sleepovers, play dates, or trick-or-treating. After I posted it to the Facebook page, a Montclair Mom sent me a direct message. It read,

> *I really want to thank you for the link. I am really shocked and disgusted because I actually know one of them!!! He is the step grandfather of one of (my) daughter's friends. I cannot believe it and obviously had no idea. My daughter has spent the night at their house too. Yuck!!!!! Sorry, but I had to share my disgust and appreciation.*
> —Anonymous Montclair Mom, August 10, 2013

I absolutely loved my community and wanted to help educate them on criminological issues that could affect their families. I aspired to do my part and assist in keeping our neighborhood safe. In addition to sharing information on general criminal justice resources, I would periodically talk about human trafficking, which was my subject matter area of expertise.

However, like many Americans, I was still somewhat naive in my understanding of how human trafficking happened in real life. Although I could recite all of the human trafficking statistics and laws from memory and knew about every documented knowledge gap, there was nothing that could have prepared me for my first suspected human trafficking encounter, especially since it was on the front steps of my family's home, in a neighborhood like Montclair.

* * *

Friday, September 6, 2013

My daughter walked in the house from school just as I finished sautéing the meat sauce for spaghetti dinner. Her track practice started promptly at 5:30 p.m. that evening, so I needed to feed the kids early. The chaos of dinnertime seemed insurmountable. My husband still wasn't home from work yet, and there was so much that needed to get done.

Leaving the house was a monumental task with four children—two under the age of two—much less getting everyone fed and out of the door in 30 minutes.

Almost as soon as I sat my kids down to eat at the dinner table, I heard a knock. *Not now*, I thought, annoyed at the dinnertime interruption. I quickly made my way down the stairs of my split-level home with the intent of sending away any uninvited guest.

As soon as I opened the front door, a young African American girl in a tight purple shirt and long colorful acrylic nails started her solicitation pitch, "Hi, my name's Kayla,[1] and I'm here selling magic in a bottle, called Mama's Cleaner."[2] Like most homeowners, I didn't particularly care for door-to-door sales people, especially when I was in the middle of feeding my children dinner, but I decided to hear her out. "This stuff's highly concentrated; you only need eight caps diluted into two liters of water. The product sells itself. Just show me a stain, take me to it, and watch me do it! Miss, what stains are the hardest for you to get out?" she asked. Before I could take a breath to respond, she began squirting the translucent red cleaner on the siding of my house, took out a rag from her pant pocket, and wiped off some algae. "See!" she exclaimed, showing how easily the stain was removed.

I was in such a rush, and I really wasn't interested in purchasing her $40 bottle of concentrated cleaner, but I had recently learned of the pervasive human trafficking exploitation in solicitation crews, so I decided to continue talking with her about her involvement with this business. I asked a series of questions that were designed to shed light on whether Kayla had control over her finances, as well as how she was living and traveling.

I learned that she lived in North Carolina and was allegedly staying at a Super 8 motel while she was working in Virginia. She told me that she shared two motel rooms with 15 other youth, including runaways and homeless men and women, who were also part of her crew. Each day, when they left for work, she told me that her boss collected the keys to the motel rooms.

The circumstances of her employment were suspicious to me and included several red flags of a human trafficking situation, according to numerous resources. During our 30-minute conversation, she explained how her employer controlled her housing, transportation, communication, and money. When she told me that she hadn't eaten all day and was thirsty, I invited her into my home for dinner with my family.

As we broke bread with my children, I shared my concern for her situation. She explained that her father had encouraged her to join this crew after her mother had died the year earlier. Wanting for her to gain an out-sider's perspective on the potential peril she was facing, I read out loud an excerpt on solicitation crews from the National Human Trafficking Resource Center website.

> *Victims of human trafficking have been found in sales crews or peddling and begging rings, where they work long hours each day soliciting money or selling products such as magazine subscriptions, trinkets, or cleaning products.*
>
> *Traffickers confiscate most or all of the victim's earnings make the victims dependent on the controller for transportation and housing. Violence, sexual assault, sexual harassment, pressure tactics, and abandonment in unfamiliar cit-ies are common.*
>
> *Begging and peddling rings may include U.S. citizens, immigrants, adults, or children. Sales crews typically recruit U.S. citizen youth ages 18 to 25, with promises of travel, a care-free life, and the ability to make a lot of money.*
>
> *A 'crew' consists of an average of 3 to 40 youth, under the direction of a manager, who moves the crew from city to city every few weeks. Crewmembers receive a small daily stipend of $8 to $15 or less to cover the cost of meals and personal items.*[3]

"Do you see why I am worried about you?" I asked. I felt that the description summarized her situation to a T.

While she appeared to be reeling with the newfound awareness of her possible exploitation, I was incredulous at the circumstances of our meeting. Despite having studied human trafficking for six years, the first potential victim I encountered was on the front steps of my home. Advo-cates always told me that human trafficking is everywhere, hidden in plain sight, and if you don't see it, you're not looking. But I never took those clichés to heart until that moment. Although I had gone through years of graduate-level coursework on trafficking in persons, I had turned away dozens of solicitors just like Kayla without giving them a second thought. How many other victims might I have unknowingly encountered? How many times did the average American happen upon a victim of human trafficking with inaction?

My neighborhood is similar to many communities across the United States. People are largely misinformed on how the human trafficking phe-nomenon may be affecting them. To gain a better understanding of how human trafficking permeates every rung of society, it is important for people to become aware of who these victims are, how they are recruited, and under what circumstances human trafficking crimes may be encountered.

This book provides the first on-the-ground account of the various types of human trafficking hidden in communities across the United States. Herein, I incorporate direct quotes from human traffickers and human trafficking survivors, as well as from the men who fuel the demand for the commercial sex industry. By providing an up-close look at human trafficking enterprises disguised within our neighborhoods, the intent of this project is to better equip average citizens with the capacity to identify human trafficking and become modern-day abolitionists.

Notes

1. Pseudonym used here to protect the identity of the potential victim.
2. Cleaning product name changed to protect the identity of the potential victim.
3. Sales Crews, Peddling & Begging Rings. (n.d.). *National Human Trafficking Hotline*. Accessed April 21, 2017, https://humantraffickinghotline.org/what-human -trafficking/labor-trafficking/sales-crews-peddling-begging-rings.

Preface

Although the term human trafficking is relatively modern, the encompassed crimes have been occurring in the United States for centuries. Human trafficking generally refers to the use of force, fraud, coercion, or deception for the purpose of exploitation or the exploitation of anyone under the age of 18. This definition generally includes two forms of human trafficking: labor trafficking and sex trafficking.

In the United States, labor trafficking is defined as the recruitment, harboring, transportation, provision, or obtaining of a person for labor or services through the use of force, fraud, or coercion for the purpose of subjection to involuntary servitude, peonage, debt bondage, or slavery.[1] Although the chattel form of slavery that once existed is no longer legally permitted, labor exploitation is still pervasive.

Sex trafficking, on the other hand, is defined as when a commercial sex act is induced by force, fraud, or coercion, or in which the person induced to perform such act has not attained 18 years of age.[2] Prior to the popularization of the term "sex trafficking," these victims were called "white slaves" throughout the early to mid 1900s, but often considered prostitutes, even if they were children.[3]

The modern concept of human trafficking didn't start becoming internationally popularized until the year 2000.

On October 28, 2000, the U.S. Congress enacted the Trafficking Victims Protection Act (TVPA), which set up formidable actions to combat trafficking in persons. Specifically:

1. Coordinate and monitor anti-trafficking activities through an interagency task force;
2. Prevent human trafficking through vocational training, education, and human trafficking public awareness campaigns;

3. Protect human trafficking survivors by not detaining them in correctional facilities, providing them with medical care and other assistance, and protecting them and their families from revictimization and/or deportation; and

4. Strengthening prosecution and punishment of human traffickers.[4]

Less than two months after the TVPA was adopted in the United States, the United Nations met in Palermo, Italy, and adopted the Protocol to Prevent, Suppress and Punish Trafficking in Persons, Especially Women and Children, Supplementing the United Nations Convention Against Transnational Organized Crime—colloquially known as the Palermo Protocol. The purpose of the protocol was threefold:

1. To prevent and combat trafficking in persons, paying particular attention to women and children;

2. To protect and assist the victims of such trafficking, with full respect for their human rights; and

3. To promote cooperation among states' parties in order to meet those objectives.[5]

Since 2000, there has been a substantial increase in public awareness of human trafficking. There are more anti-trafficking task forces, hotlines, and survivor services than ever before. However, there are still critical gaps between the human trafficking narrative, reality, and policy, which inhibit our ability to prevent new crimes, prosecute offenders, and protect survivors.

Although more Americans are aware of the human trafficking concept, few understand how this crime manifests in real life. The fictionalized narrative of an innocent victim who is kidnapped and forcefully held against her will is not the reality for most human trafficking cases. Typically, victims are coerced, defrauded, and deceived into an exploitive situation, where they are manipulated into complacency, which may or may not accompany intermittent physical abuse. As such, while more Americans have heard about human trafficking, they may not understand the realities enough to educate others about this pernicious crime, much less advocate for changes to policy.

In addition, although the penalties for human trafficking crimes have increased on the books, offenders are infrequently convicted for these offences. Instead, behind the headlines, human traffickers are pleading guilty to lesser, tangentially related offenses and receiving shorter punishments, while victims continue to be erroneously criminalized and denied services. Unfortunately, the reality for human trafficking survivors is that they are often misidentified and revictimized, even post "rescue," due to the inadequacy of trauma-informed services.

The intention of this book is to take each reader behind the headlines. I want you to see firsthand where the rubber meets the road on anti-trafficking policy and practice in the United States. In order for you to understand modern day slavery, you must be exposed to the realities of how the human trafficking scourge has permeated American commerce, culture, and communities. Only then will you be equipped with the knowledge needed to become a modern-day abolitionist and effectuate change.

In addition to utilizing primary court documents, peer reviewed research, and media accounts on major human trafficking cases, much of the material for the book comes from direct observations, as well as interviews with human traffickers, victims, and consumers of the commercial sex trade.

For example, between 2014 and 2015, I sent written inquiries to convicted human traffickers who were incarcerated in federal prison. In each initial letter, I wrote:

> *Hello,*
>
> *I am contacting you because you were convicted of a crime related to human trafficking. Human trafficking is defined as the recruitment, harboring, transportation, provision, or obtaining of a person for the purpose of exploitation through the use of force, fraud, or coercion, or performed by a child under the age of 18. In the United States, this crime typically involves sex trafficking or debt bondage labor. Your case is listed in the Michigan Law Center Human Trafficking Database as an example of a human trafficking conviction. I am hoping that you may be willing to answer a few questions for me, as I am trying to learn more about human trafficking from someone who has been convicted of this crime. I can write you back if you have any questions for me.*
>
> *Here are my questions for you:*
>
> 1. *Please describe your crime.*
> 2. *How did you recruit/target your victim(s)?*
> 3. *In your opinion, how can the United States effectively prevent human trafficking?*
> 4. *Why did you engage in the crime of human trafficking?*
> 5. *Why weren't you caught sooner?*
>
> *I understand if you do not feel comfortable answering my questions. However, I would greatly appreciate it if you could still reply so that I at least know that you did receive this letter.*

Although the early responses were relatively banal, over the course of six months, I exchanged over 2,000 written inquires with convicted human traffickers, including domestic sex traffickers, colloquially referred to as "pimps," and international sex traffickers.

Although true-life cases are directly referenced throughout the book, Chapters 1 and 8 include direct quotes from the human traffickers I personally interviewed, with their true identities concealed through pseudonyms. Long quotes and stories are featured in order to illustrate the mannerisms used by traffickers, as well as the disconnection between their projected and true self-identities.

Anonymous quotes are also featured from sex workers. In 2016, I fielded a snowball sample survey, soliciting the opinions from consenting prostitutes on the topic of commercial sex marketing online, specifically regarding the criminalization of Backpage.com and the intersection between sex trafficking and commercial sex work. Nationally networked sex worker rights activists, such as Norma Jean Almodovar[6] and Billie Joe McIntire,[7] shared the survey within their respective networks. Over the course of one month, 31 sex workers responded. Quotes from the anonymous respondents are featured in Chapter 19.

Finally, this book includes direct quotes from my interviews with commercial sex consumers, which are prominently featured in Chapter 22. In 2016, I conducted online and in-person interviews with more than 30 commercial sex consumers I met through Craigslist.org. These data were supplemented with quotes sampled from commercial sex information exchange forums, such as RubMaps.com, USASexGuide.info, and InternationalSexGuide.info, which are featured throughout the book, prominently in Chapters 5, 6, 9, and 20. Data from these men are used to better understand how Americans fuel the commercial sex industry in the United States and in various countries around the world.

Given the clandestine nature of the crime, it was imperative to triangulate data from multiple sources in order to paint a more complete picture of these pernicious crimes. These data, taken from case files, media reports, quantitative and qualitative online surveys, in-person interviews, written inquires, and content analyses of postings on virtual commercial sex forums are used herein to reveal the human trafficking industries that were previously hidden in plain sight.

This book contains graphic material, including offensive language. Reader discretion is advised.

Notes

1. Victims of Trafficking and Violence Protection Act of 2000. PUBLIC LAW 106–386. https://www.state.gov/documents/organization/10492.pdf.

2. 22 U.S. Code § 7102 - Definitions | US Law | LII / Legal Information Institute. Accessed April 21, 2017, https://www.law.cornell.edu/uscode/text/22/7102.

3. For example, see *The Maiden Tribute of Modern Babylon*, published through Pall Mall Gazette in July 1885.

4. Victims of Trafficking and Violence Protection Act of 2000, Pub. L. No. H.R. 3244 (2000). http://www.state.gov/j/tip/laws/61124.htm.

5. Protocol to Prevent, Suppress and Punish Trafficking in Persons, Especially Women and Children, Supplementing the United Nations Convention Against Transnational Organized Crime. (2000).

6. Author of *Cop to Call Girl*, published by Simon and Schuster in 1993.

7. Executive Director of the Social Wellness Advocacy Network (SWAN) Colorado and Member of the National Human Trafficking Survivor Network.

PART 1

Sex Trafficking

This isn't the movie *Taken*. Liam Neeson isn't going to show up in a black Audi and Versace suit to rescue his innocent victim daughter from gun-wielding Albanian mobsters. Sex trafficking across America is a more clandestine activity, hidden within the commercial sex industry that has flourished in our country for centuries, as well as in plain sight under the veneer of legitimate businesses.[1]

Understanding the reality of sex trafficking begins with insight into the market, as well as the perpetrators, victims, and customers. The difficulty lies in distinguishing consenting prostitutes from sex-trafficked victims.[2]

Today, commercial sex is advertised both in the street and online. For example, in Washington, DC, during the dark hours of early dawn, women in platform heels and lingerie solicit customers on 10th and K Streets. There, willing sex workers walk alongside sex-trafficked victims, without distinction. However, this is dying practice. Given the growing public awareness about sex trafficking and the resulting increased law enforcement, more marketing is taking place online.[3]

Upper-crust clientele may peruse sex workers on websites that provide screening services for high-end "adult companionship." An average Joe, on the other hand, can find more economical options under the escort or adult sections on other sites. After screening for law enforcement, in-call providers will give customers an address for the exchange, while outcall providers will go to a location provided by the customer—a home or hotel, for example.[4]

The central distinction between consenting prostitution and sex trafficking is the use of force, fraud, or coercion for the purpose of exploitation. This can happen in a number of ways, which infrequently involve conventional kidnapping. For example, a woman managing an erotic massage parlor may import women from South Korea and hold them in indentured servitude to repay an inflated visa debt, such as in the case of "Peach Therapy" in Virginia. The business proprietor, Susan Lee Gross (a.k.a. Ju Me Lee Gross), was sentenced to two-and-a-half years for bringing women in as sex workers to her Annandale-based massage parlor and laundering the proceeds from the illegal activity, according to the Department of Justice.[5]

There are also domestic sex traffickers—colloquially referred to as pimps—who feign love and affection for new recruits, filling a void in their lives through the provision of food, shelter, clothing, fellowship, and/or esteem, before coercing or deceiving their victims into the commercial sex industry. Then, the trafficker may use threats, drugs, and/or violence to maintain compliance. Both of these types of sex trafficking involve creating a virtual tether between the offender and the victim, instead of a physical chain, as depicted in Hollywood portrayals.[6]

Sex traffickers can be best described as wolves in sheep's clothing. They manipulate their victims into believing they are heroes or Casanova lovers.[7]

This is the reality of sex trafficking in cities across the United States. Unlike Hollywood depictions, sex trafficking victims in real life are difficult to differentiate from consenting prostitutes. This failed distinction has led to the erroneous criminalization of sex trafficked victims and the unsuccessful prosecution of sex traffickers. Understanding this reality is key to combating the human trafficking scourge in our country.[8]

However, when a woman or man has the agency to choose a profession in sex work, it is important to understand that she or he should not be considered a victim of sex trafficking. Conflating the two does a disservice to the women and men in each situation. For example, Christina Parreira is a PhD student at University of Nevada, Las Vegas and chose to engage in sex work at Alien Cat House—a legal brothel—while pursuing her degree. She is also an advocate for sex-positive sex work, which denounces the criminalization of consenting prostitutes. Sex workers and advocates such as Parreira demand *rights, not rescue*. She is, for all intents and purposes, a consenting prostitute, not a victim.

Where possible, it is important to distinguish consenting sex workers from sex-trafficked victims; however, it is extremely difficult to assess agency without in-depth information. With that being said, while consensual prostitution is not sex trafficking, the two go hand in hand and are discussed herein as such. It is important to better understand who is procuring commercial sex services and where, because sex workers are at high risk of being trafficked by third parties.

Notes

1. Kimberly Mehlman-Orozco, "Consenting Prostitutes or Trafficked Victims?" *The Baltimore Sun* (June 19, 2016): accessed July 6, 2017, http://www.baltimoresun.com/news/opinion/oped/bs-ed-sex-trafficking-20160619-story.html.
2. Ibid.
3. Ibid.
4. Ibid.
5. Ibid.
6. Ibid.
7. Ibid.
8. Ibid.

CHAPTER ONE

Runaways, from the Frying Pan into the Fire

There is NOTHING that can be done about children being used as prostitutes. It happens. Just like some children use and deal drugs. It's a part of life. Let's say a young girl is 16 or 17 and she has no family, money, or food. So the young lady has to fend for herself. She is already sexually active, roaming the streets surviving. She does so with no guidance. Without proper guidance, one will be reckless. But, remember, she is a survivor. Willing to do whatever it takes to survive. There is truly no way to ever stop it. It has been going on since humans started walking on earth! That is why only .01% of traffickers get caught. America is not looking to stop it. To Uncle Sam we are all pawns on his chessboard, but pussy will be getting sold until the creator ends the world.[1]

—James,[2] convicted juvenile sex trafficker

Two adult black men in a blue Lincoln approached 12-year-old Allison on November 2, 2002, as she was walking along the sidewalk near a public library on Malcolm X Avenue in Brooklyn, New York. From the passenger's seat, James instructed his co-conspirator, Juan, to drive the car alongside the girl until she slowed her gait. From this very first interaction, his intention was to recruit Allison into the commercial sex trade.

To accomplish this singular objective, James used tactics indigenous to many domestic sex traffickers, who refer to themselves as "pimps" in the United States. He initiated his recruitment by telling Allison that she was pretty and offering her a ride. When she declined his advances, he persisted, presenting his character as one worthy of trust. Recognizing that she was a young runaway, alone and in need, he offered to provide her with clothing, as well as food and drinks at a party. Allison was enticed by his proposition but still wary of the incentive for his kindness. Looking at her surroundings, without anywhere to sleep, she eventually accepted his assistance, hesitantly approaching the passenger side of the car and entering the vehicle.

Raised in a home where she was unwanted, considered a "throwaway kid," Allison was a perfect target for recruitment into the commercial sex trade. Without social and financial resources to support her and with few life prospects of her own, she was in dire need—physiologically, socially, and emotionally. All James had to do was fill some of her needs to build a bond with her.

Instead of forceful kidnapping, James's recruitment strategy began with urbane manipulation. He attempted to portray himself as a classy and knowledgeable individual, with a wealth of substantive and practical advice that could benefit Allison and her future. "I encourage you to practice the 5 'Ps': **P**roper **P**reparation **P**revents **P**oor **P**erformance," he coached. But in reality, it was all a façade to build Allison's confidence in his character. Human traffickers are rarely direct in their speech and keep their motives hidden. "I never let my right hand know what the left is doing," James would say.

After a car ride full of euphemisms and tried-and-true mantras for recruitment, James and Juan brought Allison to a motel on Queens Boulevard, where the men introduced her to two of their older female sex workers. One of the women, known as "Pebbles," was caramel-skinned and full figured, with curly auburn hair and a round face. She dressed in a salacious manner, with a black and white short animal print dress and stilettos. Her breasts were nearly popping out of the bust of her dress, exposing her black bra and a large tattoo, which read the nickname "Slick"[3] in cursive. Allison awkwardly smiled up at her, uncomfortable but feeling a little safer with two other women in the dilapidated motel room.

James provided Allison with a fast-food meal and a clean outfit, similar to the type worn by Pebbles, before plying her with drugs and alcohol. She initially declined because she had no interest in getting drunk or high, but he wouldn't stop until she was inebriated. Although Allison knew that it was wrong to indulge in illicit substances, she relished the feeling of inclusion, so in the face of peer pressure, the 12-year-old girl consumed every mixed drink and smoked every joint passed in her direction. The substances numbed the emotional pain, which had plagued her for most of her childhood, and alleviated the fears of her current situation. She thought she was having a fun time. Little did she know this was all just bait before the inevitable switch.

Once Allison was intoxicated, James's demeanor changed, and the welcoming reception ended. He instructed Pebbles to assist in taking the girl's clothes off, as she lay on the polyester motel bedding in a haze. James retrieved his 35-mm camera and inculcated the older sex worker to begin sexually engaging the minor. If he ever had difficulty in keeping Allison under his control, he would need pictures for blackmail, so he snapped photographs as he watched Pebbles perform cunnilingus on the child. Afterward, 27-year-old James raped 12-year-old Allison himself, to formally begin the process of "turning her out."

* * *

November 7, 2002

Five days after meeting, Juan drove Allison, Pebbles, and James from New York to Washington, DC. There, 12-year-old Allison was instructed to sell her body for sex, soliciting customers by walking up and down 13th and K Streets, NW, an area known as the local "track," "strip," or "ho stroll." Allison was provided with marijuana and told to sell herself for $90 to $100. On the second night, however, police identified her as a victim of child sex trafficking.

At approximately 1:00 a.m. on November 9, 2002, a Metropolitan police department officer stopped another juvenile victim who was being sex trafficked by James. She gave a fake name and told the officer she was 19 years old. However, after further questioning, she revealed her true identity and that she was only 17. The officers transported her to the First District Police Station until her parents could be contacted and pick her up.

Upon witnessing the police confront the juvenile, James changed hotels and then left town. Police later stopped his accomplice Juan, who was with Allison. In the vehicle, they recovered the 35-mm camera that James used to take the pornographic photos of Pebbles and Allison.

Upon learning of her victimization, the officers attempted to reunite the child with a guardian and have her returned home, but there was no family or social worker to retrieve the little girl. Instead, Allison was transferred to Oak Hill—a juvenile detention center—where two inmates later sodomized her with a toothpaste tube.

When she was released, Allison ran away again, so prosecutors had her detained as a material witness. According to court documents, she didn't avail herself for counseling and therapy, so she was never treated for the trauma she had endured.

Although James was offered a plea bargain for 10 years in prison, he took his case to trial, where he was convicted on all charges. He was the first person tried in DC under the federal anti-trafficking statute and sentenced to life in prison. However, his life sentence didn't end the cycle of victimization and criminalization for Allison. She re-entered the commercial sex trade following the trial and may very well still be exploited to this day.

* * *

Unfortunately, Allison is not alone. Despite their status as victims, juvenile survivors of sex trafficking rarely receive needed social service intervention. Instead, they are repeatedly arrested and detained for crimes related to their victimization, namely involvement in the commercial sex industry. According to the Office of Juvenile Justice and Delinquency Prevention (OJJDP), there were approximately 700 juveniles arrested for prostitution and commercialized vice in 2014.[4] These prostituted kids typically grow up in dysfunctional environments, being in and out of various parts of the social services system, including private nongovernmental organizations (NGOs), foster homes, and runaway shelters. Yet, despite having high risks and experiencing multiple forms of traumatic victimization, these children often fail to receive directed services and are typically forced into a revolving door of exploitation and arrest.

For example, on January 31, 2013, Aarica S.[5] was arrested in Los Angeles, California. At the age of 17, she was charged with prostitution after she agreed to have unprotected sex with an undercover police officer in exchange for $60. During her court proceedings, Aarica explained that she was a victim of human trafficking, and the charges against her should be dismissed.

In support of her claim, Aarica testified that her father raped her when she was only three years old. Her childhood was harrowing from then on. At the age of 14, a friend introduced her to a pimp, who trafficked her into the commercial sex trade. After the pimp and his uncle raped her, she ran away and aborted the child with whom she was impregnated.

At the age of 16, another pimp recruited her. Although he gave her food and shelter, the pimp would physically abuse her if she didn't make enough money for him. She was indoctrinated to believe that she was the "property" of her pimp. By the time of her arrest, Aarica had been trafficked by approximately 10 different pimps, running away each time the abuse became too much to bear.

At trial, Aarica testified that she didn't have a pimp controlling her when she was arrested. After being trafficked on and off for over three years, she had been free for three months, living with her grandmother. However, since she admitted on cross-examination that she didn't have anyone directly exploiting her at the time of her arrest, the court treated Aarica as a criminal, not as a victim. Despite the fact that the Californians Against Sexual Exploitation Act (CASE Act) states that "Because minors are legally incapable of consenting to sexual activity, these minors are victims of human trafficking whether or not force is used,"[6] prosecutors working under Attorney General Kamala Harris, who presents herself as a paragon of anti-trafficking reform, pursued a criminal conviction against this teenage girl.

Juvenile victims of sex trafficking are frequently arrested for crimes related to their victimization.

The case of Aarica has been repeatedly used as legal precedent in the State of California to facilitate the criminalization of other human trafficking victims. Prosecutors interpreted the ruling to suggest that juveniles can choose to engage in sex work and should be punished accordingly. However, like Aarica, many of the juveniles who were being prosecuted had long histories of mental and physical abuse, as well as sex trafficking and exploitation. Unfortunately, sex traffickers are so skilled in recruiting that they can even make juvenile victims appear to be consenting delinquents or co-conspirators.

* * *

Domestic sex traffickers are proficient in recruiting runaways because they are typically raised in similar environments to their victims. These offenders also come from broken families and enter the commercial sex industry as juveniles. Similar to their victims, domestic sex traffickers are likely to have experienced abusive situations, drug-addicted parents, poor health and education backgrounds, and few life prospects. Others are literally born into the commercial sex trade as the children of sex workers and/or traffickers. With these experiences, human traffickers are able to relate to their victims in a way that law enforcement and victim service providers may not understand, giving offenders an advantage in maintaining the victimization without interference.

To better understand methods of domestic sex trafficker conscription, I conducted multiple interviews with James as he was appealing his conviction. From our interviews, I learned that James was only 13 years old when he recruited his first sex worker. He was relatively open in disclosing information about his crimes, but more importantly, his prose provided insight into how he may converse with a potential victim.

> *Against the rules of the pimp game, I am going to enlighten you about the intriguing lifestyle of pimps, players, macks, and ho's. That life is behind me now, but internally I will always be connected to the game. It takes an open-minded person to be able to fathom the life of a ho and/or pimp. The media has made the game look bad, just as they do with everything. If you truly want to know about this, please try to look at things openly, without closed eyes. If that makes sense. I hope that you do not feel as if I am glorifying. Pimping costed me life in prison. I am 100% against the game, but it will always be in me. I have 2 young daughters, 17 and 21. I would not want either of them to become a ho/whore! But, in reality the possibility is there. Pimping and hoing has been going on since the world began.*

When asked about methods of recruitment, James alluded to the fact that most domestic sex traffickers use deception and coercion, as opposed to force, in order to gain the victim's "consent" for exploitation. Although he claimed that there are six different types of pimps (see Table 1.1).

Table 1.1   Domestic Sex Trafficking Typology

Typology	Description
Gorilla Pimp	*Beats his hoes and makes them do what he wants them to.*
Understanding Pimp	*Compromises with his hoes and gives them a little lead way. Personally, hoes should never be able to have any say so about nothing that a pimp says or does. At least that is how I operated.*
Hard Pimp	*Works his hoes until she is all worked out . . . Making them no good to him in my opinion.*
Soft Pimp	*Thinks with his dick. He just wants to fuck all of his hoes. He is weak minded if you ask me. Tricks think with their dicks, making them prey. Real pimps are not moved by a ho's pussy or her good looks. Only the money that she can earn with her pussy, mouth, butthole, titties, and hands moves a pimp.*
Money Pimp	*Strictly about his paper (money). All of his hoes are part of his corporation. Money is the objective and nothing else. He may never once have sex with any of his hoes. The only thing that his penis stand at attention for is the greenback currency, and the more that he has gives him the ultimate nut.*
Simp	*A fake fraudulent imposter.*

Through the eyes of a convicted sex trafficker like James, a victim who is exploited though coercion or deception is considered as "consenting" to her exploitation, and in his opinion, it is her "choice" to be victimized. Utilizing coercion and deception to recruit victims, as opposed to force, is also a tactic that facilitates the development of a trauma bond between victim and offender. The trauma bond, or strong emotional attachment between the abused and abuser, helps maintain victim compliance and inhibits the ability for successful prosecution by undermining the credibility of the victim.

A whore is not a target, because in the field of pimping and hoing, a ho/whore 9 times out of 10 will choose her pimp. It is a way of life. The choice ultimately is always the female's. She has to want the same thing as the pimp in order for their unionship of pimping and hoing to be a success. When a pimp recruits another female to represent him and his family (all his ladies are his family), she offers him money and buys her way into the family. I am not quite sure what you know or have heard, but I assure you this much, a true pimp is always a purse first when it comes to a female. I do not care how beautiful she may look or if she is sexually enticing; she has to pay a pimp. If a whore understands that, I accept her as my girl. If she does not, I let the next pimp have her.

For people who are not in an exploitive situation, it may be difficult to imagine being manipulated into oppression, but this happens with frequency. Victims such as Allison come from destitute circumstances where they may actually perceive exploitation as an improvement to their life. While this is a sad testament of their socioeconomic opportunity before victimization, it is the stark reality of juveniles targeted by domestic sex traffickers.

Why does a prostitute need a pimp? To guide her, to love her, to protect her. The pimp is her father that she never had. He is that big brother that she misses, or the boyfriend from back in the day. The pimp is that husband that she fantasized about over and over. He is the popular guy in school that never paid her attention in class. To her, he is what Christ is to a Christian . . . The blood that pumps in her heart and keeps her legs moving. Without him, there's no her. You must understand, a ho was put on earth to be pimped by her pimp . . . Not all pimps, players, or macks possess the same characteristics. But, what we all have in common is a unique way of life and love for women and how they are able to use what they have to get them, and us what we need (notice I said NEED); we all need money to survive!

James was not unique in his perceptions of "the pimp game." Other domestic human traffickers whom I interviewed shared his beliefs. For example, a convicted juvenile sex trafficker named Michael also told me that he began trafficking as a juvenile from a lower socioeconomic upbringing. Michael was serving over 20 years in federal prison for sex trafficking a minor and transportation of a minor with intent to engage in criminal sexual activity.

Michael was in his mid-30s when he met his 16-year-old victim. He trafficked her across the Midwest and East Coast.

In his first correspondence with me, Michael included a picture of himself. He was a smaller-built black male with a short, faded hairstyle. In the photo, he was kneeling down on concrete turf, wearing a pair of gray Champion shorts, a white undershirt, and black New Balance sneakers. Both of his arms were covered with tattoos, and his smile revealed a gold, diamond-studded grill that shined in the sunlight. He posed in front of a gray cinder-block wall—it was a quintessential prison photo.

In his response to my questions, Michael wrote,

> Listen real good, I been to every state in the United States, I have seen the kind of stuff in the sex trade that people would never believe.
>
> My mother was a big time hooker. When I was growing up as a kid I lived in a house with two other hookers, my mother's pimp, and my brother and sister. Our basement was turned into a brothel. Tricks came in day and night; I would watch my mother walk the track jump in and out of cars day and night fucking and giving blowjobs. My mother's pimp was . . . my role model. As a kid he would send his prostitutes into my room at night. At the time I didn't think of it as rape or child sexual abuse. There was young runaways, older women, and all in the house. By the age of 14 I had been to Alaska, California, Las Vegas, Texas, Chicago, and with my own eyes I seen the life that chose me. My sister got pregnant at 15-years-old, so my mother told me and my brother, who was into gangs, that we were grown enough to take care of ourselves.
>
> (My mother's pimp) gave me my first hooker and I never looked back. My sister went on welfare and I went to a motel with a runaway and an older hooker named "Big Mama". She taught me how to pimp, have sex, how much money to take from a woman and how much not to take, she showed me how to pick up hookers, how to catch any women in the sexual business and outside of the business. Women and money became my drugs of choice.

Like James, Michael felt as though he helped his victims and denied forcing them into the commercial sex industry. Domestic sex traffickers tend to portray themselves as heroes and lovers, despite the fact that they are coercing their victims into exploitive situations. Michael believed that since part of the money was used for the women he exploited, his victims were consenting. He explained,

> *I have bought over 10 women breast implants, nose jobs, cars, houses you name it . . . This girl on my case, I took shopping, to the hair salon, to the doctor, you name it. She wore nothing but the best clothes and shoes. I swear, never did I once lay one hand on this girl or force her to do nothing. In all reality, I was fool for helping her.*
>
> *I could get out and run into a thousand missing girls in the sex trade. Business is a phone call away with who you know, hotels, motels, clubs, parties, strip clubs, escort lines, help wanted ads, you name it . . . From New York to Cali, to Boston, Atlanta, Houston Texas, Hawaii, Alaska, Las Vegas . . . Florida, you name it.*

Ultimately, victims of domestic sex traffickers are recruited in a way that makes them feel like their life circumstances are being improved. While they may be exploited and sex trafficked, they are provided with shared housing and basic sustenance. These kids, who often come from the margins of society, are made to believe that they are consenting co-conspirators, and the criminal justice system treats them accordingly. However, the reality is that they are being surreptitiously victimized. Regardless of whether they appear to be consenting, a child should never be criminalized for her or his involvement in the commercial sex industry. Moreover, anyone exploiting a child in the commercial sex industry should be held accountable for his or her crimes. Unfortunately, this is extremely difficult to effectuate in practice.

* * *

Given the clandestine nature of human trafficking crimes, as well as the trauma bond that often exists between victims and offenders, fewer than 0.01 percent of traffickers are ever convicted for their offenses. Research suggests that complainants in human trafficking cases still struggle to gain credibility in the eyes of police, prosecutors, and jurors. The majority of human trafficking survivors have engaged in behaviors that may be perceived as being inconsistent with claims that they have suffered abuse, which can be a consequence of rape trauma syndrome (RTS), child sexual abuse accommodation syndrome (CSAAS), and/or trauma bonding.

Human trafficking survivors who suffer from RTS may experience a credibility gap in courts because the symptomology includes discrepant, delayed, or failed reporting; promiscuity and sexual dysfunction; substance abuse; and/or desensitization to violence. As such, this may make them unconvincing witnesses, especially under cross-examination in a courtroom. Similarly, human trafficking survivors who suffer from CSAAS may exhibit behaviors that are counterintuitive for how a victim may be expected to behave. These human trafficking survivors may keep their victimization a secret or have a delayed or unconvincing disclosure; they may retract the report of their victimization; and they often feel helpless and entrapped, leading to accommodation.

In fact, some victims, who are colloquially referred to as the "bottom" or "bottom bitch," can even engage in behaviors that may facilitate the recruitment, trafficking, and control of other victims. Although these women are victimized and exploited themselves, they have been manipulated for so long and indoctrinated into their own exploitation to such an extent that they behave like co-conspirators. Ultimately, the trauma bond that is often forged between sex traffickers and their victims can make it more difficult to hold the perpetrator accountable and lead to the erroneous criminalization of victims.

Trauma bonding facilitates victim control and obedience. This bond is forged through a combination of emotional manipulation, feigned affection, physical and emotional abuse, and common goals. For victims, the attachment to the trafficker serves as a coping mechanism. However, it also undermines their credibility, considering it leads to their distrust of law enforcement, family, and service providers, which in turn contributes to their failure to report their victimization or delayed reporting, as well as omissions, errors, and discrepant accounts.

To address the issue of the victim credibility in court, an increasing number of prosecutors have begun to rely on expert witness testimony to educate jurors and restore credibility to complainants' accounts. Expert witnesses educate jurors on the impact of human trafficking victimization and the complex reactions of victims due to the trauma bonding with their offender. Expert witness testimony can be used to clarify the distinction between prostitute and sex trafficking victim, human trafficker and human trafficking survivor.

A general outline of the expert witness testimony that I have provided in multiple human trafficking cases across the United States is included in Appendix B.

Notes

1. Quotes featured in this chapter were taken from Dr. Mehlman-Orozco's interviews with convicted human traffickers.

2. Pseudonyms used throughout this chapter, due to the direct quotes from convicted human traffickers.

3. Tattoo is also a pseudonym.

4. Kimberly Mehlman-Orozco, "Why Do We Criminalize Young Victims of Sex Trafficking?" *The Crime Report* (January 17, 2017): accessed July 6, 2017, https://thecrimereport.org/2017/01/17/why-do-we-criminalize-young-victims-of -sex-trafficking/.

5. In Re: Aarica S., No. B248010 (California Court of Appeals, February 21, 2014).

6. Californians Against Sexual Exploitation Act (2012): accessed July 6, 2017, https://www.post.ca.gov/Data/Sites/1/post_docs/HumanTraffickingProp35Text .pdf.

CHAPTER TWO

Happy Beginnings, Sad Endings

According to media reports, 400 federal and local law enforcement officers raided 11 suspected brothels in the San Francisco area during "Operation Gilded Cage."[1] The raid led to the arrest of 27 suspects and recovery of more than 100 female sex workers. U.S. Attorney Kevin Ryan described the traffickers' treatment of the victims as "horrific, demeaning, and oftentimes brutal."[2] Brad Schlozman, acting assistant attorney general for civil rights, called the raid "one of our biggest" nationwide and stated that law enforcement had unraveled a "sophisticated criminal enterprise."[3] The raid commanded headlines from across the United States and was heralded as a successful operation in combating the scourge of human trafficking.

News agencies reported that one of the raided businesses, King's Massage, had served as the primary entry point for girls who were new victims to San Francisco's erotic massage parlor industry. Although the business was within walking distance from Westfield San Francisco Centre Mall, most area residents were not aware of the alleged indentured sexual servitude that was occurring. Mechanic Carlos Lopez, who worked next door to the spa at Performance Auto, told reporters, "It looks like a normal business. I'm surprised something like this could happen. It's crazy."[4] He had no idea until dozens of FBI agents raided the old brick building, pulling out beautiful young girls in handcuffs and chasing down management at full speed.

The officers initiated Operation Gilded Cage after two women came forward in August 2004, detailing the sexual exploitation they had allegedly faced.

According to the media and court documents, from 2001 to 2004, the sex trafficking ring targeted women who were living in impoverished areas of South Korea. Recruiters Wu Sang Nah and Sung Yong Kim claimed to work for a legitimate company—YJY Travel and Tour—offering the women lucrative jobs as waitresses and bar hostesses in America.[5] However, the girls' American dreams quickly faded into broken promises.

After being smuggled from South Korea to Canada, and then into the United States, the women were picked up by a networked transportation company—Yang's Taxi—and taken to King's Massage. Each woman was allegedly assessed smuggling fees, ranging from $10,000 to $15,000, and their employer placed them in perpetual debt bondage, controlling and charging for their housing, transportation, communication, sustenance, and finances.[6] In order to repay the debts, the women were taught English phrases for various sex acts and told how to service customers.

At the time of the raid, law enforcement officers seized more than $2 million in cash, three ATM machines, and several vehicles.[7] They arrested over two dozen suspects, including purported kingpin Young Joon Yang, who was charged with conspiracy to harbor aliens, sex trafficking, conspiracy to launder money, and transporting women across interstate lines to engage in prostitution.[8]

Acting Special Agent in Charge Arthur Balizan said, "This cooperative enforcement action is a testament to the FBI's commitment in investigating sophisticated human trafficking cases. These alleged illicit activities erode our social fabric and feed the coffers of many criminal enterprises."[9]

San Francisco Police Department Deputy Chief of Investigations Morris Tabak stated, "The San Francisco Police Department is proud to have joined forces with U.S. Attorney Kevin V. Ryan, the FBI, and the rest of our federal partners to combat the scourge of human trafficking, also known as modern slavery. There is no place in the world for human trafficking, especially here in San Francisco."[10]

Although this case was described as a success and one of the largest sex trafficking rings ever prosecuted, the reality was that many of the charges were eventually dismissed, and none of the 29 defendants were ultimately convicted of sex trafficking (see Table 2.1).

According to court documents, of the 29 prosecuted defendants, the lengthiest imposed sentence was about 12 months credited for time served and 36 months of supervised release; the largest amount of restitution was $609,840.[11] The alleged kingpin, Young Joon Yang, was only sentenced to time served, three years of supervised probation, and an assessment fee of $400. Although the defendants were successfully

Table 2.1 *United States v. Yang et al.* **Sentencing Summary**

Defendant	Indicted	Sentenced
Young Joon Yang	Conspiracy to bring in and harbor aliens	Time served; three years of supervised release; assessed $400 fee and fine waived
	Money laundering conspiracy	
	Mann Act conspiracy	
	Conspiracy to use facility in aid of unlawful activity	
	Sex trafficking; aiding and abetting	Dismissed
Wu Sang Nah	Conspiracy to bring in and harbor aliens	Time served; three years of supervised release; assessed $100 fee and fine waived
Sung Yong Kim	Conspiracy to bring in and harbor aliens	Dismissed
	Sex trafficking; aiding and abetting	Dismissed
Hang Joe Yoon	Money laundering conspiracy	Dismissed
Myong Su Ahn	Money laundering conspiracy	Dismissed
Nam Young Lee	Money laundering conspiracy	Dismissed
Fred A. Frazier	Conspiracy to bring in and harbor aliens	Dismissed
Truong Du Nguyen	Conspiracy to bring in and harbor aliens	Dismissed
Ahdi M. Nashashibi	Conspiracy to bring in and harbor aliens	Dismissed
Young Joo Lee	Conspiracy to use facility in aid of unlawful activity	Time served; three years of supervised release; assessed $200 fee and fine waived; forfeited $3,011 in U.S. currency and $1,600 postal money orders

(*continued*)

Table 2.1 (*continued*)

Defendant	Indicted	Sentenced
Min Young Bang	Interstate travel in aid of racketeering	Time served; three years of supervised release; assessed $100 fee
	Mann Act conspiracy	Dismissed
	Conspiracy to use facility in aid of unlawful activity	Dismissed
In Seung Kim	Mann Act conspiracy	Seven months in custody for each count, to run concurrent; three years of supervised release, with conditions; $200 special assessment
	Conspiracy to use facility in aid of unlawful activity	
Seyun Kim	Interstate travel in aid of racketeering	Time served; three years of supervised release; assessed $100 fee; forfeited $3,009 in cash
	Mann Act conspiracy	
	Conspiracy to use facility in aid of unlawful activity	
Eugene Yi	Willful failure to file tax returns	One year of probation; pay income tax for 2004, as determined by IRS, and $25 special assessment
	Mann Act conspiracy	
	Conspiracy to use facility in aid of unlawful activity	
Chang Soo Youn	Willful failure to supply information	Two years of probation; three months of home detention; $2,316 in restitution and $25 special assessment
	Mann Act conspiracy	
	Conspiracy to use facility in aid of unlawful activity	
Mo Sook Yang	Conspiracy to use facility in aid of unlawful activity	Dismissed without prejudice

Name	Charge	Sentence
Keun Sung Lee	Interstate travel in aid of racketeering	Three years of probation; six months of home confinement; assessed $100 fee and $20,000 fine
	Conspiracy to use facility in aid of unlawful activity	
Myung Jin Chang	Interstate travel in aid of racketeering	Time served; three years of supervised release; assessed $100 fee and $3,000 fine
	Conspiracy to use facility in aid of unlawful activity	Dismissed
Won Seok Yoo	Conspiracy to use facility in aid of unlawful activity	Dismissed without prejudice on government's motion
Jimmy Gong Yan Lee	Interstate travel in aid of racketeering	Three years of probation; 10 months of home confinement; assessed $100 fee and $2,000 fine
	Conspiracy to use facility in aid of unlawful activity	Dismissed
Aesun Kim	Interstate travel in aid of racketeering	12 months and one day in custody; three years of supervised release; assessed $100 fee and fine waived
	Conspiracy to use facility in aid of unlawful activity	Dismissed
Hyeon J. Park	Interstate travel in aid of racketeering	Three years of probation; three months of home confinement with electric monitor; assessed $100 fee and fine waived
	Conspiracy to use facility in aid of unlawful activity	Dismissed
Anthony Gar Lau	Conspiracy to use facility in aid of unlawful activity	Dismissed
Mi Young Sim	Interstate travel in aid of racketeering	Three years of probation; six months of home confinement with electric monitor; assessed $100 fee and $40,000 fine; forfeited $415,000, with credit $5,100.00
	Conspiracy to use facility in aid of unlawful activity	Dismissed

(continued)

Table 2.1 *(continued)*

Defendant	Indicted	Sentenced
Kum Pae Yi	Making and subscribing false tax return Conspiracy to use facility in aid of unlawful activity	Three years of probation; assessed $100 fee and fine waived; restitution $1,276.36, payable to the Department of Treasury
Han Lee	Interstate travel in aid of racketeering Conspiracy to use facility in aid of unlawful activity	Four months in custody; three years of supervised release; four months of home confinement; assessed $100.00 fee and $40,000 fine; forfeited $609,840 Dismissed
Hye Cha Kim	Tax evasion Conspiracy to use facility in aid of unlawful activity	Three years of probation; ten months of home confinement with monitor; assessed $100 fee and payment of restitution to Department of Treasury (amount not stated)
Jin Ah Kang	Interstate travel in aid of racketeering Conspiracy to use facility in aid of unlawful activity	Three years of probation; three months of home confinement; assessed $100.00 fee and fine waived
Yon Suk Pang	Conspiracy to use facility in aid of unlawful activity	Dismissed

charged with bringing in and harboring aliens, money laundering, and a Mann Act conspiracy, the charges that carried the longest sentences—sex trafficking and aiding and abetting of sex trafficking—were dismissed.

* * *

Erotic massage parlors such as King's are located in proximity to nearly every community across the United States. Despite the increasing amount of law enforcement conducting raids on these illicit industries, many of these massage parlors enjoy the same level of impunity as what occurred in Operation Gilded Cage.

Regardless of the indicted charges, these business owners are rarely convicted of sex trafficking. Instead, they plead guilty to tangentially related offenses that carry more lenient punishments, such as money laundering. Following the conviction, the erotic massage parlor will typically reopen, sometimes in the same location under a different business name or occasionally in a new location. Given the financial and social capital from the networked businesses, bouncing back from a conviction is a relatively fluid process, like a game of Whac-A-Mole. This is perhaps one of the reasons that human trafficking is the fastest growing crime in the world—the financial gains are high, and risks of punishment are low.

In 2013, I conducted a systematic review of massage parlors advertised and reviewed through online sex marketplaces, such as AdultSearch.com, RubMaps.com, and USASexGuide.info. If you aren't familiar with these websites, they are essentially forums for commercial sex consumers to share information with others who are interested in procuring sexual services.

For example, AdultSearch.com is described on the website as, "The world's only adult search engine with listings & reviews on escorts, strip clubs, erotic massage parlors, sex shops, adult websites, and adult entertainment."[12]

RubMaps.com provides a similar service and operates with the tagline "where fantasy meets reality." "RubMaps is your #1 massage parlor locator. The site is updated daily with the best massage reviews from your area, which include body to body massages, prostate massages, massages with happy endings, nuru massages and hot massages,"[13] reads the website description.

USASexGuide.info also provides a comparable service and is described as "a FREE forum for the exchange of information between men who are looking for sex with women."[14]

By searching these websites, I identified 102 suspected erotic massage parlors located in my home state of Virginia. The advertisements and reviews posted online provided a wealth of information on the erotic massage industry. For example, using the extant data from the advertisements and reviews, I determined that the average house fee for these alleged erotic massage parlors in Virginia is $60, which is paid to the business. Additional services are then negotiated with the masseuse. The standard is $40 for a genital massage and $100 and up for other services, including sexual intercourse. At the time, credit cards were accepted at most Virginia-based erotic massage parlors (79 percent).

According to the massage parlor descriptions, 96 percent of the masseuses were Asian, including women from Korea, China, Thailand, Philippines, and Japan. Consumer reviews suggested that most women masseuses providing erotic services at these massage parlors were in their late 30s to early 50s.

To arrange erotic services, the "John," also known as a "hobbyist" or "monger," would describe initiating the sexual exchange by groping the female masseuse. If she didn't pull away, he would purchase his desired erotic services by using hand signals to negotiate price (for example, four fingers = $40). Once a nonverbal price agreement was met, the masseuse would continue the sexual encounter. This process was likely to evade detection from law enforcement, the rationale being that a police officer would not initiate an illicit transaction in that manner. Instead, law enforcement would be more likely to solicit a verbal agreement for the exchange of money for sex, which could be more easily used as evidence and a catalyst for an arrest.

Alternatively, the use of table showers was also perceived as an indication of commercial sex because it facilitates the opportunity for inappropriate touching. In the words of one "John," ". . . technically, you are only paying to be washed by a Japanese woman . . . being that you are both naked, in close proximity . . . the sex is expected."[15]

Another interesting aspect of the advertisements was the fact that 34 percent of the suspected commercial sex massage parlors advertised "new staff," "new girls," or "new management." This was noteworthy considering that many of the businesses had been in operation for multiple years, and the nature of the sex trafficking industry encourages movement of victims from one brothel to another. This practice facilitates the traffickers' control over the victims by restricting knowledge about their surroundings. It also provides new women or "variety" for regular patrons.

In addition to the advertisements, the men who patronized these establishments provided detailed descriptions of the services they received and the women they encountered.

One reviewer stated, "[The mamasan] said the young girls [were] new to the country and worked as part of a crew (which had darker implications), but all the older women were working off gambling debts. [The mamasan] said they were all gambling addicts and were in the AMP [Asian Massage Parlor] trade because they couldn't pay them off [any] other way . . ."[16]

Multiple reviewers implied that these businesses were networked, cooperating with others out of state. Patterns extrapolated from the qualitative data in the advertisements through stylometry suggested that the women arrived in San Francisco or New York and were then moved to other locations once acclimated to the sex industry. Suspected networks tended to have locations in the DC metropolitan area, New York, Florida, and California. These suspected networks included as many as 18 "branches" in various out-of-state localities, which spanned as far as Manila, Philippines.

One consumer inquired in an online forum, "At some point you have to ask why there are practically zero therapists under 32 in the entire D.C./NoVA/Maryland area AMP/AAAMP scene . . . [Asian Massage Parlor/Asian American Apartment Massage Parlor]."

A senior user responded, "Most of the time, in NY area they are paying off their debt (in getting to the US) . . . The real deal is the girls once used up (or been busted too much) that circuit must move on. They hit Boston, some go west but then they are finally fresh here in NOVA and DC they are no longer a spring chicken . . ."[17]

Compartmentalizing business assets within a large network may help explain how erotic massage parlors are able to continue operating despite setbacks from arrests, seized assets, and forfeitures. According to one "John," "If you chat it up with the girls you will find that most of the AMPs [Asian Massage Parlors] are owned by only a few people. I know one lady (name redacted) who owns and runs four parlors in the Tidewater area . . ."[18]

I felt that the data I had gleaned from these publicly available materials was rich and could be used as a tool. I compiled the information into a report and began sharing it with law enforcement agents, who agreed.

On May 15, 2013, a sheriff in Minnesota responded, "Thank you for the information. The document you provided is a great tool to educate others. We are in the process of developing an ad-hoc task force to deal with this situation as well as expand our community education efforts. What would be involved in developing a local version of this study?"[19]

On October 4, 2013, a special agent of Homeland Security Investigations with Immigration and Customs Enforcement (ICE) in New York wrote to me, "I came across your report 'Massage Parlors and Commercial Sex . . .' regarding commercial sex networking through Asian Massage Parlors in the United States. I am currently involved with investigating this form of sex/labor trafficking, particularly the 'network' aspect. Would it be possible for you and I to discuss your . . . work in this area? I am hoping to gain a better understanding of the bigger picture behind the actual parlor location, in an effort to dismantle the network, instead of just shutting down the parlors piecemeal, which usually results in them re-opening shortly thereafter."[20]

On September 23, 2014, a fire marshal's office code enforcement unit supervisor in Virginia wrote, "I have read your study of online advertising for massage parlor and commercial sex establishment in Northern Virginia. Has this study been updated or amended since the original publications? Are any of the maps cited in the publication reproducible? As most commercial establishments require annual inspections, instruction on recognizing various aspects of the commercial sex trade, as well as recognizing signs of human/sex trafficking, may result in local fire marshals involving law enforcement to appropriately investigate suspected cases. Any data you have that can be shared would be of great assistance."[21]

Given the positive reception from state and federal law enforcement agencies across the country, I wanted to see if this information could have more of a direct impact in my local community. During the course of my review of the online advertisements and reviews for commercial sex massage parlors, I discovered that many of them had already encountered the police.

In 2011, the Northern Virginia Human Trafficking Task Force teamed up with Immigration and Customs Enforcement (ICE), the Federal Bureau of Investigation (FBI), and the Polaris Project in an initiative to crack down on commercial sexual exploitation and potential human trafficking in Virginia. In one raid, officials checked 23 businesses and filed charges against seven of them, primarily for licensing violations. My search of online commercial sex advertisement and review websites indicated that 86 percent of the cited locations continued to post massage ads, which suggested sexual services were still being provided. One of those businesses—Peach Therapy—was located in my hometown of Annandale, Virginia.

* * *

Peach Therapy was situated at the end unit of a brick business complex, which was adjacent to my childhood grocery store. It operated next to legitimate IT companies, law firms, and counseling centers, all of which had uniform gold-plated signs emblazed with each business's legal operating name in front. The neighboring community paid little attention to that end unit until it was raided in 2011 by law enforcement agencies working with the Northern Virginia Human Trafficking Task Force.

In October 2012, the owner, Susan Lee Gross, pled guilty to transporting women from South Korea to work as prostitutes at the massage parlor. According to the official Department of Justice press release, Gross was bringing girls from South Korea to New York and trafficking them down I-95 to my Virginian suburb for the purpose of commercial sexual exploitation.

The investigation that led to her arrest, which was conducted by U.S. Immigration and Customs Enforcement, the Internal Revenue Service Criminal Investigation Division, the Naval Criminal Investigative Service, and Fairfax County Police, was touted as a victory against the sex trafficking scourge. "Peach Therapy was nothing but a front for a prostitution ring," U.S. Attorney Neil H. MacBride said in a statement, "This conviction is the result of an ongoing investigation into the sale of sexual services at Northern Virginia massage parlors as part of my office's crackdown on sex trafficking in the region."[22]

However, one week after Gross's guilty plea, a woman in heavy makeup and hot pants answered the door at Peach Therapy and assured *The Washington Post* reporter Tom Jackman that the business was still open.[23] In fact, Peach Therapy continued posting advertisements suggestive of sexual services (in the adult section) on Backpage.com and other websites. "Our Staff smile will warm you," their advertisement promised, "and our hands will melt your stress and tension away! Sensation Asian ladies to choose from."

Eventually, the massage parlor called Peach Therapy ceased to exist at that location and was replaced by another—Bada Spa—that continued posting similar advertisements on websites known to cater to sex-for-hire clientele. Curious, I went to go see for myself.

During the spring and summer of 2013, I conducted systematic social observations of Bada Spa. My first visit was a weekday afternoon, and I parked my SUV facing the entrance from a lower tier of the parking area. I watched as man after man went in and out of the massage parlor.

On each occasion that I returned, at different times and days of the week, all I saw was 100 percent male clientele, of various age groups and races/ethnicities, entering and exiting the establishment—one, after another, after another, occasionally exiting after only 20 minutes of being inside. Some of the men arrived in vehicles with government license plates, others with stick-figure families embossed on the rear windshield of their vanity-plated cars. I didn't see a single female customer go into the massage parlor for services during my observations.

On several occasions, I took pictures or video and even approached a few of the men to ask questions. "Excuse me, sir. Did you know a massage parlor at this location was recently prosecuted for human trafficking?" I would ask. Some of the men would hurry off without saying a word. Others brazenly told me they were patronizing the business for sexual services but didn't think the women were trafficked and made it a point to tell me that the parlor no longer offered "full service," only "happy endings."

One older man with white hair even posted about our encounter on USASexGuide.info. He wrote,

> *Today I decided to visit Bada Spa. As I was leaving I noticed a woman in a gold SUV across in a lower parking lot talking on her phone. As I got closer to my car she pulled a camera out of her car and aimed it at me! I kept walking past my car to another part of the complex. About five minutes later I returned to my car not seeing the woman or her car. As I started to leave she pulled out of another parking space closer to the spa . . . and whipped up a camera again . . . recommend that anyone visiting Bada [to] park in a distant lot. Not many businesses near the spa, so it's pretty obvious where you're visiting if you park right in front.*[24]

This was incredulous to me.

Nearly two months following Susan Lee Gross's sentencing to 30 months in prison and forfeiture of nearly $250,000, there was still a business operating at the same location, under a different name, where men were claiming to receive sexual services. Yet, this fact didn't stop trafficking policy makers, law enforcement officials, and service providers from continuing to tout the conviction as a "win" in the war against sex trafficking. Around that same time, I attended a local anti-trafficking event and listened to Frank Wolf (R) Member of the U.S. House of Representatives from Virginia's 10th district as he mentioned the human trafficking prosecution of Peach Therapy, while multiple news agencies recorded his speech and took down notes. Representative Wolf portrayed the conviction as a prime example of the efficacy of his federally funded efforts to combat human trafficking locally. However, the reality was that the proprietor had received a slap-on-the-hand sentence, and the commercial sex industry continued to flourish locally.

I felt like he didn't really care. To me, it seemed like he was just bragging about a hollow victory for public accolade. I started to become jaded.

Despite the previous conviction and investigation for sex trafficking, the massage parlors at that same location, with the same phone number and goodwill of the business, continued to post advertisements on Backpage.com under the adult section for body rubs. The business also continued accumulating reviews on websites such as RubMaps.com, from 54 men claiming to have patronized their location in pursuit and/or receipt of sexual services between September 9, 2011, and February 12, 2017. One man's review read:

> *I went in this place and it looked really good. Everything is clean and well organized. I paid my house fee, then I got Mimi. She's average looking with some perky tits in a tight shirt, so that was cool. I followed her into a room and got undressed. The room was smaller, but it looked fine to me. She came back and was putting oil all over my back giving me a massage. She was really good about it and I was definitely enjoying myself. She took her time and really worked hard on my neck. I told her I sit at a computer all day, so she knew exactly where to rub me down with the oil.*
>
> *I finally was on my back, then she began to give me a hand job. When her hands started to touch my cock, it was so nice to feel that finally. She was really doing a good job, and she was full of energy. She had both of her hands working at the same time. I also got frisky and started to rub those nice tits she had. They were firm, but her nipples were the best part. I loved feeling her nipples get harder and harder. That is what made me cum so hard with lots of intensity. When I finished, she milked me dry. I was very satisfied with the session. I will be back here again.*[25]
>
> —Commercial Sex Consumer, November 8, 2016

I brought these facts to the attention of Representative Frank Wolf, Congresswoman Barbara Comstock, as well as the local police and vice squad who were in charge of combating sex trafficking locally. The Northern Virginia Human Trafficking Task Force had just received a $1 million grant from Department of Justice's Office of Justice Programs to combat human trafficking. In addition to their funding, leading anti-trafficking agencies and federal law enforcement supported them, so there was no dearth of resources at their disposal, yet they didn't appear to act on this information.

At the time of this writing, there is still a business at that same location that uses the same telephone number as Peach Therapy, but it now goes by the name Sun Therapy. This business still posts advertisements on websites that are frequented by commercial sex consumers. For example, under the women-for-men dating section of Backpage.com, the massage parlor's advertisement reads:

GRAND OPENING!!!
New Management!!!
Relaxation
Beautiful Asian staffs!!!
Table Shower
~~~O.o~~~ PROFESSIONAL ASIAN STAFF ~~~O.o~~~
** NEW MANAGEMENT & New Young staffs**
** ORIENTAL RELAXATION **[26]

Next to the text of the massage parlor advertisement, which was posted on April 21, 2017, there was a black and white video of two young Asian women dancing in heels, black hot pants, and black bras. The audio of the video featured the song *Youth*, by Troye Sivan. The context of that song on the advertisement's video carried even more inappropriate and suggestive innuendo. In part, the chorus is:

My youth is yours
Runaway now and forevermore[27]

While I cannot say definitively what type of business operates at that location, massage parlor advertisements featuring scantily clad young women dancing suggestively in a post under the women-for-men dating section of Backpage.com is highly suggestive, in my opinion.

These types of advertisements are all over the Internet, and you may be shocked by what businesses you find them being posted for. Appendix A features acronyms and terminology to help readers decipher the argot that is often used in commercial sex advertisement and review websites, should you choose to take a look for yourself.

Notes

1. Jaxon Van Derbeken and Ryan Kim, "Alleged Sex-Trade Ring Broken Up in Bay Area/Police Say Koreans in Massage Parlors Were Smuggled In—SFGate," *SFGate* (July 2, 2005): accessed July 6, 2017, http://www.sfgate.com/bayarea /article/Alleged-sex-trade-ring-broken-up-in-Bay-Area-2624979.php.

2. Carolyn Marshall, "Agents Said to Dismantle a Korean Sex Ring," *The New York Times* (July 2, 2005): accessed July 6, 2017, http://www.nytimes.com/2005 /07/02/us/agents-said-to-dismantle-a-korean-sex-ring.html.

3. David Rosenzweig and K. Connie Kang, "Raids on Brothel Rings Net 45 Arrests," *Los Angeles Times* (July 2, 2005): accessed July 6, 2017, http://articles .latimes.com/2005/jul/02/local/me-smuggling2/2.

4. Jaxon Van Derbeken and Ryan Kim, "Alleged Sex-Trade Ring Broken Up in Bay Area/Police Say Koreans in Massage Parlors Were Smuggled In—SFGate,"

SFGate (July 2, 2005): accessed July 6, 2017, http://www.sfgate.com/bayarea/article/Alleged-sex-trade-ring-broken-up-in-Bay-Area-2624979.php.

5. Ibid.

6. Ibid.

7. Ibid.

8. Ibid.

9. U.S. Department of State, "U.S. Agents Crack West Coast Human Smuggling, Trafficking Ring: Forced Prostitution Alleged in San Francisco, Los Angeles Arrest," *IIP Digital* (2005): accessed July 6, 2017, http://news.findlaw.com/scripts/printer_friendly.pl?page=/wash/s/20050701/20050701182254.html.

10. Ibid.

11. *USA v. Yang et al.*, No. 3:05–cr–00395–JL (U.S. District Court California Northern District, January 14, 2009).

12. Find Escorts, Strip Clubs, Sex Shops | Adult Search Engine. Accessed April 21, 2017, https://adultsearch.com/.

13. Ibid.

14. "USA Sex Guide," accessed April 21, 2017, http://usasexguide.info/.

15. *Virginia Massage Parlor Reports* (August 7, 2011): accessed July 6, 2017, http://www.USASexGuide.info.

16. *Virginia Massage Parlor Reports* (August 19, 2013): accessed July 6, 2017, http://www.USASexGuide.info.

17. *Virginia Massage Parlor Reports* (August 18, 2013): accessed July 6, 2017, http://www.USASexGuide.info.

18. *Virginia Massage Parlor Reports* (July 4, 2011): accessed July 6, 2017, http://www.USASexGuide.info.

19. Anonymous Sheriff in Minnesota. Utility of Commercial Sex Advertisement Information in Human Trafficking Investigations. Personal correspondence, May 15, 2013.

20. Anonymous Special Agent of Homeland Security Investigations with Immigration and Customs Enforcement (ICE). Utility of Commercial Sex Advertisement Information in Human Trafficking Investigations. Personal correspondence, October 4, 2013.

21. Anonymous Virginia Fire Marshal's Office Code Enforcement Unit Supervisor. Utility of Commercial Sex Advertisement Information in Human Trafficking Investigations. Personal correspondence, September 23, 2014.

22. U.S. Immigration and Customs Enforcement, "Former Massage Parlor Owner Pleads Guilty to Prostitution, Money Laundering," (October 25, 2012): accessed July 6, 2017, https://www.ice.gov/news/releases/former-massage-parlor-owner-pleads-guilty-prostitution-money-laundering.

23. Tom Jackman, "Annandale Massage Parlor Peach Therapy Was a Full-Blown Brothel. Is It Still?" *The Washington Post* (October 29, 2012): accessed July 6, 2017, https://www.washingtonpost.com/blogs/the-state-of-nova/post/annandale-massage-parlor-peach-therapy-was-a-full-service-brothel-in-heart-of-fairfax-county-is-it-still/2012/10/29/95303d2e-1f26-11e2-ba31-3083ca97c314_blog.html.

24. *Virginia General Reports* (May 22, 2013): accessed July 6, 2017, http://www
.USASexGuide.info.

25. *Sun Therapy Spa* (November 8, 2016): accessed July 6, 2017, http://www
.RubMaps.com.

26. *Sun Therapy Spa* (April 21, 2017): accessed July 6, 2017, http://www.Back
page.com.

27. Sivan, Troye (2015). *Blue Neighbourhood*. Google Play.

CHAPTER THREE

Disposable Wives

Anyone know which country I can buy a sex slave from, or go to fuck one who will do absolutely anything I command her to do?[1]
—Anonymous Commercial Sex Consumer, Philadelphia,
Pennsylvania, July 21, 2013

Indle King wasn't an attractive man by conventional standards. He was obese, bald, and his typical wardrobe included a pocket protector, members-only jacket, and budget-framed glasses. He attempted to use his advanced degrees in business to appeal to women, but he didn't have an amicable personality, which made dating on his own accord difficult, especially with women who fit his tastes in physical appearance.

Despite his unattractive looks and lacking personal qualities, Indle was only interested in young, tall, and physically fit exotic women—the type of women who would typically ignore someone like him. He quickly decided that if he couldn't naturally attract his ideal woman as a partner, he would buy one. And luckily for him, purchasing a wife was rather economical—about the same price as a reliable used car.

Indle's first wife was procured through a classified advertisement in a Russian newspaper. Dreaming of a life in America, Ekaterina "Katya" Kazakova agreed to marry him. Indle was content with his purchase and often boasted about the stunning beauty of his 5'9" wife, with porcelain skin and long, dark hair. Yet, their relationship quickly soured. After only four years of marriage, Indle's wife divorced him amid allegations of abuse. "He hit me in the head with his fist . . . threw me against the wall and continuously pounded my head,"[2] she recounted in an Ohio court. He was furious, as the divorce cost him more than $55,000.

Despite the failure of his first marriage, Indle was determined to obtain another wife, so he signed up for a mail-order bride service. In no time, the 38-year-old divorcee met his second wife, 18-year-old Anastasia, a native of Kyrgyzstan. She fit the profile of Indle's type, with blonde hair that reached down to her svelte waist, ivory skin, a round Slavic face, and beautiful smile. She was a conventional Russian beauty, and Indle thought she would make the perfect-looking wife to bear his children.

Anastasia accepted Indle's proposal, and six months after they met online, she came to live with him in Seattle, Washington, where they were married by a justice of the peace. It was the first time she had left her home country, and she was anxious to soak up everything she could in this new adventure abroad.

Their prenuptial agreement outlined the arrangement. In exchange for U.S. citizenship, Anastasia would bear Indle's children. However, after arriving in America and meeting her future husband, she changed her mind.

Indle had boasted of wealth during the online courtship, but the reality was that he was financially struggling. Indle was fired from his job, and his cars were being repossessed.[3] All the while, he was extremely controlling of his new wife.

Anastasia expressed to Indle that she wanted to go to school and work. She felt that she needed time to grow as an individual before becoming a mother. In response to her request for independence, Indle became jealous and suspicious of her intentions. He allowed her to work, but she had to deposit her money to his account, and only he was allowed access to the bankcard. Each day, he would drop her off and pick her up from work. Restricting her access to finances and transportation gave Indle additional leverage over Anastasia.

Just as with his first wife, almost immediately after the wedding, the relationship began to deteriorate. Anastasia kept a diary in a safety deposit box, where she detailed instances of domestic violence, invasion of privacy, and sexual assault. One year into the marriage, she still hadn't given him a child, as he had requested. In fact, Anastasia insisted that they continued sleeping in separate bedrooms, which infuriated Indle.

Anastasia had become disgusted with her husband and confided in a coworker that she wanted a divorce but feared the consequences. She needed to be married for two years before she would qualify for U.S. citizenship. If Anastasia left Indle after the first year, she would have to return to Kyrgyzstan, so she stayed in the marriage.

Financially struggling and with his marriage quickly deteriorating, Indle advertised rooms for rent in his house for short-term tenants.

Daniel Larson became one of the renters. Daniel had a criminal history of sexual assault crimes, which scared Anastasia, but Indle didn't seem to mind. The two men got along famously, while Anastasia felt trapped almost like a prisoner in her own home at times.

During their second year of marriage, Anastasia wanted to get away from Indle, so she left Seattle to visit her parents in Kyrgyzstan. While she was away, Indle filed for divorce on August 21, 2000. He also had reignited his search for a mail-order bride online, this time to replace Anastasia. A few weeks later, however, he followed her to Kyrgyzstan.

While in Kyrgyzstan, Anastasia told her parents of her plans to divorce Indle, considering that she could now apply for permanent residency in the United States.[4] Indle, on the other hand, put on a show for the family, pretending like everything was fine in their marriage. Anastasia's parents dropped the couple off at the airport on September 22, 2000, and that was the last time they ever saw or heard from their daughter again.

Anastasia was supposed to call her parents when she arrived home, but she didn't. She also missed her shift at work and didn't show up at the University of Washington, where she was scheduled to begin her fall semester of classes. When concerned family and friends called the home, Indle would hang up on them. They alerted authorities, and nearly 10 days after her disappearance, Anastasia was declared a missing person.

Upon arriving at Indle's home, police knocked on the door and could hear movement, but no one immediately answered. They walked around to the back of the house and found the sliding glass door partially open. The police entered and discovered Indle inside.

Upon questioning, Indle told the police that he and Anastasia had gotten in a fight during the layover in Moscow. According to him, he returned home, and she stayed in Russia. Indle also informed the police that Anastasia was having affair with a man named Serge, which he alleged was the reason why she declined to return home.

During that visit with police, Indle showed them a home video from Kyrgyzstan. In the video, Indle was wearing sunglasses and a plaid shirt, kissing Anastasia on her cheek, as she pulled away. Anastasia had her long blonde hair in a ponytail and was wearing a beautiful black blazer and white blouse. The video showed the couple waving, dancing, and smiling. It was his attempt at deceiving the police about the nature of their relationship. He wanted them to believe that he was a loving husband and she was a consenting wife.

Although this narrative didn't explain why Anastasia hadn't contacted any of her friends or family in over one week, the police didn't have enough evidence to detain Indle or further question his version of events until

early October, when they obtained more evidence to undermine his credibility. The flight manifest showed that Anastasia was on the plane from
Moscow to Seattle. In addition, customs records verified that she and Indle
both passed through within one minute of each other. Finally, a shuttle
driver reported dropping the couple off at their home, together, at approximately 2:30 p.m. on September 22, 2000.[5]

When police told Indle of those facts, he acted in disbelief that she was
on the plane with him. At that point, he became the prime suspect for
police, and they put him under surveillance.

While under surveillance, Indle led police to Daniel Larson, his former
renter, who was incarcerated at Snohomish County Jail for taking inde-
cent liberties with a 16-year-old girl at the Alderwood Mall restroom.[6]
Police noticed that Larson had been visited by King multiple times, which
was odd considering that Indle had described their relationship as
landlord-tenant, not friends.

Police also made a visit to Daniel Larson on December 28, 2000. After
being questioned, he confessed what happened to Anastasia.[7]

According to Larson, as soon as Indle and Anastasia arrived at the
Seattle airport from Moscow, Indle called to alert him, "We are on our
way home, be ready." He was angry with Anastasia about her desire for
divorce and had conspired with Daniel to murder her. After the couple
arrived home, Indle called Anastasia downstairs and lured her into the
garage.[8]

"Why?" she asked.

"Give me a kiss," Indle demanded.

As soon as she approached, Indle grabbed Anastasia in bear hug, and
Daniel came from behind to wrap a necktie around her. Anastasia was
kicking and fighting, as 270-pound King pinned his 20-year-old wife to
the ground in the hallway of their home, while his 21-year-old housemate
accomplice strangled her to death.

According to Daniel, it took about a minute for her to lose conscious-
ness. In a recorded interview, he divulged to investigators, "Indle told me
to put the tie around her neck; otherwise, he would bring Anastasia into
his room and shove her on the bed, grab his gun, and shoot her and me."
Daniel obeyed Indle and continued pulling the tie tighter until Anastasia
stopped moving.

After they killed her, Indle instructed Daniel on how to dispose of
Anastasia's body. Daniel helped him wrap her in a rug and put her in the
backseat of her car. They then drove her body through stop-and-go
afternoon traffic to the Tulalip Indian Reservation.[9] Indle removed Anastasia's clothes and cut off her blonde ponytail before burying her face

down in a grave, under a dirty mattress at an unsanctioned dump on the reservation.

After being questioned and admitting to the murder, Daniel led police to the location, through thick brush, where they recovered Anastasia's corpse.

Indle was arrested the following day and eventually sentenced to 28 years in prison for Anastasia's murder. Her parents subsequently worked with legislators to pass the International Marriage Broker Regulation Act of 2005, which requires background checks for U.S. citizens attempting to bring women into the United States through mail-order bride services. The hope of the law was that the background check could reveal any criminal background or restraining orders filed by previous partners.

* * *

The mail-order bride fantasy is portrayed as a young, obedient, exotic woman who connects with an American man through an online international marriage brokerage (IMB) firm. However, in reality, mail-order brides can be defrauded and deceived into coming to the United States, and subjected to physical and sexual exploitation once they arrive. If a mail-order bride is coerced, deceived, or defrauded into an exploitive situation, she can become a victim of trafficking.

Mail-order brides can be especially vulnerable to sex trafficking due to their immigration status and lack of language skills, deficient employment opportunities, and strained familial support. Consumer spouses who order a bride may believe that they have bought and own a person to control, abuse, and exploit as they please.

For example, take the case of Abeba,[10] who also testified in support of the International Marriage Broker Regulation Act of 2005.

Abeba was born in Addis Ababa, Ethiopia.[11] She was going to college and working part-time when she met a classmate who was involved with an online dating website. Her classmate explained that the men could be pen pals, and she could practice her English.

Abeba eventually began writing to a man who initially described himself as a consultant. A few weeks later, he changed his story and told her that he was a doctor. He explained that he didn't want others to know that he was a doctor because he didn't want a woman only interested in him for money.

After exchanging a few letters, the man began calling Abeba every other day. He told her that he was in love, and Abeba expressed to him that she felt the same way. Eventually, the man began sending her money, clothes, and different kinds of gifts. When he asked Abeba to marry him, she said yes.

After a few months of communicating, the man came to visit Abeba in Ethiopia. She felt that he was handsome, a good Christian, caring, generous, and loving. Her family and friends were so happy for Abeba when she became his wife in an Ethiopian ceremony. It seemed like a blessing.

Abeba's new husband told her that he would apply for a fiancé visa. Although they had already married, he explained that these visas could be processed more quickly. After a few months, she received the application from the American embassy. Her husband filled out the paperwork for her, and Abeba eventually received permission to travel to the United States.

However, after only three days of being in the United States, everything changed. Abeba's husband took her money and identification and began abusing her physically and mentally. He drugged her, so that she would sleep for long periods of time. He would threaten her by showing her scary movies and explaining that in the United States murderers who are rich don't have to go to prison. Abeba thought she was going to die and didn't know what to believe. Her husband told her that if she went outside and the police found her, they would arrest her and put her in jail.

After a few weeks of being tortured and in fear for her life, Abeba decided to look for help. While staying at a motel, she approached the front desk staff and asked them to call the police, who eventually brought her to a women's shelter.

Several days later, her husband committed suicide.

Following her testimony in support of the International Marriage Broker Regulation Act of 2005, Senator Sam Brownback (R)-Kansas explained that Abeba's statement was evidence that her husband brought her to the United States under fraudulent claims and intended only to use her as a sex slave. Subsequently, Abeba was granted a T-visa, which is a nonimmigrant (temporary) visa provided for human trafficking survivors under the Victims of Trafficking and Violence Protection Act (VTVPA).[12]

Experiences like those of Anastasia and Abeba are not isolated. Each year, thousands of women are granted permanent residency visas as a result of reported abuse. However, some claim that these women may be crying wolf, and their husbands are the ones who are being financially exploited by the mail-order bride system through falsified accusations of abuse in order to obtain permanent residency[13] or accepted money and gifts under false pretenses.[14] For example, 69-year-old Jerry Mentzel alleged that his 24-year-old mail-order bride from Tangiers, Morocco, whom he met on RoseBrides.com, scammed him out of $100,000 prior to their two-week marriage.[15] Or take David Brannon, who is one of hundreds of American men who claim their foreign wife exploited the trafficking laws in order to secure T-visas or U-visas, intended for victims of crime. Brannon claimed that his wife falsely alleged that he had threatened and pushed her in order to receive a green card and other benefits.[16] Regardless of whether either claim is true, it is clear that mail-order bride arrangements can breed exploitive situations, which begin with coercion, fraud, and deception.

* * *

The American mail-order bride concept began in the 1600s. Single European women were recruited to immigrate to the colonies and marry surplus bachelors, who were prospecting land and natural resources.[17] At the time, these mail-order brides were referred to as "Jamestown brides," "King's daughters," and "casket girls." They were credited with facilitating the survival and sustainability of the new American colonies. The original settlers had planned to make their fortunes and return to England. By starting families in America, the colonists established the roots that were necessary for the colonies' survival.[18]

Men would place advertisements in newspapers and magazines, and interested women would respond for a relatively short period of time before making the trip to the United States for the wedding. The new brides were offered the opportunity to equally share their husband's wealth and return to England if they should so choose. Colonial mail-order brides enjoyed greater property rights and equality than their contemporaries living in Britain.[19]

Since that time, the mail-order bride dynamic has changed exponentially. While the advertisement process is fundamentally similar—by sharing personal details of attributes and desires—the incentives for procuring a mail-order bride are very different. While prospective husbands in colonial America had once turned toward international advertisements, due to the dearth of local women available for courtship, twenty-first century mail-order bride services generally cater toward male desires for domestic and sexual servitude, as well as obedience from young and physically attractive women.

Currently, there are hundreds of online international marriage brokerage agencies that boast hundreds of thousands of young women from around the world. Although many of these agencies claim to be no different than any other online dating website, statements from consumers of the commercial sex industry suggest a more nefarious intent. The mail-order bride system may be a mechanism for these men to evade law enforcement and procure cheaper and more obedient sexual service.

One commercial sex consumer explained:

> *The police are just a regular part of the milieu of our hobby, akin to static in the background. That is until a political bureaucrat orders the police to crack down on our hobby. Then the hobbyists, the providers, and the intermediaries will feel the pressure of local law-enforcement as they make a symbolic cleanup of the streets.*
>
> *It will be a few more years before I can afford my Eastern European mail-order bride, then I shall take a two-year hiatus as I pay attention to violating her unspoiled body. I chuckle at the thought of me saying "never say never" because I know better than that.*
>
> *24 months is what I estimate it will take me to tire from abusing this young clean tight Eastern European's vagina as I penetrate her with one or possibly two penises in her tight vagina. I am self aware that I am a vile individual, but I laugh in irony.*[20]
>
> —Miami, Florida, September 7, 2016

Although the concept of mail-order brides dates back to the colonial era in the United States, there are some important differences between the practice in the 1600s and mail-order brides today. First, mail-order brides who traveled to the United States during colonial times did so out of necessity. The original settlers were predominately male and, therefore, did not necessarily have the opportunity to find a wife locally. Conversely, men who procure mail-order brides today explain the rationale as being rooted in social and sexual obedience.

Second, mail-order brides in the 1600s were described as enjoying greater freedoms in America than in their country of origin. That is not necessarily the case now. While some modern mail-order brides may experience greater financial stability, they often describe being treated like a slave and living under more intense forms of social control. As such, while the mail-order bride concept may have begun as a mechanism for facilitating the connection of couples who are internationally separated, some now utilize these services as a conduit for procuring a sexual or domestic slave.

Third, during the colonial era mail-order brides were allowed to change their mind and rescind the marital arrangement. They could leave their husband and remain in the United States or return to their home country without harsh consequence. Today's mail-order brides may feel coerced into enduring an emotionally, physically, or socially oppressive relationship because they fear deportation and returning to financial hardship.

Ultimately, while some mail-order brides may find love and/or healthy relationships through international marriage brokerage firms online, the dynamic is also conducive to sex trafficking and other forms of exploitation. While laws such as the International Marriage Broker Regulation Act of 2005 and Trafficking Victims Protection Act attempt to safeguard women from abusive or oppressive relationships in the United States, some countries have taken additional steps to further restrict mail-order bride services. For example, the Senate and House of Representatives of the Philippine Congress passed Republic Act No. 6955, also known as the Anti-Mail Order Spouse Act, which made it illegal to match Filipino women for marriage to foreign nationals on a mail-order basis.[21] The intention of the act was to "prevent the exploitation of Filipinos, and protect them from unlawful practices, businesses, and schemes which offer Filipinos for marriage to unscrupulous foreign nationals and expose them to abuse, exploitation, prostitution, and violent situations." Given the potential for human trafficking through mail-order bride services, other countries should strongly consider following suit.

Notes

1. *Philadelphia Forum* (July 21, 2013): http://www.USASexGuide.info.
2. Lewis Kamb and Robert L. Jamieson Jr., "Mail-Order Bride's Dream of a Better Life Ends in Death," *Seattle Post* (February 2, 2001): https://archive.li /fV0ir.
3. Anne Koch, "A Search for Status and Mail-Order Wives," *The Seattle Times* (February 25, 2001): accessed October 18, 2015, http://community.seattletimes .nwsource.com/archive/?date=20010225&slug=indleking25m0.
4. David Foster, "Slain Bride's Parents Tormented by 'If Onlys,'" *Los Angeles Times* (April 7, 2002): accessed October 18, 2015, http://articles.latimes.com /2002/apr/07/news/mn-36626/2.
5. "Timeline: Anastasia Solovieva and Indle King Jr.," *The Seattle Times* (February 22, 2002): accessed October 18, 2015, http://community.seattletimes .nwsource.com/archive/?date=20020222&slug=timeline22m.
6. Anne Koch, "A Search for Status and Mail-Order Wives," *The Seattle Times* (February 25, 2001): accessed October 18, 2015, http://community.seattletimes .nwsource.com/archive/?date=20010225&slug=indleking25m0.
7. "Timeline: Anastasia Solovieva and Indle King Jr.," *The Seattle Times* (February 22, 2002): accessed October 18, 2015, http://community.seattletimes .nwsource.com/archive/?date=20020222&slug=timeline22m.
8. Ibid.
9. Ibid.
10. Pseudonym was used to protect the identity of the victim.

11. Human Trafficking: Mail-Order Bride Abuses, Pub. L. No. 108–695, §
Subcommittee on East Asian and Pacific Affairs of the Committee on Foreign
Relations United States Senate (2004): accessed March 16, 2017, https://www
.gpo.gov/fdsys/pkg/CHRG-108shrg96804/html/CHRG-108shrg96804.htm.

12. Victims of Human Trafficking: T Nonimmigrant Status. USCIS. Accessed
April 21, 2017, https://www.uscis.gov/humanitarian/victims-human-trafficking
-other-crimes/victims-human-trafficking-t-nonimmigrant-status.

13. Frances McInnis, "A Husband Spurned: Are a Small Number of Immigrant Wives Faking Domestic Abuse to Stay in the Country?" *Slate* (November 8,
2010): accessed March 21, 2017, http://www.slate.com/articles/double_x
/doublex/2010/11/a_husband_spurned.html.

14. Marty Griffin, "Mail-Order Bride Scam Victim Tells His Story to Federal
Agents," *CBS Pittsburgh* (November 4, 2015): accessed October 18, 2015, http://
pittsburgh.cbslocal.com/2015/11/04/mail-order-bride-scam-victim-tells-his
-story-to-federal-agents/.

15. Ibid.

16. Frances McInnis, "A Husband Spurned: Are a Small Number of Immigrant Wives Faking Domestic Abuse to Stay in the Country?" *Slate* (November 8,
2010): accessed November 14, 2016, http://www.slate.com/articles/double_x
/doublex/2010/11/a_husband_spurned.html.

17. Marcia Zug, "Lonely Colonist Seeks Wife: The Forgotten History of America's First Mail-Order Brides," *Duke Journal of Gender Law & Policy,* 20(85) (2012):
85–125.

18. Ibid.

19. Ibid.

20. *Miami Florida Forum* (September 7, 2016): accessed March 13, 2017, http://
www.USASexGuide.info.

21. An Act Providing Stronger Measures Against Unlawful Practices, Businesses, and Schemes of Matching and Offering Filipinos to Foreign Nationals for
Purposes of Marriage or Common Law Partners, Pub. L. No. 10906 (2016).

CHAPTER FOUR

Child Sex Tourism

Stereotypical stories of American sex tourism involve an old, white-male pedophile traveling abroad to molest children. The quintessential culprit is someone like Richard Arthur Schmidt.

In April 1984, Schmidt was 41 years old when he was charged with multiple third- and fourth-degree sex offenses, as well as child abuse and assault and battery in Queen Anne's County, Maryland. After he posted bond, he was again arrested several months later for almost identical crimes in Talbot County, Maryland. This time he was held without bond.

However, Schmidt—a former school teacher—ultimately received only minor punishments for these offenses, which allowed him the freedom to continue violating multiple children in the United States between 1984 and 1986. During those three years, he was charged with fondling and simple assault against children, child abuse and rape, and perverted practices and strong-arm assault in the abuse of a child.[1] He wasn't punished with any remarkable length of incarceration until 1987, when he was sentenced to 18 years in prison after he was convicted of sexual assault and sexual offenses involving a 12-year-old boy. Schmidt served 13 years and was released on parole in 2000.

It didn't take long for him to make unauthorized contact with a minor in violation of his parole. However, before Schmidt could be re-incarcerated in the United States, he traveled to the Philippines in June 2002 and obtained employment as a school instructor. International sex tourism gave Schmidt even greater access to minor victims and the ability to circumvent punishment. A clandestine network of taxi drivers and business owners was used to connect children from indigenous families and remote areas of the

Philippines to sex tourists in areas such as Boracay, Angeles City, Olongapo, Puerto Galera, and Surigao.[2]

Schmidt didn't waste any time in finding young boys to molest. Local authorities quickly arrested him; yet, this wasn't the United States. Access to corrupt judicial officials was more readily available, and Schmidt knew that he could just purchase his freedom whenever he got caught. While on pre-trial release, he again absconded and decided to further minimize his risk of incarceration by continuing his sex tourism in another country.

In December 2003, Schmidt fled to Cambodia where he quickly made friends with several local children, some of whom worked as shoeshine boys. Similar to the Philippines, Cambodian and Vietnamese children were moved from rural areas in Cambodia to tourist destinations, such as Phnom Penh, where these kids were trafficked into brothels or indirect sex establishments, such as beer gardens, massage parlors, salons, or karaoke bars.[3] Some children were sold into the commercial sex trade by their parents in order to pay off a debt,[4] while others were impoverished and/or homeless and engaged in survival sex to meet basic physiological needs.

Schmidt asked the boys to call him "Rick" and invited them to his apartment to play video games and learn English. He gave them money, food, clothing, and toys[5] to help befriend them and gain their trust.

Police in Phnom Penh quickly took notice of the single man traveling alone, as child sex tourism was a critical concern in the region. The local authorities contacted U.S. federal law enforcement[6] after they observed Schmidt, whom they described as a tall, lanky American, socializing with Cambodian children.

Cambodian authorities arrested Schmidt for sex offenses, but he was released on police watch. Two days later, he raped another young boy.[7]

At that point, U.S. federal law enforcement became involved. When the agents arrived to arrest Schmidt on federal charges, he was found with a 12-year-old boy in his riverside guesthouse. The boy later told agents that Schmidt asked him to take a shower and then lay on top of him naked.[8] Upon searching Schmidt's apartment, the agents recovered a digital camera, Sony PlayStation, baseball gloves, and children's clothing. In addition, the agents also found the documentation regarding the child molestation charges against Schmidt in Philippines.[9]

Schmidt was handcuffed to an Immigration and Customs Enforcement agent and extradited back to the United States in February 2004. The U.S. Protect Act allowed Homeland Security agents to pursue him as a child sex tourist and return him to his hometown of Baltimore, Maryland, so that he could be prosecuted in federal court.

Schmidt was indicted on 10 separate charges, but eight of them were eventually dismissed in exchange for his guilty plea for two offenses: (1) travel by U.S. citizen in interstate and foreign commerce with intent to engage in sexual act with a minor and engaging in illicit (2) travel by U.S. citizen in interstate and foreign commerce to engage in illicit sexual conduct with a minor. For these two crimes, which the court described as encompassing "extensive and grotesque sex offenses involving young boys," Schmidt was sentenced to 180 months (15 years) in federal prison. In addition, he was required to be supervised for life, and part of his conditions of post-release supervision included restrictions from owning or using a U.S. passport; owning or using a computer; all contact with minors, especially males; coming within one mile of a school; and possessing any child or adult pornography.

* * *

Child sex tourists abuse both young girls and boys,[10] but regardless of their gender preference, these men are typically chronophiles, meaning that they are attracted to children who fall within a specific age range. For example, a nepiophile or infantophile is a sex tourist who is attracted to infants and toddlers aged zero to three, and a hebephile is a sex tourist who is attracted to children in the midst of puberty, aged 11 to 15. A considerable proportion of pedophiles are attracted to children ages four to 10 years.

According to the United Nations International Children's Emergency Fund (UNICEF), over 1.2 million children are trafficked each year, most of them into the commercial sex trade.[11] Americans who travel to developing countries to engage in commercial sex acts with children fuel the child sex tourism (CST) industry. Some child-advocacy groups estimate that as many as 25 percent of all sex tourists abroad come from the United States.[12] Cases have been brought against various successful businessmen, such as a pediatrician, a retired Army sergeant, a dentist, and a university professor. Developing countries are targeted by these sex tourists, who are looking for anonymity and the availability of children in prostitution. The devastating consequences for the victimized minors include long-lasting physical and psychological trauma, disease (including HIV/AIDS), drug addiction, unwanted pregnancy, social ostracism, and possibly death.

Sex tourism is also fueled by weak law enforcement and corruption. Previously, U.S. authorities could not intervene unless they could prove that the international predator ventured into another country with the intent to harm or molest a minor. The Protect Act, which was signed by

President George W. Bush on April 30, 2003,[13] waived the intent require-
ment, making it so that a pedophile could be prosecuted on U.S. soil if it
could be proven that he or she had attempted to have sex with a child in
another country.

Despite this advancement in international policy, offenders still do not
necessarily receive particularly harsh punishments, given the severity of
their crimes. For example, 70-year-old military veteran Michael Lewis
Clark was the first American convicted under the Protect Act. In June 2003,
local authorities arrested Clark in Cambodia for engaging in illegal sexual
activity with two boys, aged 10 and 13.[14]

Clark had resided primarily in Cambodia since 1998 but would take
annual trips back to the United States, where he maintained real estate, as
well as bank and investment accounts. He would also use his trips home
to the United States as opportunities to visit with family.

Following his yearly trip in May 2003, Clark returned to Cambodia,
where he came to the attention of Action Pour Les Enfants, a nongovernmental organization (NGO) whose mission is to rescue minor boys who
have been sexually molested by non-Cambodians. According to the organization, some of the street kids reported Clark was regularly molesting
young boys.

On June 28, 2003, a member of the NGO observed Clark take two
boys from the riverfront of Phnom Penh to a local guest room, prompting
them to alert the Cambodian National Police.

After the police arrived at the guesthouse and knocked on the door,
Clark answered, before attempting to shut the door on them. The police
ended up forcing their way inside, where they discovered Clark with the
two boys, whom were all naked. He was charged with debauchery in
Cambodia before the U.S. federal government took jurisdiction.[15]

On July 11, 2003, Immigration and Customs Enforcement (ICE) Deputy Attaché Gary Phillips, who was stationed in Bangkok, Thailand, was
informed of Clark's arrest. One week later, he and other colleagues from
ICE and the U.S. Embassy in Phnom Penh interviewed Clark's victims.

The 10-year-old boy told the agents that he was homeless when he met
Clark through his friend.

According to the child, Clark directed the 13-year-old boy to lie on his
back and then kneeled on top of him before instructing the boy masturbate
him with his hand. At the same time, the 10-year-old boy was instructed to
insert his index finger in Clark's anus. This activity continued until Clark
ejaculated onto the 13-year-old boy's chest.

The 13-year-old boy corroborated the information provided by the
10-year-old. In addition, three other teenage boys came forward, stating

that Clark had sexually engaged them on multiple occasions, by instructing them to lie on a bed, kneeling above, and masturbating until he ejaculated onto each boy's chest.

Ten days after interviewing the boys, ICE agents met with Clark under the supervision of the Department of Prisons in Phnom Penh. Although he initially denied being a pedophile, Clark later admitted that he had been involved in sexual activity with children aged 10 to 18 years since he began traveling in 1996.

Clark stated that he paid the boys $2 each for engaging in sexual activity with him and corroborated the boys' accounts of what had occurred on June 28, 2003. In addition, he also admitted to showering with the boys, instructing them to lather soap on his rectal area, and rubbing soap on their rectal areas. Clark stated that he told the boys to dry themselves off with a towel and get on the bed in the room before engaging them as the children had described. He also attempted to coerce the 13-year-old to perform oral sex on him, but the child refused.

In addition to those crimes, Clark eventually confessed that he had molested as many as 50 children since 1996, and in recent years, he may have caused more serious damage to some of his victims. He also admitted that he attempted to bribe a Cambodian judge with $3,500 in order to obtain his release and had already made a $500 down payment to initiate this process at the time of his interview with ICE agents.

After his confession, Clark was extradited to Seattle in March 2004.

According to his indictment, Clark was only officially charged with two crimes: (1) travel in foreign commerce and engaging in illicit sexual conduct with a minor for directing the 10-year-old victim to digitally penetrate Clark's anus and (2) travel in foreign commerce and engaging in illicit sexual conduct with a minor for instructing the 13-year-old victim to masturbate Clark by touching his penis with the young boy's hand.[16]

Clark pleaded guilty to both counts, and for these crimes, he was only sentenced to 97 months (approximately eight years) in federal prison and five years of supervised release thereafter.

While jurisdictional barriers, stark economic disparities, and pervasive judicial corruption continue to impede efforts to combat child sex tourism in countries such as the Philippines and Cambodia, the burgeoning illicit online marketplace for commercially sexually exploited children has added an additional complexity to this scourge affecting kids from around the world. For example, NGOs and other anti-trafficking nonprofits describe a pervasive issue of very young Filipino children being sold by family members and coerced into performing sex acts, filmed in private residences or small Internet cafés, for live broadcasts to paying foreigners around the world.[17] However, in 2015, only 42 people were convicted for human trafficking in the Philippines, of which five were for online child sex trafficking.[18]

In order to better address the issue of child sex trafficking and tourism online, NGOs have begun to implement innovative undercover sting operations. For example, Terre des Hommes, an international organization that develops and implements projects designed to improve the living conditions of disadvantaged children,[19] designed a computer avatar of a 10-year-old Filipino girl, whom they called "Sweetie," and used her to infiltrate online commercial sex forums and entrap international sex tourists online. In a little over two months, Terre des Hommes documented the interactions of over 20,000 men attempting to coax their avatar of a little girl into taking off her clothing for money via webcam.[20] From these virtual interactions, the company was able to provide law enforcement with the virtual identity of more than 1,000 men from approximately 70 countries.[21]

Notes

1. Lynn Anderson and Michael James, "New U.S. Law Puts Maryland Man in Court as 'Sex Tourist,'" *The Baltimore Sun* (February 29, 2004): accessed July 6, 2017, http://articles.baltimoresun.com/2004-02-20/news/0402200073_1_predator -homeland-cambodia.

2. Office to Monitor and Combat Trafficking in Persons. Philippines. U.S. Department of State 2016 Trafficking in Persons Report. Accessed July 6, 2017, https://www.state.gov/j/tip/rls/tiprpt/countries/2016/258843.htm.

3. Office to Monitor and Combat Trafficking in Persons. Cambodia. U.S. Department of State 2016 Trafficking in Persons Report. Accessed July 6, 2017, https://www.state.gov/documents/organization/258878.pdf.

4. Tim Hume, Lisa Cohen, and Mira Sorvino, *The Women Who Sold Their Daughters into Sex Slavery.* CNN (2013).

5. Anderson and James, "New U.S. Law Puts Maryland Man in Court as 'Sex Tourist.'"

6. U.S. authorities are designated to investigate suspected acts of child sex tourism.

7. *United States v. Richard Arthur Schmidt,* No. 16–6567 (U.S. Court of Appeals, Fourth Circuit, January 4, 2017).

8. Anderson and James, "New U.S. Law Puts Maryland Man in Court as 'Sex Tourist.'"

9. Ibid.

10. Depending on the area, as much as 50 percent of sex tourism can be committed against boys.

11. UNICEF. Fact Sheet on Commercial Sexual Exploitation and Trafficking of Children. (n.d.): accessed July 6, 2017, https://www.unicef.org/indonesia /Factsheet_CSEC_trafficking_Indonesia.pdf.

12. Eric Lichtblau and James Dao, "U.S. Is Now Pursuing Americans Who Commit Sex Crimes Overseas," *The New York Times* (June 8, 2004): accessed July 6, 2017, http://www.nytimes.com/2004/06/08/us/us-is-now-pursuing-americans -who-commit-sex-crimes-overseas.html.

13. Orrin Hatch. Prosecutorial Remedies and Other Tools to End the Exploitation of Children Today Act of 2003, Pub. L. No. 108–21 (2003): accessed July 6, 2017, https://www.congress.gov/bill/108th-congress/senate-bill/151.

14. *United States of America v. Michael Lewis Clark,* No. 04-30249 (U.S. Court of Appeals, Ninth Circuit, January 25, 2006).

15. Ibid.

16. *United States of America v. Michael Lewis Clark,* No. CR03-0406L (U.S. District Court, Seattle, Washington, April 26, 2004): accessed July 2, 2017, http:// www.leagle.com/decision/20041442315FSupp2d1127_11345/U.S.%20v.%20 CLARK.

17. Office to Monitor and Combat Trafficking in Persons. Philippines. U.S. Department of State 2016 Trafficking in Persons Report. Accessed July 6, 2017, https://www.state.gov/j/tip/rls/tiprpt/countries/2016/258843.htm.

18. Ibid.

19. "Home." Terre des Hommes. Accessed July 6, 2017, http://www.terrede shommes.org.

20. Angus Crawford, "Computer-Generated 'Sweetie' Catches Online Predators," *BBC News* (November 5, 2013): accessed July 6, 2017, http://www.bbc.com /news/uk-24818769.

21. Ibid.

CHAPTER FIVE

Adult Sex Tourism

In addition to sex tourism for children, many American men travel abroad to procure sex with adult women. While some of these women may be consenting sex workers, others are victims of sex trafficking who are being forced, defrauded, coerced, or deceived into sexual exploitation. The average hobbyist or monger, as they call themselves, cannot tell the difference between a victim of sex trafficking and a consenting prostitute, or even if they can, they typically don't care.

One sex tourist in Manila, Philippines explained,

> Mongering is basically finding poor desperate women in failed states and fucking them on your terms. Take these same women out of their impoverished hopeless environment and bring them to your countries in the west and then try your luck with them . . . Mongering involves exploiting weakness and despair. The levels of exploitation vary on the degree of deviancy among individual mongers but at the end of the day every monger is just an individual part of the international mongering machine, a machine whose individual parts share and analyze information on where to find these vulnerable women and fuck the shit out of them for the lowest possible price much like the circuitry in a central processing unit. Unlike a CPU there are no rules or algorithms when it comes to mongers' behavior. Each individual does what he pleases as far as the circumstances and the girls will permit . . . It's hardly a game between gentlemen and ladies. Sometimes the hooker will win and rob or extort the monger, and other times the monger will get away with giving the girl a bareback cream pie or running off without paying as agreed. It's a predator and prey relationship with interchanging roles.[1]

Despite the oftentimes inherently exploitive nature of international adult sex tourism, the practice is often discussed as a "boys will be boys" indiscretion. Although incidents involving public figures soliciting commercial sex services abroad are perceived as an embarrassment, there is an element of gendered acceptance. This sentiment may be a testament to the evolving public opinion on sex work between consenting adults.

In recent years, there have been several high-profile examples of public figures patronizing commercial sex workers abroad. For example, DeAndre Jordan, DeMarcus Cousins, DeMar Derozan, and possibly others from the 2016 U.S. Olympic basketball team made international headlines when pictures of them surfaced inside a well-known brothel in Brazil—Termas Monte Carlo.[2] Although the players claimed they had no idea that the business was a brothel, men posting on commercial sex websites didn't believe them. According to the commercial sex customers online, it is unlikely for someone to walk into that business without knowing it's a brothel, especially considering that there is no signage in front of the establishment.

> *Right! They went here by "mistake." Of course that makes sense, especially since they are staying on a luxury cruise liner. I'm sure there are "spas" on the boat LOL![3]*
> —Anonymous Sex Tourist in Brazil, August 6, 2016

Moreover, some commercial sex patrons online alleged that this was not the first time that U.S. athletes had frequented brothels in Brazil.

> *Does anyone else remember that time period, maybe 2002–2004 when you would always see Pro US athletes in L'uomo, Monte Carlo and Centaurus? They were like the proverbial bull in a china shop. They would give you the head nod like you just think you see me here trying to fit into this robe or wearing my street clothes because no termas robe in the world is going to fit on my 6'9" oversize frame.[4]*
> —Anonymous Sex Tourist in Brazil, August 6, 2016

Ultimately, the Olympic athlete brothel scandal quickly receded from headlines. Despite speculation, there was no way to prove that the athletes knew it was a brothel, much less had purchased commercial sex services. However, there were many other Americans who visited Brazil for the Olympics and were intent on procuring sexual services.

> *The Olympics is about to start and there were a lot of mongers announcing they were going to Rio. It would be nice to read some reports about the monger situation in Copacabana.[5]*
> —Anonymous Sex Tourist in Brazil, August 5, 2016

Internationally, high-end brothels are glamorized, and it is assumed that all of the girls working at these establishments are consenting and aren't being exploited. As such, celebrities feel comfortable patronizing these businesses. For example, on November 1, 2013, Justin Bieber was pictured exiting a Brazilian brothel named Centaurus.[6]

Another example of high-profile American commercial sex patronage involved Secret Service agents in Cartagena, Colombia, in 2012. According to media reports, although Secret Service agent Arthur Huntington was married to his wife of almost 20 years, who homeschooled their two teenage sons and ran a neighborhood Bible-study group, he regularly engaged in extramarital affairs.[7]

Huntington landed in Colombia on April 11, 48 hours before President Barack Obama was scheduled to arrive in Cartagena. After checking into Hotel Caribe, he headed out with colleagues for dinner before making their way to club Tu Candela. There, 41-year-old Huntington met 24-year-old Dania Suarez, a high-end escort whom he decided to bring back to his room. During the ride home, he stopped at a store to purchase condoms, and Suarez explained the fee for her sexual services—$800.[8]

Upon arriving at the hotel, Suarez and Huntington engaged in sexual intercourse in his room before falling asleep.

The next day, Suarez requested her payment, but Huntington refused and claimed he didn't know that she was a sex worker. Instead, she alleged that he provided her with only about $30 in local currency and yelled, "Let's go, bitch. I'm not going to pay you," while shoving her out of the hotel room door.[9]

Suarez was furious. She began yelling and threatened to call the police, prompting Huntington's colleague Joe Bongino, who was also married and had slept with a local that night, to emerge from his room. In attempt to resolve the issue discretely, Bongino went from room to room, asking other agents for "scoots," the term they use for local currency, or any U.S. dollars they could spare. Bongino came up with $250 in mixed currency and gave it to Suarez, which satisfied her enough to leave the hotel without further incident.[10]

Eventually, the media was alerted to the transgression, and during the investigation that followed, it was discovered that nine men paid or solicited prostitutes, including two Secret Service supervisors. Shadowing the debacle, the Secret Service issued 10 new rules governing conduct on trips, including not drinking alcohol within 10 hours of duty and not visiting "nonreputable establishments."[11] However, this hasn't stopped members of the Secret Service from procuring commercial sex services in the United States and abroad.

For example, reports surfaced alleging that Secret Service members solicited sex workers in Puerto Rico and Amsterdam in 2014,[12] and a member of Vice President Mike Pence's Secret Service detail was allegedly suspended by the agency after he was charged with soliciting a prostitute in Maryland in late March 2017.[13]

While these situations brought international attention to the concept of sex tourism, they may have involved consenting sex workers instead of sex trafficked victims. However, the reality is that every day American men are obtaining sexual services from women in underdeveloped countries around the world. Although international sex tourism is often publicly framed through the lenses of sexual freedom and legality, sex trafficking situations, especially in underdeveloped nations, are ubiquitous.

At times, sex tourists will describe evidence of physical abuse on the women, such as burns and scars. Other men will describe women being drugged. Even in situations that may seem superficially consensual, there is a larger question of financial coercion that can lead to trafficking and sexual exploitation. Reading about the depravity involved with some of these encounters, which come directly from the men who claim to procure these services, illustrates this concept of exploitation through financial coercion and exposes the apathy toward clear indications of abuse.

The following provides first-hand accounts and opinions of English-speaking sex tourists, including Americans, who purchased sexual services with women around the world.

On international forums, such as InternationalSexGuide.info, sex tourists often describe demeaning acts with women; for example, forcing the women, whom they referred to as "the help" or "sex slaves," to eat bread covered in semen from various men, as well as defecating or urinating on the women. Others describe stretching orifices to the point of causing soft tissue tears and inflicting pain in other fashions. In addition to degrading treatment, some women were lied to about the use of prophylactics, which contributed to the growing number of children fathered by sex tourists.[14]

According to one sex tourist in Bangkok, Thailand,

> "Rice growers" will do anything for money. Just give 'em a bit more, and you can abuse them against their wishes . . . When someone says "I will take care of her," it means that he is going to offer more money and make it financially worth her while to do whatever he wanted to do.[15]

Sex tourists in the Philippines, Thailand, Indonesia, Japan, and China reported multiple women with similar signs of abuse, such as cigarette burn marks on their backs, shoulders, wrists, and breasts, as well as knife wounds on their arms and buttocks. Some men speculated that pimps or traffickers caused the wounds, while others claimed they were self-inflicted during bouts of depression. Yet, despite the clear and concerning evidence of abuse or self-harm, many of these men still took advantage and purchased cheap sexual services from the women.

While there was some variation in the types of sexual experiences reported, international sex tourists often describe procuring or attempting to obtain services without condoms, such as BBBJ[16] and/or BBFS.[17] From the outside looking in, the lack of desire to use protection with commercial sex workers may seem counterintuitive. However, many sex tourists are not particularly afraid of contracting sexually transmitted diseases from sex workers for several reasons. First, they believe the statistical probability of men contracting a serious STD from engaging in heterosexual sex with a woman is extremely low.

One sex tourist asserted,

> A man has a 1 in 214 chance of contracting HIV from an HIV-positive female from heterosexual unprotected sex, while a woman has a 1 in 14 chance of contracting the virus from unprotected sex with an HIV positive man.[18]

Many of these men were not concerned with the health of the sex worker and, therefore, were willing to forego protection, especially since they would most likely not be legally or financially responsible for any child that may be conceived.

Second, multiple sex tourists described rituals for attempting to minimize the likelihood of infection, such as washing, urinating, or pouring alcohol on their genitals post-coitus. Given these beliefs, although the women would frequently attempt to use protection, many sex tourists would coerce them with money to omit condom use.

Even if a sex worker adamantly objects to unprotected sex, some men reported removing the condom mid-coitus without her knowledge or consent—an act termed "stealthing." While some commercial sex consumers feel that stealthing is a form of rape, others believe that "when a provider accepts money for sex, it is never rape."[19] When and if the sex worker discovers the protection is gone, the hobbyist will deny responsibility by telling her that it accidentally came off during sex, typically in a "doggie-style" position. As a result, despite deceiving the sex worker and forcing the nature of the sexual interaction upon her, the commercial sex consumer will typically be treated as innocent of wrongdoing, while the sex worker is left to deal with any resulting sexually transmitted diseases or unintended pregnancies.

While some men portrayed the sexual acts as occurring with willing and enthusiastic women, others described less than consensual experiences, suggesting human trafficking. For example, one sex tourist in Yogyakarta, Indonesia, claimed to have ventured through "a warren of dark grimy alleys, seemingly of misery and despair" to a "dingy, dark hovel," where he had sex with woman who laid there like " 'starfish,' wincing."

Or take the experience of this sex tourist, who picked up a girl from an expat bar called TopGun in Jakarta, Indonesia. He claimed, "She had cigarette burn marks all over her breasts and ass."[20] When he asked who had victimized her, all she could muster in English was, "Bad man."

Typically, when sex tourists encounter situations of suspected trafficking, they turn the other cheek despite the red flags. At best, they refuse to engage with the victim sexually, pay her for her time, and send her on her way. At worst, they sexually exploit the woman and speculate about who had perpetrated the abuse (boyfriend/husband, pimp, or mamasan) after the fact. Regardless, sex tourists traditionally do not care to become involved for various reasons.

In fact, many commercial sex consumers are disbelieving of the hardship and abuse faced by the sex workers. Instead, they accuse the women of fabricating stories for sympathy money.

For example, one sex tourist, who I'll refer to as James, obtained services from a young woman in Bandung, Indonesia, who told him that she had just recovered from a coma, after going over a cliff in a bus. She explained that it was a very bad accident, and her best friend had been killed. "Riiiiight!! Tell the dick cos' the heart don't wanna know," he thought. In his words, all he wanted to do was, "spray paint her larynx."[21] Once back at the hotel, she performed fellatio on him, which he described as being done "hammer and tongs." However, during the sexual act, he grabbed the back of her head and three feet of hair came off in his hands.

That was when he came to the realization that she was telling the truth and had been in a coma. There was a six-inch gash in her scalp, with cotton sewn in, and 30 to 40 stitches to prove it.

Unfortunately, men like James, who claimed to have been an active monger in Asia and the Middle East for over a decade, don't have much empathy for commercial sex workers, even if they are victims. They may be resistant to accepting the harsh realities faced by the women they purchase sexual services from due to the cognitive dissonance that could result. Alternatively, they may be fully aware of the heartening circumstances that befall these women, but they just don't care.

For example, another sex tourist described acquiring sexual services from a woman in Calcutta, India, who fell victim to circumstance and was financially coerced into the commercial sex industry. Upon entering the small, dirty bedroom where they were supposed to have sex, the woman revealed to him that she had once been a supervisor in Mumbai. Due to her spondylitis, however, she had to leave her job. She physically could not continue working on a computer. After a series of failed attempts to find gainful employment thereafter, she ended up in Paritosh Den—a budget brothel. "Such is life," she said, as her voice cracked. With a smile on her face and a tear unspilled in her eye, she explained, "Once I had everything in life, see where I ended up."

However, the customer could not have cared less. Her unfortunate life story had eaten away 15 of the 30 minutes he had paid for sex with her. So, the sex tourist told her to undress and proceeded to "manhandle" her body "before banging her with full force with her legs up to her shoulders."

Upon completion, according to the sex tourist, he "had the decency to wipe the tear that had rolled by her eyes. Still a smile on her face."[22]

Another dynamic that sex tourists seem to pay little or no attention to is the fact that many international commercial sex industries have women imported from other countries and rotate them out every few months. Although prima facie this may not seem alarming, it could be a red flag for sex trafficking. Women from impoverished nations who do not speak the language in their country of residence and have no social support system tend to be more exploitable.

For example, one sex tourist in Volgograd, Russia, described procuring services with African girls.

> When I got there, a Russian woman was there, along with two African girls. Seems like she was in charge of them. After minor chat with the Russian, she took me to a different room with the bed, locked the door and started undressing . . . She reached for a condom in her handbag, but I convinced her to go raw . . . and ended with CIM.[23]
>
> Sometime later I went to the place again for the African. This time there was only one African and three other Russians (including the Russian from earlier) . . . (The) African girl . . . was mostly lying on the bed and not moving, then telling me you can't touch there, here, etc . . . When I was done and headed for the bathroom, there were two Russian men in the living room. It seems they were waiting for the African. And one of the Russian women (who looked like the leader) was telling the African in a loud and angry tone to hurry up and get prepared. I kind of felt sorry for her. Never went back to the place.[24]

According to online reports, Chinese women were found in the commercial sex industry in areas around the world, including Afghanistan,

Iraq, and Spain. Women from Serbia, Romania, Bulgaria, Austria, Spain, Moldova, Argentina, Poland, Hungary, and Czech Republic were found in the FKK sex clubs in Germany. Sexual services from Thai women could be purchased in countries around the world, including South Africa and India. Women from Ukraine, Uzbekistan, Lithuania, and Nigeria were found in the commercial sex trade in Dubai, while women from Uzbekistan and Tanzania could be purchased in Abu Dhabi. However, despite the international diversity of women involved in the commercial sex trade, few sex tourists question the immigration patterns, much less the social and financial isolation that may accompany the expatriation.

Instead, international commercial sex consumers focus on the services that could be purchased at each location, with the most beautiful woman, at the cheapest price.

To brag about the breadth of their experiences, numerous men would routinely take pictures of their sexual conquests in various stages of undress. Many of the women appeared to be aware of the photographs, while others may have been photographed secretly without their consent.

For example, one sex tourist in Ukraine posted topless pictures of a young blonde woman wearing white underwear and dark sunglasses. The photos depicted her in various positions—bending over on a bed and sitting, as well as with her legs open on a chair.

In response to the post, another sex tourist inquired, "What the heck has happened to that girl? She has some pretty severe scars right across the chest and arm. Victim of domestic violence?"

In response, the sex tourist who copulated her wrote,

> *Katya would not allow her uncle any child-buggering privileges, so instead, she became his human ashtray and personal carving board.*
>
> *Fortunately, her abuser spared her face, breasts, ass, and genitals, so she was a perfect pleasure to spend a few evenings with. The sunglasses were supposed to hide her identity, though the scars will certainly be a give-away, if anyone else can peg her.*[25]

Given the fact that many of these women appeared to be survivors of various forms of abuse, it is not surprising that multiple sex tourists described instances in which the women recoiled from touch and were recalcitrant to certain sexual requests.

For example, an American sex tourist in Prague described acquiring services from a 24-year-old Czech girl with long black hair. Initially, he described her as being standoffish before giving him a BBBJ in the shower. When he flipped her over and began kissing her breasts and stomach, he said that she began squeezing her legs together and became "fidgety" and "uncomfortable." In response, he "stopped and yelled at her that if she doesn't want kissing or licking anywhere on her body just fucking say so before we get up here." After which, he bragged that he took it out on her, "just rammed the poor girl hard . . . Not really enjoying it, but fuck her. I'm paying you, you lied (and) don't want to do anything. Let her have it."[26]

Many sex tourists perceive that any and every sex act can be purchased for the right price. These men recognize that they have the upper hand for value and availability in economically depressed nations, which is why they travel overseas. Each illicit exchange is typically treated as binding and enforceable by hook or crook.

Although some sex tourists will try to convince themselves that they are buying sexual services with a fully consenting participant, the reality is that women entering the sex trade in or from economically depressed countries often don't have the agency to truly make that choice.

One French sex tourist in Germany explained,

> Don't (tell) me they choose, but they are obliged because they were born in poor country: Romania, Bulgaria, Moldova, and they may have to (feed) children or to help family because of alcoholic or left father or most often to give money to BF/pimp to buy his car. Unfortunately, I can't change the world. I can just try to help my favs . . . Not their choice but "C'est la vie" as say Romanian girls about their life, so far from their child dreams.[27]

Even in areas like Germany, which is said to have gone through a sexual revolution leading to the legalization and regulation of prostitution, women are being imported from third-world countries to satiate the sometimes-taboo or sadistic sexual needs of tourists for the most economical price.

Germany's FKK clubs are described as upscale brothels that boast pools, saunas, excellent food, and gorgeous young women from around the world. Their existence is supported in part by the premise that legalizing and regulating commercial sex reduces sex trafficking, since both sex workers and consumers would theoretically choose to work for—and patronize—legitimate proprietors. This is called a replacement effect.

However, available evidence suggests that the legalization of prostitution results in an opposite, scale effect. This basically means that expanding the prostitution market increases the illicit sex trafficking market as well. One study examining the impact of legalized prostitution on human trafficking inflows in 150 countries concluded that countries where prostitution is legal experience a higher incidence of human trafficking.[28] As such, it is more likely that the FKK clubs in Germany have created a protective veneer for sex trafficking enterprises, allowing them to exploit women with even greater impunity.

Ultimately, it is important to understand that not everything is as it seems in the commercial sex industry. Although a sex worker may appear to be consenting, there are a number of factors that could contribute to her exploitation through force, fraud, coercion, or deception. While prostitution should not be legalized[29] because of its positive impact on the sex trafficking market, decriminalizing[30] sex workers and providing social services to this marginalized population could assist in empowering these women in standing up against situations of abuse.

Notes

1. *Forum in Manila, Philippines* (October 31, 2011): accessed July 6, 2017, http://www.InternationalSexGuide.info.

2. Mike Matvey, "DeMarcus Cousins, DeMar DeRozan, and DeAndre Jordan, and Maybe More USA Basketball Players, Showed Up at Rio Brothel," *NY Daily News* (August 5, 2016): accessed July 6, 2017, http://www.nydailynews.com/sports/basketball/trio-usa-basketball-players-showed-rio-brothel-article-1.2740295.

3. *Forum in Rio de Janeiro, Brazil.* (August 6, 2016): accessed July 6, 2017, http://www.InternationalSexGuide.info.

4. Ibid.

5. *Forum in Rio de Janeiro, Brazil.* (August 5, 2016): accessed July 6, 2017, http://www.InternationalSexGuide.info.

6. Amos Barshad, "The World Cup of Dirty Dreams: Inside Brazil's Most Infamous Brothel," *Rolling Stone* (June 26, 2014): accessed July 6, 2017, http://www.rollingstone.com/culture/news/the-world-cup-of-dirty-dreams-inside-brazils-most-infamous-brothel-20140626?utm_source=email.

7. Shane Harris, "Secret Service Prostitution Scandal: One Year Later," *The Washingtonian* (March 25, 2013): accessed July 6, 2017, https://www.washingtonian.com/2013/03/25/secret-service-prostitution.

8. Ibid.

9. Ibid.

10. Ibid.

11. Ibid.

12. Khaleda Rahman, "Secret Service Sex Scandals Revealed Four Years after Colombia," *Daily Mail Online* (July 21, 2016): accessed July 6, 2017, http://www.dailymail.co.uk/news/article-3701926/Secret-Service-sex-scandals-revealed-four-years-Colombia.html.

13. Elizabeth Landers, Mary Kay Mallonee, and Peter Morris, "First on CNN: Secret Service Agent on VP's Detail Caught after Meeting with Prostitute at Maryland Hotel," CNN (April 6, 2017): accessed July 6, 2017, http://www.cnn.com/2017/04/05/politics/secret-service-agent-prostitute-maryland-hotel/index.html.

14. Dave Tacon, "Philippines' Generation of Sex Tourism Children," Aljazeera (March 12, 2015): accessed July 6, 2017, http://www.aljazeera.com/indepth/inpictures/2015/03/philippines-generation-sex-tourism-children-150305120628971.html.

15. *Forum in Bangkok, Thailand.* (March 31, 2010): accessed July 6, 2017, http://www.InternationalSexGuide.info.

16. Bare back blow job. See Appendix A for more information.

17. Bare back full service. See Appendix A for more information.

18. Accessed July 6, 2017, http://www.InternationalSexGuide.info.

19. Bareback Beauties Forum in Los Angeles, California. (April 26, 2017): accessed July 6, 2017, http://www.USASexGuide.info.

20. *2003–2006 Photo Gallery.* (May 21, 2006): accessed July 6, 2017, http://www.InternationalSexGuide.info.

21. *2002–2006 Jakarta Reports.* (June 25, 2004): accessed July 6, 2017, http://www.InternationalSexGuide.info.

22. *Calcutta Forum.* (May 12, 2014): accessed July 6, 2017, http://www.InternationalSexGuide.info.

23. Cum in mouth. See Appendix A for more information.

24. *Volgograd Forum.* (November 17, 2014): accessed July 6, 2017, http://www.InternationalSexGuide.info.

25. *Ukraine Photo Gallery.* (July 19, 2009): accessed July 6, 2017, http://www.InternationalSexGuide.info.

26. *Prague Forum.* (November 20, 2012): accessed July 6, 2017, http://www.InternationalSexGuide.info.

27. *Germany FKK Forum.* (August 8, 2015): accessed July 6, 2017, http://www.InternationalSexGuide.info.

28. Seo-Young Cho, Axel Dreher, and Eric Neumayer, "Does Legalized Prostitution Increase Human Trafficking?" *World Development* 41 (January 2013): 67–82.

29. Legalization is when a particular criminal activity is no longer against the law.

30. Decriminalization is when an activity is illegal, but the punishment is not as severe, or police may use their discretion more frequently and "turn a blind eye" to the practice. In this case, I am suggesting that sex workers should be decriminalized, so that they would be more inclined to report the men and women who may exploit or abuse them.

CHAPTER SIX

Human Trafficker Deployment

At DynCorp International it is our commitment to conduct business honestly, ethically and in accordance with best practices and the applicable laws of the U.S. and other countries in which we operate. We are guided at all times by the highest standards of integrity, whether dealing with customers, co-workers or others.[1]

—DynCorp International Website

Texan Ben Johnston, a six-year Army veteran, did what many former military men do after they complete their service; he went to work for a top government contracting firm—DynCorp. For over 50 years, DynCorp had provided maintenance support for the U.S. military through contract field teams and was one of the federal government's top 25 contractors, securing $2 billion per year in funding.[2]

Ben began a three-year U.S. Air Force contract with DynCorp as an aircraft-maintenance technician for Apache and Blackhawk helicopters at U.S. Army Camp Comanche in Tuzla, Bosnia.[3] He quickly realized that many of his co-workers were different from him; some of the men were lazy or incompetent, and others were unprofessional, occasionally coming to work intoxicated. Ben ignored the exposure to what he perceived as pervasive government fraud, waste, and abuse, until one day in early 2000.

Johnson began seeing his co-workers out on the streets of Dubrave, at company functions, and at corporate dinners with very young girls.[4] He learned that these girls weren't from Bosnia. Human trafficking syndicates were importing the adolescents from Russia, Romania, and other countries, specifically for DynCorp employees and the Serbian mafia.[5] Ben recoiled with disgust as he listened to one of his fellow helicopter mechanics brag about a preteen he had purchased from a local brothel. "My girl's not a day over 12," said the man in his 60s, by Johnston's estimate.[6] The U.S. military contractors were allegedly purchasing the teens for $600 to $800.[7]

Johnston later complained to managers at DynCorp and the Army Criminal Investigation Command (CIC), but instead of intervening, the Reston, Virginia-based military contracting firm fired Ben. News of the incident became public in 2002 when Johnston settled his wrongful termination lawsuit for an undisclosed sum of money.

Johnston's settlement came within hours of DynCorp losing its first whistleblowing case, filed by Kathryn Bolkovac. In 1999, while Bolkovac was working in a police station in Bosnia as part of a U.N. mission, she came across an international sex trafficking operation. Girls from Ukraine and Moldova, among other countries, were lured away with false promises of working as a waitress, a maid, or a nanny before being humiliated, beaten, and raped into dead-eyed submission in the commercial sex trade.[8]

Not only did Bolkovac discover that this was happening, but she also uncovered that peacekeepers were purchasing sexual services with the women and facilitating their exploitation. Bosnian and U.N. police, including DynCorp employees, were patronizing the brothels where these women were being trafficked. Some were even employed by the traffickers, receiving compensation for giving warnings on raids and returning girls who had escaped.[9] Shortly after Bolkovac reported her discoveries, she was terminated for allegedly filing falsified time sheets.

Although both Ben Johnston's and Kathryn Bolkovac's whistleblowing on the illegal activities of DynCorp employees ended with their vindication and a substantiation of their claims,[10] it failed to curb the abuse of sex-trafficked women by military contractors. Eight years later, illegal activity within DynCorp was exposed again when an employee was shot and killed while traveling in an unsecure car, performing a high-risk mission in Iraq.[11] His death was attributed to a site manager who had misappropriated an armored car to transport prostitutes from Kuwait to Baghdad hotels operated by DynCorp.

Ultimately, it isn't rare for peacekeepers to engage in sex tourism, and it isn't limited to government contractors either. The U.S. Military has a very long and troubled history of members engaging in sex tourism overseas. Although it could be assumed that supporting sex trafficking through consumerism or protection would tarnish the reputation of military and government contractors whose employees engage in these activities, there are often very little or no consequences. For example, despite the three public instances discussed above involving DynCorp employees' engagement with sex trafficking consumerism, the company received $2.5 billion of the nearly $4 billion spent by the State Department for Afghan reconstruction from 2002 to 2013.[12] In fact, they continue to receive government contracts to this day.

* * *

I spent a year in Kosovo—the worst place I have ever been, including Iraq—and can proffer the following advice for booty:

Kosovo is truly the asshole of Europe. Women can be had at Ferazi and some other shady ass places around Prishtina, but the girls there have been trafficked, and if you are caught you can kiss your contractor or UNMIK[13] job good bye. That's why I'd recommend whoring in Macedonia for short time needs. It's expensive, like 300 a night, but its safe. I stayed in the Tomska Sofia and always got top quality gals.

If you can get down to Sofia, do it. It's about four hours away and the brothel girls there are 25 bucks an hour if u ditch the taxi driver.

Maybe I'm lucky or crazy, but I went to Sofia for a weekend, met a nice (sex worker), paid for her for the weekend, and convinced her to run off to Kosovo with me for six months!!! She was trafficked, but was quite pretty and spoke perfect English. Remember, Kosovo, has (or had) no immigration policies, so anyone can come without a visa. It was a pretty good experience; we were both happy for a relatively small investment on my part. Even if she wasn't, where could she have gone in Kosovo? To the DynCorp guys.

Along similar lines, I use video chat (most often when I am in war zones) and have gotten 2 of the 5 girls I asked to come visit me in Kosovo for between 2–3 months each. This, on some scale, is doable for most everybody.[14]

—Military Sex Tourist, Kosovo, September 30, 2005

* * *

Research suggests that human trafficking syndicates respond to U.S. deployment by establishing illicit businesses in close proximity to barracks (e.g., Juicy Bars in South Korea, as well as American-named establishments in Kosovo and Bosnia—Liberty Restaurant, Malibu Club, and Monroe Club).[15] Experts draw strong correlation between the number of peacekeepers stationed overseas and the number of human trafficking victims in that location.

Although the majority of international peacekeepers are not engaged in human trafficking, overwhelming evidence links the prevalence of sex trafficking to exploitation by some peacekeepers in post-conflict regions. Sex trafficking in response to peacekeeping deployments has security implications for both human rights abuses and unwitting support of organized crime. When a peacekeeper traffics or facilitates the trafficking of women and girls, or purchases sex with trafficked women and girls, he not only harms the victim but also critically damages the reputation of the United States.[16] For years, uniformed service members and civilian contractors have been implicated in procuring commercial sex services and sex trafficking with no consequence, except possibly losing a job.

Hello Mongers

I am deploying to Baghdad, Iraq in the next two weeks, I want to see if I can get one of those Hijab Girls to show little red the goods (good pussy). I can't access adult sites on my closely monitored Internet connection (yes big brother is watching), so it may be some time between reports. My Baghdad buddy says he cannot access USASG,[17] so I e-mail him periodic reports.

Going to Baghdad to get some, Hoorah.[18]
                                                        —Military Sex Tourist, January 5, 2008

Following several high-profile controversies involving military sex tourism, President George W. Bush signed an executive order making patronizing a prostitute a crime under the Uniform Code of Military Justice.[19] However, the order went largely unenforced for years, and the practice continued relatively undeterred. Perceptions of impunity can be demonstrated through the candid online postings of sexual exploits from men who claim to be members of the U.S. military, even in combat zones.

During the early 2000s, safety and trust issues between American military and local support appeared to inhibit commercial sex procurement in Afghanistan. On October 5, 2002, one man, claiming to be stationed at the Bagram Air Base, which is 35 miles north of Kabul, Afghanistan, wrote,

I have been in this shit hole for four months now and have been trying to get a piece since day one . . . a local worker told me that I could go to Kabul with him, and he would set up a 'date' for me with a young lady. It would cost 40 bucks for a couple hours. Although this was tempting, I had to pass it up because I can't trust too many people over here . . . it is still like the Wild West.[20]

Instead, colleagues recommended that he travel to neighboring countries to purchase sexual services. Another self-proclaimed military sex tourist wrote, "If you are with the military at Bagram, try to take a hop to Kyrgyzstan (Bishkek), where there are tons of Russian women who will screw your brains out for $14."

Two years later, the military sex tourists in Afghanistan felt more comfortable venturing off base and discovered sexual services from Asian women in local restaurants.

> *Tried the Chinese Bar, Shanghai Restaurant in Wazir Akbar Khan. About four girls working, all Chinese, and would rate them all 4–5. Chose one named Fifi (definitely not French). Cost was $100, and that would probably have lasted the night, but I was pretty loaded and just wanted to get home and get to sleep after the deed. Service was basic with no GFE[21] and nothing memorable. I don't think I would repeat. Price is high for level of service, so you are probably better off saving money for use in Dubai or Baku.[22]*

Eventually, the media caught wind of the Chinese brothels in Kabul. Nearly six years after the brothels in Wazir Akbar Khan were first discussed on InternationalSexGuide.info, a Reuters article exposed the lucrative commercial sex industry in Kabul to the larger public. The story claimed that the young girls working at the business had fled high unemployment in China. After the Taliban were removed from power in 2001, well-paid foreigners flocked to Afghanistan, which created a demand for commercial sex.[23]

Following the media coverage and government response, many of the brothels closed. One self-proclaimed military sex tourist explained,

> *There is a reason why (the InternationalSexGuide.info Kabul) thread is dead. There use to be Chinese restaurants where girls would be hidden upstairs in a room about 10 or more 1–5 at best (in the looks department), and you could pick one and fuck for like $20 bucks but the pseudo moral police and government deported a lot of them and closed down the shops.[24]*

After leaving Kabul, military sex tourists went on to purchase commercial sex services in a variety of other countries. Posters on the Kabul InternationalSexGuide.info thread later claimed to have obtained sexual services in Germany, Slovakia, Czech Republic, Netherlands, Spain, and Morocco, among other countries.

For decades, members of U.S. armed forces have traveled around the world, purchasing sexual services from women (and men) in undeveloped countries. Some of these self-proclaimed military men brag about their sex tourism as "free trips abroad paid for by Uncle Sam." Many men claimed to prefer women overseas because they are described as being more beautiful and obedient, as well as less expensive, than sex workers in the United States.

Historically, military sex tourism was a clandestine activity that was only shared with fellow service members. However, the popularization of commercial sex advertisement and review websites has provided forums for better understanding the extent and dynamics of sex tourism from men who allege to be members of the U.S. military.

For example, one man, whom I will refer to as Leeroy, claimed to be a member of the U.S. Navy, and between April and September 2010, he posted messages on InternationalSexGuide.info suggesting that he had obtained sexual services in six countries: Japan, China, South Korea, Singapore, Philippines, and Thailand.

His posts on the InternationalSexGuide.info message board began with him asking for referrals for sex services in Pusan, South Korea, followed by Yokohama and Tokyo, Japan. Later, he posted descriptions of his sexual exploits.

> Some Chinese guy greets us at the door, discuss business . . . We wait about five minutes, then he called us into our rooms, where our lady of the evening was waiting. I walk in to a 30ish looking Chinese women (she told me she was 26), decent looking, a little on the chubby side. We make small talk for a bit. Takes me to the shower, and bathes me quickly while naked. Once we get back to the room, pretty much just got down to business. BBBJ,[25] CFS.[26] Get done, made friendly conversation afterwards. Overall, a very good value for what was paid.[27]

Following the services purchased in Japan, he asked for commercial sex referrals in Singapore. While in Singapore, he bragged about spending $1,100 U.S. dollars on sexual services from two women in one night before his ship required him to return for curfew. He stated the first sexual service he received was at a Holiday Inn.

Prior to arriving in Thailand, Leeroy expressed a common fear among military sex tourists. "I am personally terrified of accidentally bringing home a TS (transsexual) . . . I need to get as much info on this subject as possible, to minimize costly mistakes!" he wrote.

Many military sex tourists in Asia demonstrate fear of inadvertently receiving sexual services from a transsexual. Incidents that have attracted international media attention include one story of a 20-year-old Marine, Lance Cpl. Joseph Scott Pemberton, who murdered 26-year-old transsexual sex worker Jennifer Laude in Olongapo City, Philippines, in October 2014.[28] Laude performed oral sex on Pemberton, and he broke her neck after discovering that she was genetically a male. Pemberton was sentenced to between 6 and 12 years in prison.

Ultimately, although Leeroy was in a conventional romantic relationship with a girlfriend and potentially risked his job by engaging in military sex tourism, he likely rationalized his actions similarly to many servicemen, as part of man's "intractable, inherent and atavistic propensity to spread his 'seed.'"

In recent years, both the Pentagon and the Department of State have reemphasized the importance of tough internal policies, which teach military personnel that prostitution is often a form of human trafficking, with strong ties to underworld crime.[29] However, while military policy explicitly states that hiring prostitutes is incompatible with core military values, it is unclear whether these policies are effective deterrents.[30]

Notes

1. Values, Ethics & Compliance | DynCorp International. DynCorp International (n.d.): accessed April 22, 2017, http://www.dyn-intl.com/about-di/values-ethics-compliance/.

2. Robert Capps, "Sex-Slave Whistleblowers Vindicated," *Salon* (August 6, 2002): accessed July 6, 2017, http://www.salon.com/2002/08/06/dyncorp/.

3. Robert Capps, "Outside the Law," *Salon* (June 26, 2002): accessed July 6, 2017, http://www.salon.com/2002/06/26/bosnia_4/.

4. Ibid.

5. Ibid.

6. David Isenberg, "Sex and Security in Afghanistan," Cato Institute (October 9, 2009): accessed July 6, 2017, https://www.cato.org/publications/commentary/sex-security-afghanistan.

7. Robert Capps, "Sex-Slave Whistleblowers Vindicated," *Salon* (August 6, 2002): accessed July 6, 2017, http://www.salon.com/2002/08/06/dyncorp/.

8. Nisha Lilia Diu, "What the U.N. Doesn't Want You to Know," *The Telegraph* (February 6, 2012): accessed July 6, 2017, http://www.telegraph.co.uk/culture/film/9041974/What-the-UN-Doesnt-Want-You-to-Know.html.

9. Ibid.

10. Robert Capps, "Sex-Slave Whistleblowers Vindicated," *Salon* (August 6, 2002): accessed July 6, 2017, http://www.salon.com/2002/08/06/dyncorp/.

11. Jason Linkins, "U.S. Military Contractor 'Used Armored Cars to Transport Prostitutes,'" *Huffington Post* (May 7, 2008): accessed July 6, 2017, http://www.huffingtonpost.com/2008/04/29/us-military-contractor-us_n_99175.html.

12. Jacob Siegel, "The Real Winner of the Afghan War Is This Shady Military Contractor," *The Daily Beast* (April 24, 2014): accessed July 6, 2017, http://www.thedailybeast.com/articles/2014/04/24/the-real-winner-of-the-afghan-war-is-this-shady-military-contractor.html.

13. United Nations Mission in Kosovo.

14. *Kosovo Forum*. (September 30, 2005): accessed July 6, 2017, http://www.InternationalSexGuide.info.

15. Sarah Elizabeth Mendelson, *Barracks and Brothels: Peacekeepers and Human Trafficking in the Balkans.* (Washington, DC: Center for Strategic and International Studies, 2005).

16. Ibid.

17. USASexGuide.info. See Appendix A for more information.

18. *General Reports Forum.* (January 5, 2008): accessed July 6, 2017, http://www.InternationalSexGuide.info.

19. Government Publishing Office. 2005 Amendments to the Manual for Courts-Martial, United States, 2005. Accessed July 6, 2017, https://www.gpo.gov/fdsys/pkg/FR-2005-10-18/pdf/05-20944.pdf.

20. *Kabul Forum.* (October 5, 2002): accessed July 6, 2017, http://www.InternationalSexGuide.info.

21. Girlfriend experience.

22. *Kabul Forum.* (June 16, 2004): accessed July 6, 2017, http://www.InternationalSexGuide.info.

23. Tan E. Lyn and Jonathan Burch, "Chinese Sex Workers Find Their Way to Kabul," *Reuters* (2008): accessed July 6, 2017, http://in.reuters.com/article/afghan-prostitution-chinese-idINISL12604420080519.

24. *Kabul Forum.* (July 29, 2009): accessed July 6, 2017, http://www.InternationalSexGuide.info.

25. Bare back blow job. See Appendix A for more information.

26. Covered full service. See Appendix A for more information.

27. *Tokyo Forum.* (April 18, 2010): accessed July 6, 2017, http://www.InternationalSexGuide.info.

28. Floyd Whaley, "U.S. Marine Guilty in Killing of Transgender Woman in Philippines," *The New York Times* (December 1, 2015): accessed July 6, 2017, https://www.nytimes.com/2015/12/02/world/asia/us-marine-joseph-pemberton-guilty-in-killing-of-transgender-woman-in-philippines.html.

29. Tabassum Zakaria and Susan Cornwell, "U.S. Military Faces Scrutiny over Its Prostitution Policies | Reuters," *Reuters* (April 29, 2012): accessed July 6, 2017, http://www.reuters.com/article/us-usa-agents-military-idUSBRE83S09620120429.

30. Deterrence is predicated on the notion that certain, swift, and severe punishments outweigh the potential benefits of committing an offense, thus leading the potential offender to make the rational choice to refrain from engaging in the crime.

CHAPTER SEVEN

Trafficked to La Mara

I'm sorry, but I don't think I'm gang material.
—Response from Latina who turned down MS-13 gang
recruiters in Alexandria, Virginia

On June 1, 2012, 24-year-old Rances Ulices Amaya was sentenced to 50 years in federal prison. According to the U.S. Attorney's Office press release that was posted on the FBI website, Amaya, also known by his gang nicknames "Murder" and "Blue," was convicted for recruiting and prostituting five girls "as young as 14 from middle schools, high schools, and homeless shelters in Northern Virginia and forcing them to engage commercial sex acts on behalf of MS-13."[1]

Following the sentencing announcement, U.S. Attorney Neil H. MacBride released a statement to the press: "Rances Amaya's gang name was 'Murder,' and in a real sense, he killed the hopes and dreams of teenage girls whom he systematically and sadistically victimized . . . He told these girls that he owned them and that he would hurt their loved ones if they didn't comply. They were his sex slaves, and that slavery goes to the heart of the heinous crime of sex trafficking. These girls have traumatic scars that will last a lifetime, and Mr. Amaya is justly going to spend the rest of his productive life paying for his crimes."[2]

A jury had convicted Amaya of conspiracy and three counts of sex trafficking of a child, after he had joined forces with an MS-13 associate who was already prostituting underage girls. The state's attorneys alleged that Amaya had used the violent reputation of MS-13 to keep the victims compliant. According to the press release, he was implemental in finding sex customers and would offer his fellow MS-13 gang members free sex with the underage girls.[3]

Amaya's victims were required to have sex with 8 to 10 paying customers per day, sometimes seven days per week, at motels, hotels, houses, apartments, and cars in Washington, DC and the Northern Virginia area. He charged between $30 and $120 for about 20 minutes of sex with the victims and used the money to purchase narcotics, alcoholic beverages, and to support MS-13 in the United States and El Salvador.[4]

According to the press release, Amaya raped the victims for his enjoyment, to "groom" them for the sex trafficking scheme, and to keep the teenage girls compliant. He would also provide them with cigarettes, alcohol, marijuana, and other drugs. Sometimes for punishment, he would have MS-13 "run a train" on the underage victim, which meant that multiple gang members would have sex with the girl in rapid succession.[5]

This was the narrative that was disseminated to the media and proliferated across multiple platforms.

For example, Amaya's crimes were featured in a book, *Walking Prey: How America's Youth Are Vulnerable to Sex Slavery*, and debuted in a true crime TV series. On March 8, 2016, *Gangsters: America's Most Evil* profiled Amaya's crimes. The plot summary for his episode read:

> *In the wealthiest and most populated area of Virginia, lies a deeper and darker world of a violent, international gang called MS 13. As a shot caller for MS 13, Rances Ulices Amaya aka "Blue," enslaved the lives of juvenile girls by recruiting them into a life of prostitution. Joining the gang at 13 years old, he and his gang were known to terrorize the streets with their weapon of choice, a machete. His reign of terror would come to an abrupt end as the number 13 would prove to be prophetic in his life, his 13th crime would prove to be the last.[6]*

Yet, while the coverage of Amaya's crimes was prolific, the true kingpin of the sex trafficking operation—Alonso Bruno Cornejo Ormeno—was treated as a footnote, receiving very little of the demonizing media coverage, as well as half the prison sentence.

Behind the headlines, gang-controlled sex trafficking crimes, prosecutions, and punishments are different from what people may understand as truth. Herein, I will recount Amaya's crimes through primary court documents so that you can compare and contrast the actual testimonies from witnesses and victims with the narrative disseminated through the media. This will illustrate how human trafficking crimes and the punishments received by offenders may not be as clear-cut as what the public is made to believe.

Table 7.1   MS-13 Human Trafficking Co-Conspirators

Name	Nickname	MS-13 Gang Affiliation	Sentence
Alonso Bruno Cornejo	Casper	MS-13 affiliate, called a paisa; not an official gang member, but the human trafficking kingpin of this operation	24 years in federal prison
Rances Ulices Amaya	Murder or Blue	Guanacos Locotes	50 years in federal prison
Hermes Salazar Perez	Crazy	MS-13 not specified	Immunity
William Reyes	Scooby or Little Crimen	Guanacos Little Cycos Salvatrucha	Immunity
Eric Duarte	Maldito	Parke Vista Locotes Salvatrucha	Immunity
Alexander Rivas	Casper	Virginia Locotes Salvatruchos	Immunity
Henry Alexander Herrera Larin	Looney, Lunatic, or Lunático	MS-13 not specified	Immunity

First, it is important to understand Amaya's background, which is similar to many sex traffickers and crime-involved youth. According to the presentence report submitted by Amaya's attorney and testimony, Amaya was raised by a dysfunctional family without any familial controls. Prior to his sex trafficking arrest, Amaya had a total of 12 criminal actions; 6 crimes were committed as a juvenile, and 6 crimes were committed as an adult over the age of 18.

Although Amaya was born in the United States, he was sent to live with relatives in El Salvador after the dissolution of the relationship between his mother and father. While living in El Salvador, Amaya suffered the loss of an aunt and an uncle, as well as the kidnapping of a cousin. As a teenager, Amaya was sent back to live in the United States with his mother, who was described as a virtual stranger, and her new husband an actual stranger.[7]

At this time, Amaya began to rebel and adopted a new family—MS-13 (see Table 7.1.)

* * *

U.S. District Court for the Eastern District of Virginia, Alexandria Division

February 21–22, 2012

An MS-13 gang member by the name of Hermes Salazar Perez, a.k.a. Crazy, was the first person called by the prosecution to testify in Amaya's trial. Early on in Crazy's testimony, the federal prosecutor, Zachary Terwilliger, Esq., pointed out that the state's first witness had "tres puntos" tattooed on his face. Crazy explained to the court that the three dots were symbolic of "My Crazy Life."[8]

The prosecution also pointed out that Crazy was incarcerated at the time of his testimony. He had participated in a murder in 2009 by disposing of cell phones and wiping out a gun. The prosecutor admitted that Crazy was receiving a sentence reduction for his charges of being an accessory to murder after the fact but wanted to acknowledge to the jury that it was contingent on him telling the truth. Specifically, Terwilliger asked:

What does this plea agreement require you to do, Mr. Salazar Perez?

Requires me to tell the truth.

And what happens if you lie?

My plea agreement will be ripped, thrown away, and I'll be charged.[9]

After establishing the foundation for why Crazy was testifying in this case, Terwilliger inquired how he knew Amaya, who was referred to by his gang names—Murder and Blue—throughout the trial.

Crazy claimed to know Amaya because they were both members of MS-13. Amaya was a leader of an MS-13 clique called GL–Guanacos Locotes. He used the terms *Ranflero*, which he described as meaning "the one who is driving the car," and *Corredor*, meaning "a runner," to analogize Amaya's leadership position within the MS-13 clique.

According to Crazy, after the murder in 2009, he was laying low and ran into Amaya on two separate occasions.

First, he encountered him at a get-together at the house of a girl named Becky. Crazy recalled that Amaya was at the house with two other gang members—Cuervo and Casper—and three girls—Becky and her friend, as well as a girl they picked up from high school. There, Crazy stated Amaya told him that he was pimping girls, whom he called *morras*, and selling drugs. He asked Crazy to recruit sex clients for the business in exchange for money and sexual favors.

At this point in the trial, Amaya's defense attorney interjected, "Your Honor, could we have a classification as to which Casper we're talking about? Apparently, there's two of them." Crazy clarified that he was talking about Alonso Bruno Cornejo, who had a unique and identifiable characteristic—his eyes were different colors.

On the second occasion Crazy encountered Amaya in 2009, they met at a McDonald's on Route 50 in Fairfax, Virginia. Amaya and Crazy were with Casper and another MS-13 gang member who went by the nickname Crítico. He was from a different MS-13 clique, called Pinos, which was named after an area in El Salvador.

While at the McDonald's, the men talked about going to a hotel to pimp the girls.

On each occasion that Crazy encountered Amaya, as well as during phone calls, he told the court that Amaya would ask him to get clients, friends, and paisas,[10] to pay for sex with the girls. Crazy said, "He would hook me up with some money, and he would let me have sex with the girls, too." However, Crazy denied ever providing Amaya with clients for the sex trafficking business.

During the cross-examination, Amaya's defense attorney Michael S. Arif, Esq., focused on the fact that Crazy agreed to testify so that he could get a sentence reduction for the charges related to the 2009 murder, which included robbery, extortion, and accessory to murder after the fact.

The second person to testify at trial was one of the victims, Francesca. She was born in November 1992 and was 16 years old at the time of her victimization. Francesca started running away from home when she was 12 years old, and in 2008, she was placed in a home for girls.

In 2009, she ran away again and met up with Casper—the one with the different colored eyes—and Amaya. She told the court that both men were affiliated with MS-13, but Casper was the one who recruited her to prostitute.

Casper told her that prostituting herself would "be a way to make easy money to help you."

Table 7.2   MS-13 Human Trafficking Victims

Name	Age at time of Victimization	Runaway
Francesca	16	Yes
Arlennie	16	Yes
Joanna	14	Yes
Ingrid	15	Yes

Prior to being prostituted, Francesca told the court that she was "tested out" by both Amaya and Casper, meaning that she was forced to have sex with them so they could "try out the product."

I was being asked to be tested out for having oral sex because I didn't enjoy it. So they told me you should try it, you might like it, and I was forced to. Basically—

Who?

Basically suck their dicks.

And who forced you to do that?

Blue and Casper.

And how many times specifically did Blue force you to provide oral sex?

It was about twice.

And where did that take place?

In the back seat of Casper's car.

And how did that make you feel?

Used.[11]

Thereafter, beginning in the summer of 2009, she was brought to motels, hotels, apartments, and houses where she would go with a client for 15 minutes, which would cost $30.[12] Both Amaya and Casper went to construction sites, 7-Elevens, and day-laborer sites around Culmore and Chirilagua in Virginia to recruit commercial sex consumers. On one occasion, Amaya brought his brother, gang name Bling, to have sex with her for half price.

Francesca told the court that Casper was the one who transported her to the commercial sex appointments and collected the money, but Amaya would be with him and served as a lookout. Amaya and Casper gave her beer and marijuana to make the experience less traumatic and purchased condoms for her.

However, she also admitted that at times she would attempt to obtain clients on her own and received a portion of the money earned from her sexual exploitation. Casper was in charge of distributing the money, and Francesca explained, "There was times I wouldn't get paid my half, and there was times I would." Other times, the money would be split three ways between Casper, Francesca, and Amaya.

Eventually, she turned herself into the police because she said she was "tired of prostituting and tired of being on the run."

On cross-examination, Amaya's defense attorney highlighted the fact that Francesca testified that it was Casper who was prostituting her and Casper who had gotten her involved in prostitution, not Amaya.

For all practical purposes, Casper is the one that controlled everything you did, correct?

Mostly everything, yes, sir.

Okay. And, is it fair to say that Blue answered to Casper?

Yes.

And Blue was doing what Casper told him to do?

Basically, yes.

And, so Blue was not the leader here. It was Casper.

No, the leader was Casper.[13]

He also brought up the fact that all three of them received and spent portions of the money. Francesca had access to communication and multiple opportunities to escape them. She was left in the hotel or motel rooms overnight, and she could have alerted authorities from the landline in the room or her cellphone on multiple occasions.

Did you ever call 911?

No.

But you could have?

I could have. I was just scared to.[14]

Like many human trafficking survivors, Francesca didn't present herself as a particularly sympathetic victim. In addition to having received some of the money from her sexual exploitation, she had also engaged in other criminal activities, such as drug use and car theft. Moreover, despite her sexual exploitation, she had the ability to escape, but she did not leave at the first opportunity.

Is it fair to say that you didn't want to go home?

Basically, yes.

Despite the fact that you were being prostituted by MS-13, you didn't want to go home?

Yes.[15]

Following Francesca's testimony, the prosecutor called Alonso Bruno Cornejo, a.k.a. Casper–the child sex trafficking kingpin. He was born in Peru, but immigrated to the United States as a child and became as U.S. citizen when he was five years old. At the time of his testimony, he was also incarcerated for sex trafficking of a minor, which he pled guilty to and received a sentence of 292 months, approximately 24 years.[16]

Again, the prosecutor pointed out that his witness was receiving a sentence reduction in exchange for testifying but that it was contingent on the truth.

Mr. Cornejo, what does this plea agreement require you to do?

To say the truth, nothing but the truth.

What happens if you lie?

I lose my plea agreement like I'm not going to get no time off.

What do you hope to get by testifying today?

Get some time off my sentence.

And what will immediately prevent you from getting any time off your sentence?

Lying.[17]

Casper went on to testify that Henry Herrera, a.k.a. Looney, and Amaya were both part of MS-13 and helped him sex traffic the girls. He described MS-13 as "one of the most violent gangs in Northern Virginia and over the world, basically." Casper denied being part of the gang but confessed to being a *paisa*, which he considered a gang affiliate.

Who recruited the girls for the prostitution?

I did, and Henry Herrera did, too.

Why you and Henry?

Because we were ladies' men at the time.

What about Blue?

Him, too.[18]

Casper explained that he would entice the girls into sexual exploitation by telling them how much money they could make, "Whatever her parents made in a week or two, she could make it in two days or a day. And I show her how much money we made." One of the girls he recruited was picked up right from her middle school. During his initial testimony, Casper didn't provide any explanation on how Amaya would recruit girls, but he did explain that Amaya would purchase alcohol for the girls because he was 21 years old at the time, and Casper was only 19 or 20. Moreover, Casper admitted that he would drive the girls to the appointments at motels such as Quarry Inn, Budget Inn, and Stratford Motel on Route 7 by Falls Church, Virginia. There, Casper said that Amaya would serve the purpose of security and would obtain the hotel room, since Casper didn't want his name on the paperwork.

In summation, Casper testified that Amaya would call people who wanted to have sex with underage girls, and Casper would pay him for each client he got. Amaya also would stay in the hotel at times to watch the girls and because he was homeless. Casper admitted that Amaya was following his orders.

> *If he don't listen to me then I wasn't going to give him money for helping me out and at that time he needed money because he had no way to provide for anything. He didn't work. His mom kicked him out the house. So I told him if he don't help me out, I wouldn't break him off with money . . .*
>
> *He would stay at the hotels. He would take care of the girls when I go home at night, wash them, find me clients, go buy condoms . . . he make phone calls for the clients. So I give him, because he didn't have a home, like that.*
>
> *He didn't have nowhere to stay. So at the same time, I would give him—break him off. He eat, I eat.*[19]

During cross-examination, Casper contradicted his initial statements by admitting that Amaya didn't recruit any of the girls; it was he and Henry a.k.a. Looney:

> *And which of the girls did you recruit, exactly which ones?*
>
> *I'd say, Joanna. I talked to Francesca. Henry did Arlennie. And Lupita, I had talked to Lupita, too. We both did.*[20]

The next person called by the prosecutor to testify was William Reyes a.k.a. Scooby or Little Crimen. He was originally from Long Island, New York, but moved to Virginia in 2006. While in New York, he became a member of MS-13 in 2003 after being jumped in for 13 seconds. He stated that the two rules of the gang were that you don't cooperate with law enforcement and must pay rent. The highest grade he completed in high school was eleventh.

Originally, Scooby was a member of the PLS clique of MS-13, which stood for Pelones Locotes de Salvatrucha, meaning bald-headed crazy Salvadorians. However, when he moved from New York, he cliqued over to VA chapter GLCS, Guanacos Little Cycos Salvatrucha. Scooby began cooperating with law enforcement after he was arrested on January 28, 2010, for malicious wounding, gang participation in a criminal act, and robbery. He also admitted to transporting firearms for MS-13 across state lines, having sex and receiving fellatio from underage sex trafficking victims, and being present for a murder. He didn't commit the murder, but he pushed the victim to the ground before he was stabbed to death in Prince William County, Virginia.

Like Casper, he too was given immunity to testify.

After he began cooperating with law enforcement, he was "green lighted," meaning that if MS-13 were to see him, they would kill him. As such, the government put him in protective custody where he was provided with free housing and reimbursed for the expenses he incurred while serving as an informant. The prosecution estimated that Scooby had received $2,001.50 from the government at the time of his testimony.

Most of Scooby's testimony focused on his interactions with Amaya in recruiting commercial sex customers. Scooby also testified that while he was at his house with another MS-13 gang member, Johnny Estrada, a.k.a. Lágrimas[21] from Charlotte Locos de Salvatrucha (CLS) clique, he received a telephone call from Casper and Amaya.

Please tell us what Casper said to you on that call?

He said that he was in the area of Manassas and he had girls there that were to fuck, and if I knew anybody that wanted to fuck to give him a call.

What did the defendant say?

The same thing, that they were in the Manassas area, and they had girls—Moritas.[22] They had a girl that was for fuck.[23]

Following the call, Scooby testified that he and Lágrimas went to the Super 8 off Route 28 in Manassas, Virginia. There, Casper opened the hotel room door where he revealed a teenage girl, who Scooby described as short, about 5'4", light-skinned Hispanic, with medium curly hair. While showing the girl, Scooby testified that Casper told the men, "That's a girl that's—for fuck." Scooby told the court that Casper handed Lágrimas a condom before he went into the hotel room to have sex with the girl.

Scooby testified that he recruited other commercial sex customers for Casper. One was a man who went by the gang name Sleepy and another nicknamed Puro. In order to arrange the appointment for Puro, Scooby stated that he called Amaya and told him, "I had somebody that want to have sex and that wanted to fuck, and he said that he was in the Fairfax area. He gave me an address, and I drove up there." Upon arriving at the house in Fairfax, Scooby stated that Amaya had a machete with him and would typically carry that weapon, a knife, or even a screwdriver. Before Puro went into the house, two older men dressed in construction attire came out.

Although Scooby denied having sex with any of Casper's victims, he admitted to having sex with another minor trafficked by a gang member named Crítico.

Following Scooby's testimony, the prosecution called the second victim—Arlennie. She was born in October 1992 and was 16 at the time of her victimization. She was going to an alternative school—Plymouth Hills—where she would frequently skip class with Looney and Casper. At the time, her family didn't have a home, and they were living in a shelter.

Like the other witnesses, she testified that Casper recruited her into sexual exploitation.

Around September of 2009, what business was Casper in?

Prostitution.

What was Casper's role in the business?

He was the boss.[24]

She told the court that Casper prostituted her out to six or seven men per day for approximately four months, four to five days per week. Arlennie discussed her sexual exploitation as if she were a consenting participant.[25]

How did that affect you?

I don't know. At the time, I was okay with it. I was making money.

Did you ever tell Casper that you didn't want to prostitute?

If I didn't, I didn't. Like if I told him I didn't, I just wouldn't.

What percentage of the fee were you paid?

Half.

Approximately how much money did you make per week?

Like $200, I don't know, like $200, I guess.

And what did you do with this money?

I spent it.

Did you need it to support your family?

I helped support my family.

Did your mother have a job then?

No.

Are you the oldest child of your family?

Yes.

And how many children does your mother have?

Seven.[26]

She also denied Amaya's involvement in the prostitution business. Her testimony was almost counter to the narrative portrayed by the prosecution.

Was anyone ever with Casper while he was running the prostitution business?

Looney.

Anybody besides Looney?

No.

Generally, who made arrangements with the customers?

Casper.

Where did you get the condoms from?

Casper.

Did Looney also sometimes give them to you?

Like hand them to me, yeah.

Did you ever see Blue purchase condoms?

Like once.

Who decided what the fees would be?

Casper.

Did you ever see Casper give money to Blue?

No.

In the fall of 2009, did Casper ever pick you up from school or drop you off at school?

Yeah.

Was Blue ever with Casper when he picked you up or dropped you off?

No.[27]

The prosecution attempted to reconcile her statements, which were contradictory to the state's narrative, by highlighting that she didn't want to testify and wanted to forget what happened.

Following Arlennie's testimony, the prosecution called Eric Duarte, a.k.a. Maldito, who was born and raised in Arlington, Virginia. He told the court his nickname meant "bad or evil person." He became a member of MS-13 in 2005 when he was 15 years old, by being jumped in, beaten in, for 13 seconds. As Scooby and Casper had described, the rules were simple—collect money for the gang and never snitch. The highest grade he completed was the tenth.

Maldito was a member of PVLS, Parke Vista Locotes Salvatrucha, which represented Parkview, a place in El Salvador. At the time of his testimony, he was imprisoned for charges of attempted rape, sodomy, abduction, robbery, and aggravated sexual battery, to which he pled guilty, alongside his co-defendant Henry Herrara, a.k.a. Looney.

Why did you testify today?

The government offered me immunity to all charges in this case.[28]

Maldito testified that Amaya's role in juvenile sex trafficking increased his standing in MS-13 and allowed him to send money to higher ranking gang members in El Salvador. He testified that the men specifically targeted juveniles because they were easier to manipulate, brainwash, and persuade into prostituting.

Although he did not participate in having sex with the girls, he told the court that none of the gang members would need to pay for sex with the victims, "Homies fuck for free." Maldito also testified that he had witnessed multiple gang members run a train on the victims, including Amaya, Looney, Profeta, Cucia, Romero, and Humilde.

Could you tell us what the term "train" means?

It means there's a girl and there's multiple men and one of them have sex with her and then the next one immediately has sex with her and the next one immediately have sex with her and keeps going like a train.

What is the Spanish language term for that?

Trencito.

Does that literally mean little train?

Yeah, choo-choo.

Is this a form of punishment?

It can be, yes.

What would a girl have to do to be punished with a train?

She would have to not—she would have to want to leave or refuse to keep on prostituting.[29]

Maldito testified that he had seen one of the girls, Arlennie, try to escape the sex trafficking on several occasions. She was distraught and crying and would get drunk or high to numb the feelings.

Following Maldito's testimony, the prosecution called Alexander Rivas, who was also known as Casper, to the stand. He was a member of MS-13 clique VLS–Virginia Locotes Salvatruchos. At the time of his testimony, Rivas was incarcerated for sex trafficking minors. During the course of his testimony, Rivas said that Amaya went to his apartment with one of the sex trafficking victims, Lupita, and her friend, as well as Casper, Looney, Sniper, and Crítico. There, they popped Triple C—Coricidin pills.[30]

Rivas stated that he did not have any direct knowledge of Amaya trafficking the girls.

I never seen him prostitute nobody.

You never saw him engaged in any sort of prostitution business?

No.

You never saw him take money?

No.

You never saw him arrange for customers to have sex with girls?

No.[31]

However, while he didn't implicate Amaya in running a juvenile sex trafficking ring, Rivas did admit to running his own, an admission that he was granted immunity for in exchange for his testimony against Amaya.

You were engaged in the prostitution business, correct?

Yes.

You had your own girls?

Yes.

How many girls did you prostitute?

Two.

And how long did you run your prostitution business?

Four or five months.

And what put that to an end?

When they went home.

Did you let them go home or—

Yeah.

—they ran away?

No, they went home.

Mr. Rivas, you had another individual who was prostituting these same girls that you prostituted; is that correct?

Yes.

What was that individual's name?

Casper. Paisa Casper.[32]

Following Rivas, the prosecutor called a third victim to the stand—Joanna. She had failed to appear in court in response to an earlier subpoena, which caused the court to issue a summons that resulted in her detention.

Joanna was born in January 1995 and met Casper and Looney after an eighth-grade dance at Kenmore Middle School when she was 14. In January 2009, she ran away and met up with Casper, who talked her into prostitution.

Joanna testified that she had sexual intercourse with Casper and Amaya but denied ever being forced to sleep with any of their friends. She said that Amaya was involved in the prostitution business, but Casper would drive her to the appointments, talk with the clients, and collect the money. She told the court that Amaya would stay in the car, and she never saw him receive any money. However, like the two other girls, Joanna received her share of the profit from her sexual exploitation.

Did you receive any of the money after the appointments?

Yeah, I received like half the share.

Did you see Casper give Blue any money?

No.

Did you see Casper give Mr. Amaya anything of value?

Of value? Not that I recall.

Okay. And, is it fair to say that Casper was running this whole operation?

Yeah, I believe that Casper was mostly running the operation. I mean Blue came around just to like provide basic things, like the alcohol, the condoms, basic things. But I don't really think he was like in yet.

He aided it?

Huh?

He aided it? He helped it?

Yeah, kind of.[33]

Following Joanna's testimony, the prosecution called the fourth and final victim to the stand—Ingrid. She was born in August 1994 and was 15 years old at time of crime. She testified that she would skip school often so that she could go and hang out with MS-13. She stated that the gang members—Casper, Blue, Crítico, Sniper, Crazy, and Pensativo—were "kind of like my friends." Initially, they would provide her with different types of drugs for free, but then they told her that she needed to work for it by prostituting. They told her if she didn't do it, they would harm her boyfriend.

And after all this, what did you say to their demand to prostitute?

I said, 'No.'

And then what happened?

They got physical.

Ultimately were you forced to prostitute?

Yes.[34]

Ingrid testified that Casper and Amaya would charge as much as they could for her, around $80. If clients couldn't pay $80, the lowest they would go was $50, and like the other victims, she testified that she received half of all the profits, before escaping.

How did you get away?

They left us by ourselves, and some other gang members had came over and picked us up. And I had told them that I had a client that could pay a lot of money. And I told them to stop by a 7-Eleven and that's when I ran.[35]

The last person called to testify was Henry Alexander Herrera Larin, a.k.a. Looney, Lunatic, or Lunático. He was also in jail at time of testimony for sexual battery, attempted rape, and robbery he committed with Eric Duarte a.k.a. Maldito.

Looney testified that he and Casper would get a hotel, drive around and find clients, then charge "$80 a nut" to have sex with the girls. He testified that the girls came from troubled homes. For example, Looney explained that Arlennie's family was "fucked up, man. Her mom used to get me to get her some crack." He explained that Arlennie would use the money she earned to help her family, and she was provided controlled substances and alcohol to make her black out and pass out. They called Arlennie "Big Bucks" because she would bring in a lot of money.

Looney admitted that initially he was Casper's "right-hand man" in the juvenile sex trafficking operation, and he had helped recruit by picking up the girls from school. Looney explained that he specifically targeted underage girls because "They were fresh, man. Everybody wanted to get a piece of that." In explaining how Amaya became involved in the business, Looney explained, "He was always hanging around with us, so, you know, he became affiliated with it."

Following the prosecution's witnesses, the defense provided neither testimony nor evidence, and Amaya was convicted on all charges.

Ultimately, although Amaya's conviction was touted as a victory against an MS-13 sex trafficking kingpin, testimony from all four victims as well as witnesses suggested that he was less involved than others, such as Casper and Looney, who received significant sentence reductions and immunity in exchange for their testimony. In addition, the juveniles who they victimized received no restitution for the emotional and physical pain they endured. Casper was only assessed a $100 fee for his crimes, which his mother paid for him.

Unfortunately, in many cases, sex trafficking prosecutions are more about public perception as opposed to the justness of the results. Moreover, although the narrative presented to the public portrays a clear-cut, open-and-shut type of case, the reality is, as presented through the court transcripts, the dynamics of these cases are a little more complex. The victimized juveniles also engaged in delinquency, and some seemed to be consenting to their exploitation, which is often difficult for jurors to reconcile. Juveniles, by law, cannot consent to being sexually exploited— their minor status makes them *de facto* victims of sex trafficking. However, this can often be perceived as a credibility gap in the veracity of their testimony in court.

* * *

In response to this chapter, Rances Amaya, a.k.a. Murder, wrote from his prison cell in a U.S. penitentiary in Tucson, Arizona,

> *It seems like you got all the information that is out there for the public, which some is true, and most is false. You do have something right. I didn't part take in the crime that I got found guilty of. I got frame because I did not want to cooperate. Look, the real sex trafficking kingpin as you know got less time than me. As you can see, they made this look like a victory against the MS13. Which the one that really got affected is me . . . I did not recruit nobody, and I never received money from nobody. I was not even okay with it or involved, but I have no control over somebody else actions . . . Let me give you a fact. I am no longer a member of the MS13. I have dropped out; they have green lighted me. (Agreed upon each other that if they get the chance to kill me to accomplish it.) The reason being was because I choose to change my life. The first step I did was covered up my MS13 tattoos.*[36]

* * *

Despite popular belief, Mara Salvatrucha, a.k.a. MS-13, did not begin in El Salvador. The gang actually originated in Los Angeles, California, during the 1980s.

At the time, the Salvadoran civil war resulted in refugees fleeing to the United States. Many of them settled into lower socioeconomic neighborhoods in the Los Angeles area, where they were harassed by already established black and Mexican gangs. In response to the organized crime and violence that surrounded them, some of the El Salvadoran refugees started their own gang—MS-13.

Although many of the MS-13 gang members had obtained temporary protected status (TPS) or other legal visas following the end of the Salvadoran civil war, they became deportable. The passage of the Illegal

Immigration Reform and Immigrant Responsibility Act (IIRIRA) of 1996 made it so that even persons who had obtained green cards and legal permanent residency were deportable if they had committed a crime of moral turpitude. As such, many MS-13 gang members were sent back to El Salvador.

However, following the 12-year civil war, the El Salvadoran government didn't have the infrastructure to combat the organized crime group. As such, they grew in numbers and power and spread throughout Central America, into Mexico, and back to the United States. MS-13 went from being a crime issue in one state—California—to a criminal enterprise that infiltrated all 50 states and transcended continents.

As a committed anti-trafficking criminologist, I absolutely detest the thought of any person exploiting another, especially children. However, while it is important to hold human traffickers accountable for their crimes, it is equally as important to prevent new crimes from occurring.

Unfortunately, gang members often come from the same disadvantaged circumstances as their victims. Second-generation Hispanic children are being targeted and recruited by organized crime groups while their parents are working long hours to provide for their family in their new country.

The area where Amaya lived in Northern Virginia is highly concentrated with Hispanic immigrants. I know because I also grew up there. My husband actually went to the same high school as Amaya—Thomas A. Edison. Both of us encountered gangs at one point or another during our adolescence and young adulthood.

On our first date, my husband and I were driving down Telegraph Road in Alexandria, Virginia, headed to a lounge in Washington, DC. Suddenly, a group of adolescents darted out in front of my car and began fighting in the middle of the road before some of them ran into the adjacent woods.

As the group dispersed and we inched forward, we noticed one of the teenagers lying on the ground in between two parallel-parked cars to the right of the street. We cracked the passenger side window and asked the remaining crowd if everyone was okay. In a state of panic, they told us one of their friends had been stabbed.

My husband and I pulled over to the side of the road and got out of the car, while calling 9-1-1. We went to the young boy, who appeared to be around 15 or 16 years old, and asked him if he was okay. It was February, and he had a black bomber jacket on, but we could see there was a small egg-size pool of blood on the concrete, underneath where he was lying.

We waited while the paramedics made their way to us and attempted to comfort him. I could tell he was afraid, as were his friends, while others appeared to be already plotting revenge.

These kids weren't bad people. They were just misguided and needed redirection. According to life-course trajectory theory, most delinquents will just age out of crime, regardless of what punishment they may or may not receive. Therefore, incarcerating them for long periods of time may do more harm than good.

These kids, who are skipping school and engaging in delinquency, are at high risk. Not only are they at high risk for becoming victims, but they are at high risk for becoming offenders as well. The same groups of kids that are joining MS-13 are at high risk of being victimized by them or other gangs. Truly effective anti-trafficking efforts would focus on the socioeconomic conditions that lead to both criminality and victimization. Programs that are successful in preventing people from joining gangs would also prevent people from being victimized or trafficked by them.

Notes

1. FBI—Leader of MS-13 Gang Sentenced to 50 Years in Prison for Sex Trafficking Multiple Teens. (June 1, 2012). U.S. Attorney's Office, Eastern District of Virginia. Accessed July 6, 2017, https://archives.fbi.gov/archives/washingtondc/press-releases/2012/leader-of-ms-13-gang-sentenced-to-50-years-in-prison-for-sex-trafficking-multiple-teens.

2. Ibid.

3. Ibid.

4. Ibid.

5. Ibid.

6. Gangsters: America's Most Evil Rances Ulices Amaya. Documentary, Biography, Crime (2016): accessed July 6, 2017, http://www.imdb.com/title/tt5481112/.

7. *United States v. Rances Ulices Amaya*, No. 1:11CR556 (U.S. District Court for the Eastern District of Virginia, June 1, 2012).

8. Although it wasn't discussed during his testimony, other gangs have interpreted the same three-point tattoo to mean "death before dishonor" or representing the three places gang members will end up—"dead, in prison, or in a hospital."

9. *United States v. Rances Ulices Amaya*, No. 1:11CR556 (U.S. District Court for the Eastern District of Virginia, June 1, 2012).

10. *Paisa* or *paisano* is a Spanish language term for individuals from the same country.

11. *United States v. Rances Ulices Amaya*, No. 1:11CR556 (U.S. District Court for the Eastern District of Virginia, June 1, 2012).

12. Women and children sold for sex at construction or day-laborer sites in the United States are often called "treinteras," after the Spanish word for 30 (*treinta*).

13. *United States v. Rances Ulices Amaya*, No. 1:11CR556 (U.S. District Court for the Eastern District of Virginia, June 1, 2012).

14. Ibid.

15. Ibid.

16. U.S. Attorney's Office. "MS-13 Associate Sentenced to 292 Months for Sex Trafficking Teenage Runaway Girls," FBI (November 4, 2011): https://archives.fbi.gov/archives/washingtondc/press-releases/2011/ms-13-associate-sentenced-to-292-months-for-sex-trafficking-teenage-runaway-girls.

17. *United States v. Rances Ulices Amaya*, No. 1:11CR556 (U.S. District Court for the Eastern District of Virginia, June 1, 2012).

18. Ibid.

19. Ibid.

20. Ibid.

21. Spanish language word for teardrop.

22. Spanish language word for young girls.

23. *United States v. Rances Ulices Amaya*, No. 1:11CR556 (U.S. District Court for the Eastern District of Virginia, June 1, 2012).

24. Ibid.

25. Juveniles cannot consent to engage in the commercial sex industry. Their minor status makes them de facto victims of sex trafficking.

26. *United States v. Rances Ulices Amaya*, No. 1:11CR556 (U.S. District Court for the Eastern District of Virginia, June 1, 2012).

27. Ibid.

28. Ibid.

29. Ibid.

30. Abused over-the-counter cough and cold medication that, when taken in excessive doses, produces hallucinations and feelings of dissociation.

31. *United States v. Rances Ulices Amaya*, No. 1:11CR556 (U.S. District Court for the Eastern District of Virginia, June 1, 2012).

32. Ibid.

33. Ibid.

34. Ibid.

35. Ibid.

36. Rances Amaya. Interview by Dr. Kimberly Mehlman-Orozco. Written correspondence, Tucson, AZ. April 16, 2017.

CHAPTER EIGHT

Now Recruiting for an Exciting Summer Abroad

A cunning individual is very capable of making another person believe that he or she is in control, concealing their intentions until they lead the person to the edge of the cliff.

—Serge Petrov,[1] convicted human trafficker

May 26, 2004, Dulles, Virginia

As soon as Danni Starrchenko took her first step on American soil, she felt as though she had arrived in the mecca of rags-to-riches success. She had just graduated high school the year before, and it was her first time traveling outside of Ukraine. She didn't speak much English, so she was nervous, but she had her friend Nikita Ivanov by her side.

It was an unbelievable opportunity; the girls would be able to make enough money to pay for their first year in college, while sightseeing internationally. It was all thanks to Danni's boyfriend, Serge Petrov.

Serge and his family were extremely wealthy, so he offered to pay for Danni and Nikita's travel and sponsored their J-1 visitor visas through his American company, Beauty Search, Inc. Danni had never been with someone who was so romantic and generous.

After they retrieved their baggage and navigated through customs, Danni and Nikita followed their instructions out to the front of the building, where they met Serge and his compatriot, Roman Mikhailov. The girls couldn't wait to begin working their summer jobs as waitresses in Virginia Beach, but they quickly learned that the plans had changed.

Once the girls were inside his Cadillac Escalade, Serge explained, "The waitress jobs in Virginia Beach were full, so you'll need to work in Detroit instead." The girls were disappointed, but they went along with it, determined to make the best of their summer in the United States.

Danni and Nikita were transported to the bus station, where they boarded a Greyhound bound for Michigan.

The girls didn't begin to comprehend what type of situation they were in until Serge had them inside a motel room. There, he confiscated Danni and Nikita's passports and money before telling the girls that they had three months to pay the men $12,000 each for travel and $10,000 each for paperwork. Danni's heart dropped into her stomach when she saw Serge present her with strip clothes and shoes. He instructed that she would need to work at a club called Cheetahs, Monday through Saturday, double-shifts, 12:00 p.m. to 2:00 a.m., stripping for $20 per lap dance.

"You're gonna have to make $1,000 a day, and if you're not making this money, I'm gonna find another way to make you earn this money," he ordered.

From that day forward, each afternoon Serge would transport Danni and Nikita to the club, and every night after their 14-hour shift, the girls would relinquish all their earnings during the car ride home. Both the girls and the apartment where they were kept were treated as Serge's property. Although he didn't live with them, he had a key, which permitted unrestricted access.

Serge planted listening devices to record Danni's conversations with Nikita, using the gathered information to break the girls down mentally and induce feelings of frustration and confusion. He would search through their belongings, confiscating anything that could presumably help them get away from his dominance, especially money. Controlling their housing, finances, transportation, and communication abetted the girls' isolation and deterred them from seeking out help.

He told the girls, "I never believe what I hear and only half of what I see."

To elicit Danni and Nikita's compliance, Serge used a progressive combination of isolation, debt bondage, immigration threats, lectures, explanations, and violence, which he referred to as "the system."

At first, it was only ominous warnings.

He told Danni and Nikita about what happened when one of the other girls tried to escape, with the help of her sister. He explained that a month before Danni and Nikita arrived, on April 30, 2004, he found out that one of the girls wanted to leave, so he paid a henchman $500 to fire bomb her sister's black 1997 BMW four-door sedan by pouring Heet, a methanol-based automotive dry gas, all over the car and lighting it on fire. For good measure, an additional $250 was spent to have the henchman break the windows of her sister's house. Danni thought, *I'm going to be next if I say something, so I'm just gonna stay as quiet as I can, go through it for a next day, for a better future.*

At first, the isolation and threats were enough to make Danni and Nikita submit to being raped and exploited, but eventually Danni began to challenge her captivity, which led to the abuse. The first time she broke one of Serge's rules, he tugged her down the stairs of his beautiful gray-brick suburban home and locked her in the basement for several hours as punishment. He admonished her, "If you do not comply with my instructions and work as you are told, I will stomp you so hard in the forehead that the shoe size on the sole of my boot will be imprinted."

As time passed and the immediacy for Danni's escape heightened, she thought about keeping some of her earnings to help her get away, but she would always talk herself out of it. She was too afraid of what he would do if he found out. Always having his threats in the back of her mind controlled her behavior better than a chain and lock ever could. "If I find even one dollar, something very bad will happen, and blood will come from you," he would threaten.

It seemed as if with each day that passed, Serge became less and less of the person he pretended to be, replacing his sensitivity with aggression and violence. "If you *ever* try to leave, I *will* kill you, and no one will find the body," Serge would tell Danni emphatically, while shoving a 9 mm Berretta in her face. He would consistently brag about "lighting up" the cars of enemies and shoot outs involving his AK-47 "chopper" and 100-round "apple drum" clip.

He would antagonize, "Win, lose, or draw, I'm going to make sure they remember me this day and for the rest of their life." She knew with certainty that he was telling the truth.

After considering suicide for months, Danni finally decided that she wanted to run away, thinking, *This is enough! I'll just have to see how it's gonna go.* She confided in a strip club client, who claimed to be the brother of an Immigration and Customs Enforcement agent. With his assistance, the girls began preparing to escape.

Overcoming the uncertainty of freedom was difficult. Once Danni and Nikita left that apartment, they would be without a place to live, transportation, identification, and food. There was no guarantee that the police would help them, so they needed to find a way to support themselves, at least for a few nights. Since Serge would randomly search the girls after work to ensure they didn't keep any of their earnings, their income could not be used to help them. Instead, each time they were given money at the store for groceries, Danni and Nikita would slide a few dollars into purchased candy boxes, so Serge wouldn't find it. Once they returned home, the girls would hide the money in a small cookie tin, buried under a bush outside of the apartment. After nearly nine months of saving, Danni and Nikita were able to conceal $700 in preparation for their escape.

In the dark hours of early dawn on Valentine's Day 2005, they asked the client, who they had confided in, to come rescue them from the apartment where they were kept. There was no guarantee that Serge wouldn't arrive just as they were leaving and discipline them for daring to vie for freedom. Danni and Nikita placed their possessions in black plastic trash bags, so that they could at least pretend that they were just taking out the garbage if he were to catch them in the middle of their getaway. Luckily, the client was able to rescue them without incident. He immediately brought the girls to the ICE office in Detroit.

For the first time in nine months, Danni felt like she was free but not of the terror that had haunted her for so long. ICE Agent David Ford interviewed the girls about their harrowing experience in the United States, unclear why they didn't run away immediately or ask a patron at the club for help sooner. "Just because I have a smile on my face, doesn't mean I'm here with my own wills and doesn't mean I appreciate this job and want to be here!" Danni responded in broken English with her heavy European accent. She was distraught at the thought of someone not believing her.

> It's not just easy for me to leave because I was kept. You know, 12 hours a day, at the same place, over and over again, it was terrible. It was the, the nastiest place I ever been. I felt miserable every single day. When I was going to shower, I was hating myself. I was even thinking about suicide many times because I didn't have a choice to get out. My life was in danger the whole time, and they knew where my mom is living. It was not about me; it was about her!

After securing corroboration from two other victims, Agent Ford determined that Danni and Nikita had been trafficked and issued an indictment for Serge Petrov. Two days after their escape, on February 16, 2015, Serge was arrested on involuntary servitude, immigration, and money laundering charges. It took nearly two years of plea bargaining and approximately $400,000 in attorney's fees before he pled guilty and was sentenced to 14 years in a U.S. federal prison and more than $1.5 million in restitution.

While Serge was incarcerated, his father Dmitry Petrov, who was the true kingpin of their trafficking operation, was on the lam from law enforcement for six years in Ukraine. After being placed on the FBI and ICE Top Ten Most Wanted lists from 2006 to 2011, he was finally apprehended when a change in Ukrainian political leadership created an opportunity for Interpol to capture and extradite him to the United States. Dmitry accepted a plea bargain and was only sentenced to a few years in federal prison.

* * *

The media coverage on this human trafficking operation only scratched the surface of what had actually transpired. The reality beggars belief.

This crime actually began on the bank of the Dnieper River, in the heart of Kiev, Ukraine, in a three-floor, 2,500 square meter restaurant-cabaret. The interior was elegantly designed with careful attention to detail, combining modernity with ethnic décor, ornate decoration, and expensive textiles. The business boasted over 100 dancers, 25 cooks, and elaborate live entertainment, nightly from 8:00 p.m. to 5:00 a.m. The club's entertainers included singers and burlesque dancers in plumage befit to grace the stages in Las Vegas. The girls who worked there made grand entrances through one of two backstage passageways, with each door set in the mouth of a golden lion sculpture. While the patrons looked on to choreographed dances, acrobatic routines, and synchronized strip teases, they could dine on an exotic selection of sumptuous Asian cuisine, such as pigs' ears or jellyfish.

This business was a front for an illicit brothel, which served as Petrov's source of victims, who were trafficked from Ukraine to the United States. At the time of this writing, it is still in operation and has been for approximately 25 years.

The inception of this business was similar to many criminal organizations, which now flourish in Ukraine. The collapse of the Soviet Union was like the 1800s' gold rush for illicit enterprises. It was a time when fortunes were made, and business ties were forged. Dmitry Petrov took advantage. After building relationships with leadership in both political and illicit arenas, he garnered enough financial and social capital to construct the first strip club/casino/nightclub/restaurant after the fall of the Soviet Union.

Dmitry received the startup capital for the business venture in the early 1990s from Boris Savlohov,[2] a leader of the largest organized criminal group in Ukraine, with over 1,000 members committing robberies, extortions, and contract killings. Dmitry was interested in establishing business ties with Boris given his connections with the high authorities in Kiev, which reached up to the administration of the president. Boris's upper-world connections provided a unique opportunity for Dmitry's underworld business to flourish. Boris used the money earned from extortion and racketeering to make an investment of $1 million.

At the time, most of the families who lived in Dmitry's community were part of the burgeoning lower working class, with no ability for social mobility. For so long, they had been subdued and terrified of the state—complacent from being reliant on the government yolk. Much of their natural-born life was previously spent working for state factories and agricultural collective farms, so when Dmitry Petrov began making money, people took notice. "I'm choosing to make a living through different, more creative means," he would surreptitiously explain his new fortune. Young women who were looking for financial betterment began to seek out employment at the club; Danni Starrchenko was one of these girls.

Danni grew up in a small Ukrainian town outside of Kiev. Her parents made a decent living, working as engineers, and she received training as gymnast. After she graduated from high school, 18-year-old Danni began searching for a job in the city to help support herself and finance college. She was interested in earning a degree in sports medicine but needed money. Opportunities for women were extremely limited in Ukraine at the time, so she didn't have many options.

Danni applied to a number of help-wanted advertisements, including one for a waitress position at Petrov's night club/restaurant/cabaret. During her initial interview with Dmitry, Danni was informed that the waitress positions had all been filled. Instead, he persuaded her that she should accept one of the available stripper positions, which were much more lucrative. As a small-town girl, enamored with the pomp and circumstance that welcomed the dancers of this big city club, Danni couldn't help but consider the proposition. In need of money and wanting to move out on her own, she timidly accepted the job in August 2003.

Several months later, the glamour of the position had faded, and Danni no longer felt comfortable working there. The job didn't only entail burlesque—the dancers were pressured to sleep with clients in the private VIP area for $100 each. Although she accepted a position as an exotic dancer, Danni couldn't further compromise her integrity by having sex for money. She quickly informed Dmitry that she intended to quit. Since Danni could leave at any time while in Ukraine and return to her family in a town nearby, Dmitry decided that he needed to take aversive measures to keep exploiting her.

Serge Petrov, Dmitry's son, was his most loyal henchman, who was especially skilled in gaining compliance from victims. Serge was only a few years older than Danni at the time and was very confident in his ability to maneuver with people, especially women. Dmitry asked Serge to fabricate a romantic relationship with Danni so that they could continue the exploitation by taking her to the United States, away from her social and financial resources in Ukraine.

"I'm capable of feeding her ears exactly what she wants to hear," Serge would brag.

When Danni first started working at the club, Serge was living in the United States, splitting his residency between Chicago, where his mother lived, and Detroit, where his business ventures were located. He returned to Ukraine periodically to visit family. During one trip in the winter months of 2003–2004, he made it a point to meet Danni.

It wasn't hard for Serge to catch her attention. He was a good-looking, younger man with a lot of money. Driving a brand new black Mercedes CLK430, wearing Versace clothes, and always carrying $4,000 in cash, he exuded success. During this trip to Ukraine, he took Danni out on several formal dates and showed her a good time, eventually leading to consensual intercourse.

Serge was quick to profess his love for Danni. Over dinner he told her,

> *To love very much is to love poorly. One loves that is all. It cannot be modified or completed without being nullified. It is a short word, but it contains all it means, the body, the soul, the life, the entire being. We feel it as we feel the warmth of our blood. We breathe it as we breathe air. We carry it in ourselves as we carry our thoughts. Nothing more exists for us. It is not a word. It is an inexpressible state indicated by four letters. Everything I feel for you is genuine and comes from the heart!*

At the age of 18, Danni never had a man be so romantic with her. Although she felt shy to have someone profess his love in that manner, it was like a dream. He knew exactly how to deceive Danni into making her think that he really cared, as he had done it successfully dozens of times before. He would read her cues, playing off her personality, to be exactly what she wanted while pretending that she was everything he wanted in a partner. "Listen, one thing about me that you have to understand, unlike others, I'm not afraid to go after what I want, no matter what it is, you feel me?"

Danni had coveted the attention of men in the past, which was often unrequited, so it was strange to receive it so freely and with such abundance. It felt good, like food for her soul, but she couldn't go along without doubting the sincerity of his sentiment.

For every question she posed, however, he had an answer. Each answer was formulated to manipulate her into making a pre-determined decision, while giving the illusion that she was an equal participant in the dialogue.

"You're right," he would say, "a pair of lips will say anything and actions speak louder than words."

To show her how much he cared, Serge offered to bring Danni to the United States to be with him. Since she didn't like stripping at the club in Ukraine, he also offered to pay for everything, as well as take her sightseeing and on vacations. The plan was for her to come to the United States for a few months over the summer, learn English, and work a new job as a waitress in Virginia Beach. To her, the proposition seemed like a tangible expression of what she thought was his true sentiment. He made it seem like the stars and the moon had aligned for this relationship and adventure to the United States. Serge implored, "You don't want to go through life climbing a ladder just to wake up one day and realize that it was leaning against the wrong wall."

Danni shared these feelings for him, at least for the man he pretended to be, but she doubted the longevity of their relationship and rightfully so. He assured her that no matter what, he would be there for her.

First and foremost, we are friends, no matter what. To me friendship is the truest form of any relationship, anything else is forced misconception. It's sad but true, and there are three phases to truth: First, it's ridiculed. Second, it's violently opposed, and third, it's accepted as self-evident. I'm the third one.

While she still had her doubts, Serge was so convincing and well cultured in the way he spoke. He also promised significant earning potential, which would help her finance college. She agreed on the condition that she could bring her friend, Nikita, who also unhappily worked at the Ukrainian club. Serge told her that he would arrange to pay for Nikita's travel expenses as well. Little did Danni know it was all a ruse to get her away from Ukraine and isolated under his control.

* * *

Dmitry only spent 30 months in prison for his crimes. After his release, he waited for his probation to elapse, while living on a beachfront property in Sunny Isles Beach, Florida, before returning to run the family business in Ukraine.

Serge was released from Loretto Federal Correctional Institution in Pennsylvania to a residential reentry center in December 2016. However, even while he was incarcerated in prison, Serge was able to manipulate multiple women concurrently, including his beautiful Italian fiancé from New York. In his correspondence with these women and others, he remained a chameleon in his interactions, convincingly expressing virtuous sentiments at first meet.

> At the end of the day this experience made me a better and a stronger person. The things I took for granted before will be cherished now. It's like a rebirth; you get to experience life all over again. How many people can say that? People out there are tired of monotony. They go through life like a repetitive exercise, always complaining and never content. Not realizing how fragile life is and how easily it could be turned up side down. You never truly respect and appreciate things till you lose them and I've lost almost everything, but I never lost the will and determination to persevere. I didn't buckle under this tremendous weight, but instead flourished as a person. Maybe I didn't flourish materialistically, but in the grand scheme of things you can always obtain material wealth. The question is 'can you ever obtain character?' Character is forged under pressure. Pressure alone can make you or break you.[3]

But, just as with his victims, as time progressed the façade of his personality began to fade. Politeness and kindness were replaced with violence,

> If you were a dude and I could get my hands on you, I'd beat your fucking brains in and make you remember how to measure your bitch ass words. On the streets it be either you get me or I'll get you. But since you're a dumb bitch and I don't beef nor do I gossip with bitches, IT'S FUCK YOU! Now go play in traffic!

This is the pattern of a trafficker—their system of gaining compliance: Initially amicable rapport, with a slow progression into verbally aggressive degradation. This is their method for strategically gaining control of those around them, which has proved to be a powerful tool in achieving successful mental domination and subsequent trafficking in persons. Men such as Serge are perhaps the most dangerous type of traffickers because they have the capacity to traffic anyone from anywhere at any time.

* * *

Whether it is in the United States or 5,000 miles away in Eastern Europe, human traffickers from all different walks of life use similar methods to recruit and elicit compliance from their victims, yet the viability of these tactics can differ depending on the socioeconomic status of the target. Trafficking men and women with few life prospects and without strong social networks provides for a shorter and easier recruitment process. Even if a destitute victim is only a few miles away from friends, family, or law enforcement, compliance can be gained by combining exploitation with the intermittent provision of basic human needs.

Physiologically, a human trafficker may recruit an indigent victim by providing and controlling food, clothing, and shelter or offering safety from other threats, such as abusive clients, even if they themselves eventually become violent toward the victim. Intermittently meeting the basic human needs of their victims facilitates the human trafficker's development of a trauma bond, which discourages them from seeking help, despite their exploitation. This process is different and more complex when conscripting more affluent targets.

For women and men who come from supportive families with an abundance of financial and social resources, traffickers are more inclined to remove the victim from their familiar environment before they will begin exploitation. They can transport him or her to a different part of the country or even to a networked business located in a different continent. Once the victim is removed from their home, the trafficker will maintain compliance by confiscating the victim's identification documents; controlling their communication, transportation, housing, and finances; and holding immigration and/or debts over the victim's head. However, these isolation methods are not as reliable for ensuring long-term control of victims, so the trafficker may use them in combination with physical force and emotional bonding.

Despite the socioeconomic status of the victim, most human traffickers will interact with their targets in a courteous manner, so that they will feel a false sense of safety, love, or belonging, at least at the beginning of the recruitment. The interactions can even initially build the self-esteem of the victim, meeting the fundamental human need to feel respected. Although the façade will dissipate with time, once the true intentions of the trafficker are revealed, it may be too late. Threats and violence are often used as last resorts to force the victim into compliance.

Notes

1. Pseudonyms used throughout this chapter due to the direct quotes from convicted human traffickers.

2. A pseudonym was not used for Boris because his criminal ties have been documented in other publications, and he is since deceased.

3. All quotes, including those in the narrative of this chapter, were taken from correspondence between the actual sex trafficker and Dr. Mehlman-Orozco.

CHAPTER NINE

Mentality of a Monger

Many nonprofit organizations have started to attack the demand side of sex trafficking by focusing on the buyers and end-users of human beings who fuel the market for commercial sex. These organizations believe that they can prevent modern slavery at its source, since it is the buyers who create and fuel the market for sex trafficking.[1]

However, the reality is that the demand for commercial sex is so prolific that it will never end. Eradicating it is a Sisyphean task. I have personally interviewed multiple men who admit to purchasing sex, including lawyers for nonprofit organizations, PhD economics professors, and journalists. Many of these men are educated with master's degrees and above, married with kids, and are middle to upper class. Publicly, these men are our colleagues, friends, and family, but privately they engage in sexual fantasies with purchased women. Their existence, reality, and drive for commercial sex are more complex than anti-trafficking organizations lead the public to believe. Strengthening the penalties for these men will not likely serve as a universal deterrent, considering their decision to purchase commercial sex is typically not a rational choice. Although understanding these men will help identify mechanisms for countering sex trafficking, it will not end the commercial sex trade.

For example, take "Dirk," a mixed-race,[2] young adult[3] American, who claimed to have graduated cum laude from the second- or third-most selective Ivy League college in the United States. As a young man, he participated in ROTC and went to an East Coast boarding school for two years.

Dirk stated that he worked for the emerging markets division of a huge multinational consulting firm where he earned $194k per year, along with per diem and living allowance when he was on the job. Before landing this position, he claimed to have worked as a military contractor and in law enforcement, as well as on a national political campaign.

At the height of his sex tourism (2008–2010), Dirk was based in Bangkok, Thailand, although he traveled around the world frequently, especially throughout the former Soviet Union, which he referred to as "FSU."

On September 24, 2008, he posted to the InternationalSexGuide.info forum in Geylang, Singapore, "Slummin' in Singapore. Didn't even take off my shoes, just dropped my pants to my ankles and nailed this Indian cutie for 15 minutes."[4] A picture of the girl he copulated accompanied his post. On October 6, 2008, he posted to the forum in Thailand, "I fucked a dog-ugly Paki in KL[5] a few days ago just to say I fucked a chick from Pakistan."[6]

Although his statements and self-proclaimed actions portrayed him as a misogynistic womanizer, the reality is that no human being can be explained so plainly. He, just like many men who patronize sex workers, is a complex individual, with deep and evolving ethics, beliefs, and experiences.

For example, his opinions on disproportionate sentencing for persons of color within the American criminal justice system were shaped by his experience teaching "history in the hood" while he was waiting for his security clearance for a law enforcement job. He provided his students with this panacea to their situation: "Do not do things which are punishable by incarceration, and do not associate with those that do."[7]

He claimed that a classmate of his worked with Barry Scheck's Innocence Project and alleged that most people who were exonerated were career criminals who had walked for many infractions for which they were not convicted. Although he admitted that police are often overly forceful in making arrests, Dirk believed that "police don't really set up innocent people."[8]

Although Dirk agreed that racism still existed, he felt that it could be almost totally mitigated depending on one's socioeconomic status and geographical location. He said, "The delineation of racism and classism is becoming increasingly difficult for me to identify. I don't think that America has a race problem. The only racial issue that I infrequently have today is with underclass ghetto blacks who are ignorant of the concept of the talented tenth and blame racism for their own pathological behavior."[9]

According to Dirk, "A lot of wealth is built on the misery and suffering of others . . . The best way to go from zero to hero in a flash is to be in a position to take advantage of other's misfortunes."[10] And that is exactly how he climbed the socioeconomic ladder.

Prior to the Iraq war, Dirk claimed that he had lost his U.S. government job, and his wife left him. His pockets were empty, and he was $25,000 in debt with no way to pay it. He felt that his family had disowned him, and he had no purpose in life. However, after 9/11, he took a job with what he described as a "dirt bag defense contractor" that hired him solely on the basis of his resume with no interview. He got his security clearance in order, went back to Iraq with a consulting firm at an outrageous salary, and cleared out his debt in three months.

He stated that opportunities like this were opened up for people like him because many companies and their personnel were left-leaning and refused to go to Iraq for political as well as operational security issues. That fact, coupled with the sheer size of the programs in Iraq, meant that there were vacancies that were not filled with the normal cadre of experienced professionals. As such, many young, smart but inexperienced people were thrust into jobs that would normally only be filled with senior development professionals that had long domestic careers before they went abroad.

While deployed, he admittedly gained invaluable experience, which translated into more assignments in other parts of the world, with more money and even better benefits. Dirk didn't agree with the war in Iraq, but he financially benefited from it and, therefore, was grateful. He said, "Fucked up. Maybe. But it is what it is."

While deployed in areas around the world, Dirk engaged in a significant amount of sex tourism. While much of his time on the commercial sex forums was spent bragging about his sexual conquests, he also debated the philosophy of sex tourism and explored the rationale for why men, including him, purchase sex.

> Most forum members see mongering as purely a short-term P4P[11] activity with numerous providers at a reasonable rate. Other members are on this site because they are socially frustrated and, ipso facto, sexually deprived. A few members may be sexual deviants and seek outlets for their perversion. While other members may be traveling or extremely busy professionals that desire sex, but don't have the time to cultivate healthy and normal sexual relations with partners.[12]

Interestingly, he recognized the inherent exploitation with purchasing sexual services from women in economically disadvantaged areas around the world, yet he somehow disassociated these facts from sex trafficking and rationalized continuing the practice.

Dirk on the Commercial Sex Trade

Some of us may attempt to delude ourselves about the merits of employing prostitutes, but we should all be clear that we are exploiting vulnerable fellow human beings for short-term physical gratification. Most people on this board happen to be born in prosperous nations that afford us a plethora of opportunities; yet, we go to places that are less prosperous and exploit their lack of prosperity to the umpth degree.

In many other parts of the world patronizing a prostitute is contributing to the dehumanization of another human being. This is a man's world. What's a woman really have to give? When she sells which should only be given it's a horrible phenomenon.

Ever heard the term "breaking a hoe"? That's what often happens to these poor girls that are trafficked. I worked in Kosovo and was appalled at how the women that serviced NATO, UN, and other international agency employees were treated. These girls were unsophisticated villagers from the Balkans that were sometimes tricked into what the terms of their employment would be. These girls were kept locked up like human chattel in abhorrent conditions, and gang raped by Albanian thugs until they were broken in. The ones that resisted were beaten and fucked in every which way until they had no will left.

The women in the troikas in Moscow, they used to have a scar on the small of their back. Do you know what it's from? It's from having a train run on them by their handlers for a weekend in some filthy kvartal.

Behind the façade are often tails of inhumane treatment and misery.

For 10 girls that make the big bucks in Dubai, there are two or three of them that go back without a penny in their pockets as broken people. I have first hand knowledge of an Arab fella that took a girl from Tiraspol back to his villa, raped her for two weeks, then had his father and uncle rape her for a week, then drove her to the dessert naked and tossed her out in the middle of nowhere on the outskirts of Dubai.

One of the most disgusting displays of inhumanity I have ever witnessed occurred in Baghdad, where one of my employees was kidnapped and raped as a 26-year-old virgin. When she returned to work I was shocked to find that my pro-western supposedly moderate Iraqi staff had ostracized her. I don't speak a lick of Arabic but I can tell the look of disdain when I see it. I'm not Arab, a woman, or a rape counselor so there wasn't much I could do. Anyway, I began to notice that she was the first one to work and the last one leave. Odd, but one day when I went back to office at 2100 hours I found her there and it suddenly dawned on my dumb ass—she was living in the office because her parents had kicked her out of the house for being abducted and raped.

The relevancy is this. My deputy was one of those rare people that understood both the Arabic and western perspective as he had spent years in Europe and the states, and when I asked him about this he stated that while it was unfortunate what happened to the girl but because she had "shamed" her family by being raped the family had to distance itself from her because the family honor was the more important than the individual.

Many of these Islamic hookers were dishonored and cut loose by their families in a culture where family is everything.

Maybe by patronizing them you are enabling their survival. Most of these hookers are not from capital cities, they are nothing more than unsophisticated peasants who are abused and violated on a daily basis.

You know why hookers are always yapping on the phone? Ever listen to their conversation? It's rubbish, just idleness chatter. They do this because it provides psychological distance from the act of selling one's soul. I am not totally here as I have a lifeline via an open line of communication with somebody someplace else. It helps keep their mind off their immediate reality.

That being said, life is Hobbesian: It is short, nasty, brutish, and often cruel. In many parts of the world violence, exploitation, and poverty is the norm rather than the exception. So in retrospect, life sucks for hookers but it sucks for many others too.

I also don't buy into the whole western feminist leftist mantra that women are trafficked against their will. Go to PBS's website and view the frontline series about Moldova . . . What a crock of shit, that crew is getting played like a flute. Most of these girls know that they will be working in the sex industry and willingly accept this; however, they are often incapable of knowing the depths of the depravity that they will encounter. Or worse yet, they are aware of it but accept it because the feel they must.

You can put lipstick on this pig all you want, but the fact of the matter is that prostitution is often a vile and hyper exploitive business with a very dark undercurrent to it.[13]

Sample of Dirk's Sexual Exploits

Over the course of five years, Dirk visited more than 20 countries, mongering in Colombia, Panama, Cuba, Romania, Uzbekistan, Thailand, Ethiopia, South Africa, and Afghanistan (see Appendix D for an abbreviated timeline of Dirk's sex tourism).

He posted pictures of many of his sexual conquests, including a young Uzbekistani girl, whom he claimed to have copulated for 7,000 baht in Thailand (approximately $200); four women in Medellin, Bogota, and Cartagena, Colombia, for 120,000 to 125,000 pesos each ($40 to $45); a 22-year-old Filipino girl for $200; three young women in Cuba for $30 each, and an Ethiopian woman for $70. Dirk's sex tourism lasted for years and provides insight into the experiences and mentality of a monger. The following are only a few examples of his exploits.

On December 29, 2005, Dirk posted about his experience in Sofia, Bulgaria. After getting intoxicated, he said that he invited some "semi sex slaves" from the local bordello to live with him in Kosovo. They accepted. By the time he had sobered up, they were all in a taxi about to cross into Macedonia. He claimed that the girls were gazing up at him as if he were their "knight in shining armor." The arrangement worked out well for him, even though he claimed to have stolen the girls from the Bulgarian mafia. In parting, he cautioned other mongers, "Remember, all of those clubs are owned by the same guy."[14]

Between 2005 and 2007, Dirk made multiple trips to Kyrgyzstan for work. He commented on how poor and isolated the country was. According to him, there was no economy to speak of, and all the money was either dirty or came from remittances or grants from the West. By his lights, the only way a woman could have anything remotely approaching a decent life was "to get the fuck out"—either on her own or through marriage.

Dirk explained that after 9/11, thousands of Westerners came to Kyrgyzstan to staff Manas Air Base, which is located near the capital Bishkek. He described that it was the main support hub for operations in Afghanistan, and Bishkek became the R&R destination of choice for many contractors stationed there. In addition, during the transit to Afghanistan, members of the military and contractors would layover at Manas for 12 to 72 hours. Dirk claimed that on the way in to Kyrgyzstan they couldn't leave the air base, but on the way out, they could. He explained that Operation Enduring Freedom (OEF) staff preferred sex tourism in Kyrgyzstan over other countries, "fuck Thailand . . . Yellow pussy there, yellow pussy here . . . Why fork over the extra money for the flight to Bangkok?"[15]

Throughout the mid to late 2000s, Dirk sexually toured much of the former Soviet Union. His sexual exploitation included a 21-year-old Gagauzian girl living in Chişinău, Moldova. Dirk described her as an ethnic and linguistic Turk who spoke good English, didn't go out, and was merely a student who needed money. He claimed to have received "an excellent BBBJ[16], CIM[17], and enthusiastic sex with passionate kissing," before haggling with her female pimp over the currency of payment ($ or €).

Dirk liked Tashkent, Uzbekistan, for the variety and beauty of the women—"Blonde Slavs, Central Asians, Caucasians (Georgians and Armenians), Tartars, and just about everything in between." He wrote, "as a veteran monger of Latin America, Eastern Europe, and Southeast Asia, this is my favorite place thus far." He felt that the sex workers had been "reacquainted" with their Islamic and Central Asian hospitality in Uzbekistan.

Even if there were a dearth of local sex workers, there would be imported women available for purchase in each location Dirk visited. For example, while in Ashgabat, Turkmenistan, with a few colleagues who, as he described them, were "NOT fellow hobbyists," Dirk explained,

> *Turkmen girls are brought up in a very strict, very traditional family environment where pre-marital relations with men is seriously frowned upon. You cannot confuse a Turkmen girl as they tend to wear the traditional long dress, which is often brightly color with a matching headscarf—well, more of a turban if you ask me. Not exactly fetching, but with the hair off the face you can see their sleek Asiatic facial bone structure. Many are serious knock-outs if you like the type. Of course, the problem is that they tend not to be working girls and literally disappear after dark. I was told that it is very, very rare that a Turkmen girl gets mixed up in prostitution in Ashgabat.*[18]

However, Dirk was still able to obtain services there with the imported sex workers from Russia. For $80, he was able to purchase a dark-haired Russian girl with a slim build and limited English language skills. While in the country for work, he had her perform a BBBJ and sexual intercourse in various positions after his colleagues had turned in to their hotel rooms for the evening.

In multiple countries, Dirk described procuring sex with women who were under the influence of drugs or alcohol. At times, while traveling for work, he would give the women money to purchase the drugs. For example, while in Cartagena, Colombia, he gave three sex workers 100,000 pesos, which they used to purchase two small balls of cocaine in aluminum foil and a bag of marijuana.

Back at his apartment, Dirk claimed that the girls began doing lines off *The Economist* on his table. He went on to say that the girls prompted, almost insisted, that he partake in the drugs as well, but he said that he "pulled a Bill Clinton" and grabbed the lit-up joint, which he only pretended to smoke. After utilizing Viagra, nicknamed "Vitamin V," he then claimed to have sex with the three women on and off for four hours, alternating between fellatio, vaginal, and anal sex, "without so much as a courtesy wipe."[19]

In addition to traveling for work, Dirk also traveled for pleasure and entertainment. In June 2010, he visited Johannesburg, South Africa, for the FIFA World Cup. In addition to watching the games, he visited the bordellos of Sandton.

Ever the sociologist, Dirk talked with the Afrikaans women about South Africa, race, and money. One of the girls claimed that because the salaries in South Africa were insufficient to meet a decent standard of living, 70 percent of her high school classmates were "fucking for money."

There didn't seem to be anything that could have deterred Dirk from his consumerism in the commercial sex industry. At one point, he claimed that he was drugged and robbed by two women from Nostalgia while acquiring sexual services in Moldova in late November 2006. He reported that all of his valuables were stolen, including his U.S. government-issued laptop and his camera. In addition to material for work, both his laptop and camera had photos of sex workers in Thailand, Cambodia, and Moldova. He explained that his belongings and the women who burglarized him were recovered within 72 hours; however, they were not returned to him, "due to the intransigence of the Moldovan FSB" and his hubris. He wrote, "I will not, as a former 1811,[20] give a cop money to do his job." He posted the story simply to warn other sex tourists, "Three people were killed in Moldova during the past six months due to variations of the chicanery that happened to me. Enjoy the pretty peasants in Moldova, but watch your backs boys."[21] Ultimately, he was not dissuaded from sex tourism and continued posting about his exploits with increased regularity.

After engaging in sex tourism for several years, however, Dirk began to exhibit signs of depression. He believed that his mongering was closing off his opportunities for intimacy with a potential partner. He felt that he was "unable to be a genuine nice guy any longer." He was so used to paying women to do everything he wanted that he could no longer tolerate a woman not acquiescing to his every whim. "If I say come at 2:00 a.m. and they don't, I will curse them and pick up the phone and will have one or two chicks at my apartment or hotel within 20 minutes."[22]

Dirk felt that he could do anything he wanted to women because he had money. For the one who wouldn't put up with him, there were three more who would eagerly take her place, as long as he paid for it. He stated that, "You can't be a true monger and have the same level of respect for women that you had before you entered the lifestyle." He felt that his mongering started to corrode him because he began to live for "the obtaining of pussy as cheaply and as effortlessly as possible."[23] He wrote about how his commercial sex tourism had changed him for the worse and transformed other sex tourists too, but they just didn't know it. He stated that he was, "disgusted by these women and even more disgusted at himself." The problem was that he just couldn't stop. Despite his misery, he still couldn't let go of the idea of showing off his $1,200 mobile phone, expensive watch, and $60,000 car before buying multiple women;

however, he did fully realize that engaging in sex tourism had eroded his decency and maligned his perspective toward women.

In the end, he was still alone and lonely. Despite engaging in commercial sex tourism for years, he articulated that he was truly searching for "stability with a reliable and trustworthy partner, not sex."

> *This is bad. Very bad. I am presently in a downward spiral in my life and may not be able to reverse it because of my behavior and the women I now surround myself with.*
>
> *I am so fucking sick of my lifestyle. Deluding myself that the garbage I boast about is a veritable substitute for intimacy. New country, new pussy, more money, but same hollowness inside . . . God forbid the day I start hitting the mini bar.*
>
> *I would give it all up in a heartbeat if I could.*[24]

The information shared by Dirk could easily be used to identify him with the right resources. If everything he said was truthful, his position, his personal background, the date of his robbery, and travel patterns could all be used to piece together who he is. However, anti-trafficking NGOs, legislators, and law enforcement are more concerned with shutting down these commercial sex information exchange websites rather than using them as a tool. Men like Dirk, who claim to have knowingly procured sexual services from trafficked victims, should be prosecuted and held accountable for their crimes. However, they continue with impunity, while most anti-trafficking advocates chase hollow victories for nothing more than public accolade.

Notes

1. About Global Centurion. Global Centurion (n.d.): accessed April 22, 2017, http://www.globalcenturion.org/about/about/.

2. White mother. Black father.

3. Under 30 years old, as of September 2008.

4. *Photo Gallery Forum in Singapore* (September 24, 2008): accessed July 6, 2017, http://www.InternationalSexGuide.info.

5. Kuala Lumpur.

6. *Photo Gallery Forum in Thailand* (October 6, 2008): accessed July 6, 2017, http://www.InternationalSexGuide.info.

7. *American Politics Forum* (October 6, 2008: accessed July 6, 2017, http://www.InternationalSexGuide.info.

8. Ibid.

9. *Opinion Forum on American Women* (October 28, 2008): accessed July 6, 2017, http://www.InternationalSexGuide.info.

10. *American Politics Forum* (January 1, 2006): accessed July 6, 2017, http://www.InternationalSexGuide.info.

11. Pay for play or pay for pussy. See Appendix A for more information.

12. *Opinion Forum on American Women* (October 5, 2008): accessed July 6, 2017, http://www.InternationalSexGuide.info.

13. *Opinion Forum on American Women* (October 13, 2008): accessed July 6, 2017, http://www.InternationalSexGuide.info.

14. *Other Areas Forum* (December 29, 2005): accessed July 6, 2017, http://www.InternationalSexGuide.info.

15. *General Info Forum in Kyrgyzstan* (December 20, 2007): accessed July 6, 2017, http://www.InternationalSexGuide.info.

16. Bare back blow job. See Appendix A for more information.

17. Cum in mouth. See Appendix A for more information.

18. *Forum on Links to Reports of Distinction in Turkmenistan* (September 25, 2008): accessed July 6, 2017, http://www.InternationalSexGuide.info.

19. *Cartagena Reports Forum* (November 21, 2010): accessed July 6, 2017, http://www.InternationalSexGuide.info.

20. According to the U.S. Government Office of Personnel Management (OPM), 1811 refers to positions within the federal Criminal Investigation Series.

21. *General Info Forum in Moldova* (February 13, 2007): accessed July 6, 2017, http://www.InternationalSexGuide.info.

22. *American Women Forum* (September 25, 2008): accessed July 6, 2017, http://www.InternationalSexGuide.info.

23. Ibid.

24. *Opinion Forum on American Women* (September 25, 2008): accessed July 6, 2017, http://www.InternationalSexGuide.info.

PART 2

Labor Trafficking

Unfortunately, every single American has used, consumed, worn, and purchased products of slavery at multiple points throughout their life. Modern-day slavery—termed labor trafficking—is defined as "the recruitment, harboring, transportation, provision, or obtaining of a person for labor or services, through the use of force, fraud, or coercion for the purpose of subjection to involuntary servitude, peonage, debt bondage, or slavery."[1] Anti-trafficking advocates explain that there are more slaves today than at any other time in history. Although data are difficult to come by, some claim that they are less expensive as well. In 1850, an average slave in the American South cost the equivalent of $40,000 in today's money. Today, on average worldwide, a slave costs about $90.[2]

Shockingly, this isn't just an issue with goods imported from third-world countries. Labor trafficking is also pervasive in the United States, among legal foreign nationals and undocumented migrants, as well as American citizens. For example, guest workers can be lured with the promises of steady and lucrative jobs, only to find upon arrival that they were deceived about their employment circumstances, income, and living situation. According to the International Labor Organization (ILO), nearly 21 million people are victims of forced labor globally—6 million of them are children, and 1.5 million are exploited in developed countries such as the United States.[3]

Ultimately, labor trafficking can be found in the production of our food, clothing, shoes, electronics, and gifts. Although there are often ethically produced alternatives, they are typically more expensive and have not yet gained the popularity needed to begin replacing products produced through slavery. Understanding how Americans support these industries is important to increasing informed consumerism in the land of the free and home of the brave.

Notes

1. U.S. Department of States. "What Is Trafficking in Persons?" (n.d.): accessed April 22, 2017, http://www.state.gov/j/tip/rls/tiprpt/2015/243359.htm.

2. Kevin Bales, *Disposable People: New Slavery in the Global Economy*, 2nd ed. (Berkeley, CA: University of California Press, 2004).

3. Zoe Tabary, "Malawian Housemaid Wins U.S. Human Trafficking Case after Three Years 'in Prison,'" Thomson Reuters Foundation (November 28, 2016): accessed July 6, 2017, http://news.trust.org/item/20161128110407-wbl1t/.

CHAPTER TEN

Legal and Still Exploited

Authorities called it "the largest human trafficking case in U.S. history."[1] A U.S.-based labor-recruiting firm—Global Horizons Manpower Inc.—was indicted for forcing over 400 Thai nationals into virtual slave labor with substandard wages, as well as inadequate food and housing. If the workers tried to escape, they told authorities that they were threatened with arrest, deportation, and physical violence.[2]

The trafficked workers described being lured into the United States with lucrative and long-term employment deals. One victim reported being promised a three-year contract, $8.72 per hour, and time-and-a-half overtime for compensation to harvest pineapples in Maui. Eleven other victims maintained that they were promised $80,000 Thai baht (approximately $2,000 USD) per month for eight hours of work each day in addition to any overtime pay.

According to the indictment, the recruited farmworkers were impoverished in Thailand, earning only the equivalent of $1,000 USD per year in family income.[3] As such, the exorbitant recruitment fees, ranging from $380,000 to $1,060,000 Thai baht, which was approximately $9,500 to $26,500 USD, seemed to be worth it in the long run. Many of them put up their family property as collateral for loans to cover a portion of the expenses, with the hope of earning a better salary in the United States.

However, although the conscripted workers were required to pay these substantially larger fees, each employee was allegedly told to lie to the U.S. Embassy and state that they only paid $65,000 Thai baht (approximately $1,624 USD). According to court documents, Global Horizons' Israeli-born CEO and president Mordechai Orian also concealed the scheme by failing to reveal the recruitment fees on U.S. Department of

Labor Employment and Training Administration Application for Alien Employment Certification (Form 750) and the Agricultural Food Processing Clearance Orders (Form 790).

Orian allegedly placed the workers into debt bondage with the recruitment fees and failed to uphold the terms of compensation, as well as length of employment contracts. He also supposedly directed onsite field supervisors to confiscate the guest workers' passports and visas as soon as they arrived. The workers were told that if they didn't turn over their passports, they would not work, according to the indictment.

The workers were allegedly kept under control through isolation. The rules for working on the farms included: (1) not talking to other people from Thailand outside the farm, (2) not leaving the housing location or else risk arrest, (3) not escaping or fleeing because police or Global Horizons would find, arrest, and deport the worker back to Thailand.

The workers were outsourced to farms across the United States.

While in Hawaii, laborers were housed in shipping containers with no carpet, beds, furniture, indoor plumbing, kitchen, nor air conditioning.

While working for the Eubanks family farm, 15 workers reported being housed by Global Horizons in rooms with padlocks, secured from the outside. Incidentally, according to the Eubanks Farm website, their mission is "to provide a safe, economical, and healthy supply of produce to our customers in a manner of integrity that honors our family farming heritage."[4] They may not have had any idea of the malicious labor law violations the farmworkers faced while being outsourced to their family produce business.

Others were allegedly held on properties that were guarded 24 hours per day, seven days per week. According to court documents, the perimeters were marked with bells on strings to alert if a worker tried to escape in the night. Some victims reported being threatened with death, guns, being hit or prodded with sticks, and other physical harm if they didn't work hard enough or tried to escape. "We worked and lived under terrible conditions, treated like animals in a cage," said one of the victimized Thai farmworkers, Phirom Krinsoongnoen.[5]

Some of these workers performed agricultural services for well-known produce distributors. For example, one worker reported that between March and May 2003 he harvested pineapples at a Del Monte farm. At times, he was never paid for his work. Immigration agents eventually came to the Del Monte farm and took the worker into custody for several days, along with other migrant agricultural laborers. During that time, a Global Horizons representative supposedly arrived and instructed the workers to agree to voluntary deportation back to Thailand.

Global Horizons brought the workers into the United States under the H2-A visa program, which required the company to provide the farmworkers with food and housing in addition to pay for work performed. Instead, the Thai workers were forced into debt bondage, charged exorbitant recruitment fees, denied or delayed pay, deprived of adequate food and water, and forced into unsanitary and overcrowded living conditions. The employees had their movements monitored and their passports confiscated, and if they complained, they were retaliated against.[6]

The alleged forced-labor ring was active in 13 states, and the network spanned 15 countries. It recruited workers on four continents, including women and men from Thailand, India, Nepal, and Israel, as well as from Eastern and Western Europe. However, the criminal charges against Global Horizons were eventually dropped with little explanation from the federal prosecutors—only that they couldn't prove the human trafficking allegations beyond a reasonable doubt.

Although Global Horizons CEO Mordechai Orian claimed it was because the government had been overzealous in their prosecution and he was innocent of all charges,[7] his company was eventually found liable in civil court, resulting in a $7.7 million judgment for 67 of the Thai farmworker victims in Washington state, as well as a $8.7 million judgment for victims in Hawaii.[8]

* * *

I had no idea about the labor abuses faced by *legal* immigrants until undergraduate school. It was not a class but rather conversations with a friend that opened my eyes. He had volunteered for the Coalition of Immokalee Workers (CIW), a worker-based human rights organization, located in Immokalee, Florida.

My friend had marched alongside CIW in the early 2000s while they were boycotting Taco Bell. According to CIW, fast food mega-chains were benefiting from the exploitation of farmworkers in the tomato industry.

CIW claimed that the median income of these farmworkers in the late 1990s was between $5,000 to $7,500 per year.[9] These legal immigrants were only earning 1.2 to 1.5 cents per pound of tomatoes they picked. CIW demanded, "Taco Bell increase the price it pays per pound of tomatoes by 1 cent, with the increase to be passed on, in whole, to the pickers."[10] An agreement was reached with Taco bell in 2005, and similar agreements followed with McDonald's, Burger King, Subway, and Chipotle, among others.

I, like many Americans, had never questioned how I was able to purchase fast food for such low prices. Learning how little the agricultural farmworkers earned, who labored for these companies' produce, put these prices into a different perspective. However, despite the penny wage increases, labor trafficking was still prolific among legal agricultural guest workers.

After over two decades worth of advocacy for tomato pickers, their wages only increased from $40 to $70 per day to $50 to $80 per day.[11] In addition to the continuation of depressed wages, labor trafficking cases involving legal guest workers rarely ended in a conviction, even if the abuses were brought to the attention of law enforcement.

For example, in 2010 Cabioch Bontemps, Carline Ceneus, and Willy Paul Edouard were indicted by a federal grand jury on charges of conspiracy to commit forced labor for allegedly holding over 50 guest workers from Haiti against their will in the bean fields of Alachua County, Florida. The indictment stated that Ceneus traveled to Haiti and recruited workers by promising them high steady wages ($8.82), as well as free room and board for three years, culminating in permanent residency in the United States. According to court documents, this enticed the workers to pay extremely high recruitment fees, which included their airfare but required them to incur substantial debts.[12]

Although Ceneus allegedly collected approximately $3,000 from each Haitian bean picker applicant, employees were brought into the United States under the seasonal and temporary H-2A nonimmigrant agricultural guest worker program and told to lie to the U.S. Embassy and state that they hadn't paid any fees for their jobs. Once they arrived in the United States, the workers were not paid as promised (instead earning only $3.50 per sack of beans picked) and received only sporadic work, which made it impossible to repay the debt they had incurred in Haiti.[13]

Court documents detailed how the employees had their passports confiscated, as well as how they were denied food, medical care, and adequate housing. The workers claimed that they were forced to pick in fields that were recently sprayed with harsh pesticides, causing blisters and permanent scarring. When inspectors came, the indictment alleged that Ceneus instructed the workers to put on a show and pretend like everything was okay, or else she would have them deported. At one point, co-conspirator Bontemps allegedly raped one of the workers in his employ, offered her money toward her debt in exchange, and threatened her if she were to report it.[14]

However, despite the slew of allegations that were included in court documents and publicized in the news, the Department of Justice dropped the charges on January 25, 2012, again with little public explanation.

* * *

Temporary guest worker visa programs in the United States are wrought with human trafficking abuses. Under the H-2A visa program, agricultural employers bring guest workers into the country under temporary nonimmigrant visas to work exclusively on the petitioning employer's farm. According to CIW, "guest workers under the visa program remain in the country only at the pleasure of their employer; they cannot change jobs, and they are obliged to return to their home country once their employer is finished with them, or face deportation."[15]

This temporary guest worker arrangement places a tremendous amount of power in the hands of the employers, making the workers at risk for extreme exploitation.[16] Debt bondage and labor trafficking can be found in nearly every faction of the agricultural industry, from tomato farms and citrus groves of Florida to the pineapple fields of Hawaii. Major food-buying corporations profit from the low cost of U.S. produce, which can be picked by workers in sweatshop or slavery-like conditions.

Similar to the H-2A visa program, the H-2B program allows U.S. employers to recruit and employ foreign workers for seasonal nonagricultural positions, unfilled by the domestic labor market. H-2B visas are provided for jobs in a number of industries, such as, landscaping, forestry and conservation, food processing, construction, tourism, and hospitality. Given the lack of visa oversight, human trafficking exploitation has been found across the board. Workers are lured to the United States with false promises of green cards, which allow permanent residency, and they are required to pay thousands of dollars in recruiting fees for the opportunity.

For example, every year hundreds of Mexican women are paid as little as $2 per pound to extract crabmeat for the seafood industry in Maryland. Their work contributes approximately $400 million each year to the local economy. Traveling thousands of miles from impoverished rural Mexican communities to the East Coast, H-2B workers have played a significant role in the state's historic industry since the program's advent in 1986. In 2007 alone, 56 percent of Maryland's seafood companies relied on the work of H-2B guest workers to process 82 percent of Maryland's crab harvest.[17] As Maryland crab companies and other H-2B employers push for additional H-2B visas, the current lack of oversight has left many H-2B visa-holders overworked, underpaid, and without legal representation.

In addition, similar abuses can be found in the J-1 visa program, which is supposed to provide temporary nonimmigrant visas for individuals approved to participate in work and study-based exchange visitor programs. However, an Associated Press investigation found that while Hillary Clinton was Secretary of State, students were forced to work in strip clubs instead of restaurants and live in overcrowded apartments, while others earned $1 per hour or less. According to Terry Coonan, former prosecutor and executive director of the Florida State University's Center for the Advancement of Human Rights, "It's difficult to prosecute these cases because the workers usually leave the country within a few months. That's why the J-1 is the ideal visa to exploit."[18] The AP story concluded that, the State Department did little to help workers with employment-related issues, instead claiming that it "has no authority to sanction employers."[19]

Despite being a prolific human trafficking issue, the abuses faced by legal immigrants are often overlooked by legislators.

For example, during the third and final debate of the 2016 presidential election, the candidates discussed immigration reform. Donald J. Trump argued the need for strong borders and an active deportation policy, while Hillary Clinton focused on improving border security, while offering a pathway to citizenship for the 11 million unauthorized foreign nationals already in the United States. Both presidential candidates omitted a strategy to fix the broken legal immigration process, which is a critical issue facing millions of legal foreign nationals in and traveling to the United States for employment.

Clinton suggested that a pathway to citizenship would "get everybody out of the shadows" and reduce exploitation of unauthorized migrant labor. According to Clinton, undocumented workers are underpaid, and if they complain, they are threatened with deportation. However, she neglected to acknowledge that this same problem affects legal nonimmigrants as well under the current system.[20]

For years, this type of exploitation has affected legal nonimmigrant guest workers in the United States without redress. According to the Polaris Project, which operates the National Human Trafficking Resource Center and hotline, there are six U.S. temporary visas commonly associated with labor exploitation and trafficking: A-3, B-1, G-5, H-2A, H-2B, and J-1.[21] Between August 1, 2014, and July 31, 2015, 38 percent of all human trafficking cases that referenced serious labor abuse involved victims who entered the United States *legally*, with one of those six visas. These facts should be the catalyst for reform.

Given the exploitation faced by legal nonimmigrants in the United States, truly comprehensive immigration reform must focus on more than just what to do with the unauthorized foreign national population and how to secure our southern border. Legal nonimmigrants are being trafficked and face human rights abuses, which deserves the attention of our country and leadership from our elected officials. Providing unauthorized foreign nationals with a pathway to citizenship will not necessarily reduce their likelihood of exploitation, unless we also address the critical labor trafficking issues affecting legal nonimmigrants.

Notes

1. Teresa Watanabe, "Federal Grand Jury Indicts Associates of Beverly Hills Firm in Human-Trafficking Case," *Los Angeles Times* (September 4, 2010): accessed July 6, 2017, http://articles.latimes.com/2010/sep/04/local/la-me-0904 -human-trafficking-20100904.

2. Ibid.

3. Ibid.

4. Eubanks Produce Farms. Welcome to Our Farms (n.d.): accessed April 22, 2017, http://www.eubanksproduce.com/ourFarms.php.

5. U.S. Equal Employment Opportunity Commission, "Judge Approves $2.4 Million EEOC Settlement with Four Hawaii Farms for over 500 Thai Farmworkers," (September 5, 2016): accessed July 6, 2017, https://www1.eeoc.gov//eeoc /newsroom/release/9-5-14.cfm?renderforprint=1.

6. Teresa Watanabe, "Federal Grand Jury Indicts Associates of Beverly Hills Firm in Human-Trafficking Case," *Los Angeles Times* (September 4, 2010): accessed July 6, 2017, http://articles.latimes.com/2010/sep/04/local/la-me-0904-human -trafficking-20100904.

7. Malia Zimmerman, "Exclusive: Global Horizons CEO Speaks Out about Human Trafficking Allegations—and the Justice Department's Decision to Drop the Charges," *Hawaii Reporter* (July 24, 2012): accessed July 6, 2017, http://www .hawaiireporter.com/exclusive-global-horizons-ceo-speaks-out-about-human -trafficking-allegations-and-the-justice-departments-decision-to-drop-the -charges/123.

8. Mateusz Perkowski, "Labor Contractor Held Liable for $7.7 Million," *Capital Press* (May 4, 2016): accessed July 6, 2017, http://www.capitalpress.com /Washington/20160504/labor-contractor-held-liable-for-77-million.

9. "CIW—Boycott the Bell." *CIW Online* (n.d.): accessed April 22, 2017, http:// www.ciw-online.org/tz_site-revision/breaking_news/boycott_in_brief.html.

10. Ibid.

11. Nick Archer, "Higher Wages for Florida Tomato Pickers Mean Fewer Jobs," *Economics21* (June 30, 2016): accessed July 6, 2017, https://economics21.org/html /higher-wages-florida-tomato-pickers-mean-fewer-jobs-1928.html.

12. *United States of America vs. Ceneus, Bontemps, and Edouard.* (October 19, 2010): accessed July 6, 2017, https://assets.documentcloud.org/documents/2177327/carline -hot-pickers-superceding-indictment.pdf.

13. Ibid.

14. Ibid.

15. "DOJ Officials Announce yet Another Prosecution for Forced Labor in Florida Fields, Eighth since 1997," *CIW Online* (July 7, 2010): accessed July 6, 2017, http://www.ciw-online.org/blog/2010/07/eight_and_counting/.

16. Ibid.

17. "Picked Apart: The Hidden Struggles of Migrant Worker Women in the Maryland Crab Industry," American University Washington College of Law and Centro de los Derechos del Migrante, Inc. (n.d.): accessed July 6, 2017, https://fairlaborrecruitment.files.wordpress.com/2013/01/pickedapart-1.pdf.

18. "U.S. Fails to Tackle Student Visa Abuses," *CBS News, Associated Press* (December 6, 2010): accessed July 6, 2017, http://www.cbsnews.com/news/us-fails-to-tackle-student-visa-abuses/.

19. "Culture Shock: The Exploitation of J-1 Cultural Exchange Workers," Southern Poverty Law Center (2014): accessed July 6, 2017, https://www.splcenter.org/sites/default/files/d6_legacy_files/downloads/publication/j-1_report_v2_web.pdf.

20. Kimberly Mehlman-Orozco, "Trump and Clinton Ignored Flaws in Immigration System during Debate," *The Hill* (October 20, 2016): accessed July 6, 2017, http://thehill.com/blogs/pundits-blog/immigration/302001-trump-and-clinton-ignored-flaws-in-immigration-system-during.

21. "Labor Trafficking in the U.S.: A Closer Look at Temporary Work Visas," Polaris Project (n.d.): accessed July 6, 2017, https://polarisproject.org/sites/default/files/Temp%20Visa_v5%20(1).pdf.

CHAPTER ELEVEN

Domestic Servants, Diplomatic Slaves

Domestic servants are common commodities for wealthy families in many parts of the world. To obtain visas for international servants, American-based families must provide a copy of an employment contract to the U.S. embassy of the source country, stating the compensation for the servant and a schedule reflecting in the anticipated hours of employment. However, these contracts can be easily violated, leaving many servants to be exploited for longer work hours, as well as little or no compensation.

Families who exploit domestic servants in the United States include diplomats and royalty, among others.

For example, Hana Al-Jader was the wife of Saudi Prince Mohammad Al-Saud, who received an annual stipend of $100,000 from the Saudi royal family.[1] She came to the attention of law enforcement after one of her domestic servants, Veronica Pedroza—a Filipino national—informed the Coalition to Abolish Slavery and Trafficking (CAST) that the royal family had exploited her.

Pedroza had previously worked in Saudi Arabia as a domestic servant for Al-Jader's sister. However, she moved to the United States in 2000 after Hana Al-Jader promised Pedroza a salary of $500 per month. Once in the United States, Pedroza was taken directly to Al-Jader's house in Massachusetts, where she and three other servants were required to be on call 24 hours per day, performing duties such as cooking, cleaning, and caring for Al-Jader's husband, who was disabled from an accident he had when he was 25 years old. For her labor, which spanned five months in

Saudi Arabia and the United States, Pedroza said she was paid only a total of $200.[2]

In her interviews with law enforcement, Pedroza stated that she and three other Indonesian domestic servants had their passports and immigration documents confiscated by Hana Al-Jader. She placed them in a locked metal cabinet in her bedroom, located in the basement of the house. Pedroza and the other domestic servants were instructed not to leave the house nor use the telephone without permission. Al-Jader would threaten them with arrest and imprisonment if they dared to run away.

Al-Jader told Pedroza that if she quit she would be required to pay back the money it cost to bring her to the United States. Pedroza escaped after several weeks of this servitude; however, she didn't immediately notify authorities.

Following Pedroza's report, Immigration and Customs Enforcement (ICE) corroborated that a temporary visitor business visa (B-1) was issued in Riyadh, Saudi Arabia, on January 31, 2000, in the name of Veronica Pedroza, as well as visas for three other Indonesian women: Tinamarina Amarudin, Indah Utom, and Legi Yanti Karto. These women entered the United States through New York on February 4, 2000, and were legally permitted to remain in the United States until May 3, 2000. A fourth Indonesian woman, Morniati Kadir, was also brought to the United States on a B-1 visa on February 20, 2001.

On November 16, 2004, search warrants were executed on Al-Jader's homes, while she and her family were asleep. Although none of the Indonesian servants named by Pedroza had left the country, they were not at the residence. However, two other Indonesian domestic servants were there—Trimurniyati Bt Sukadi Dzalipa ("Tri") and Rohimah Bt Lili Bakri ("Ro"). Through an interpreter, the agents learned that Tri and Ro worked for Al-Jader for little money, were not allowed to leave the house alone, and did not have possession of their own passports. Tri and Ro did not want to stay in the house, so they gathered their belongings and left to be interviewed by ICE agents and receive victim services.

When the agents searched the house for the domestic servants' passports and other personal identification documents, they were found in a safe located in Al-Jader's room, as Pedroza had claimed in her affidavit.

It was later determined that Al-Jader had filed an application to bring the two women into the United States from Indonesia to work as domestic servants at her home in Massachusetts. The contract stated that the women would be paid $1,500 per month and would work no more than eight hours per day. However, when the women arrived in Massachusetts, Al-Jader confiscated their passports to preserve her access to inexpensive labor and led the women to believe that they would be harmed if they did not work for her. The women often labored much longer than eight hours, and Al-Jader paid them only $300 per month.[3]

Al-Jader was eventually indicted on two counts of forced labor and attempted forced labor, two counts of domestic servitude, two counts of falsification of records, two counts of visa fraud, and two counts of harboring an alien in the United States. She avoided trial by pleading guilty to both counts of visa fraud and both counts of harboring an alien in the United States.

Al-Jader's attorney successfully argued that she should not face prison time, because she had six children and her husband was severely disabled and unable to care for himself, much less the children. Instead, she was sentenced to six months of home confinement and deportation after the completion of her sentence, along with a $40,000 fine to the court and $206,972 in restitution to three of her former servants: $10,000 for Veronica and $98,486 each for Tri and Ro.

Ultimately, Al-Jader's sentence didn't seem to reflect the severity of her crimes. Prior to sentencing, the judge even acknowledged,

> I see that there are a number of cases like this where foreign nationals bring domestic servants into the country and either misrepresent what they are paying and do not pay them adequately, and it should not be the case that this can happen, and someone of wealth and privilege can do it, and the only punishment is that you pay fines; that you are deported; and, in short, that the punishment is simply financial.[4]

However, that is exactly how she was punished.

The judge rationalized the sentence by saying that Ms. Al-Jader was "irreplaceable" in caring for her disabled husband. "I don't believe that it's possible to take away what has been provided by way of emotional support by you to your husband and to your children, but particularly to your husband."[5] Instead of being incarcerated, her "deterrence" was to perform 100 hours of community service by volunteering with the Embassy of the Republic of Iraq.

Wealthy individuals who labor traffic domestic servants are often able to avoid punishment through top-notch legal representation and by paying hefty fines and restitution fees, if they are ever caught.

For example, Jane Ngineriwa Kambalame enjoyed diplomatic immunity in the United States until at least January 17, 2012, after which time she became Malawi's High Commissioner to Zimbabwe and Botswana. She was accused of illegal trafficking, forced labor, and tortious treatment of Fainess Bertha Lipenga. Lipenga was allegedly forced to work from 5:30 a.m. to 11:00 p.m., seven days per week, for no pay for several months and then for only $100 to $180 per month for three years in Kambalame's Maryland home. Lipenga was not allowed to leave the house, denied medical treatment, had her travel documentation confiscated, and was threatened with deportation. Kambalame was never convicted or punished for her crimes, but was ordered to pay $1 million in restitution after Lipenga won a civil judgment against her former employer.[6]

Or take the case of Leopold Bonkoungou and Lucile Bonkoungou Ouedraogo, U.N. diplomats from the West African nation of Burkina Faso, living in New York. They had brought Fatoumata Ouedraogo–a distant relative of the wife–to the United States to work as a domestic servant and care for the couple's children, promising her a steady income, education, and permanent residence in the United States. However, after she arrived, Ouedraogo alleged that she was paid only approximately $400 over the four years she had worked with them, as well as periodically provided with $2 calling cards.[7] On two occasions, Ouedraogo claimed that Leopold sexually molested her. However, by the time she learned of her rights, Ouedraogo's former employers had left the country and could no longer be found. The case was dropped without prejudice.

Since the punishments for domestic servitude rarely involve imprisonment, affluent families are not necessarily deterred from committing these crimes in the United States.

* * *

Domestic servants can be outright sold by their parents or loved ones into slavery or deceived into debt bondage situations. Victims are kept in compliance through fear of deportation, threats against family members, or violent retaliation. Domestic servants are often forced to work between 10 to 16 hours per day for little or no pay.

Most victims of domestic servitude in the United States are foreign national women without legal or long-term immigration documentation. Their foreign national status is one of the key factors that prevents domestic servants from reporting their abuse to the authorities. Although the Trafficking Victims Protection Act (TVPA) provides the opportunity for victims of human trafficking to legally remain in the United States under the T-visa program, these visas are infrequently granted. In fact, roughly 40 percent of law enforcement officers have seen victims of human trafficking deported.

In addition, human traffickers who exploit domestic servants are rarely held accountable for their crimes. Charges are often withdrawn or lessened due to the lack of evidence and/or offenders' prestige. At the time of this writing, the Michigan Law Center Human Trafficking Database only listed

78 cases of domestic servitude human trafficking from 1986 to 2013, which represent a fraction of actual incidents of domestic slavery in the United States.

Notes

1. Josh Gerstein, "Saudi Prince's Wife Gets House Arrest for Lying to U.S.," *The New York Sun* (December 22, 2006): accessed July 6, 2017, http://www.nysun.com/foreign/saudi-princes-wife-gets-house-arrest-for-lying/45613/.

2. *United States of America v. Hana F. Al Jader,* No. 05–10085–RCL (n.d.).

3. Josh Gerstein, "Saudi Prince's Wife Gets House Arrest for Lying to U.S.," *The New York Sun* (December 22, 2006): accessed July 6, 2017, http://www.nysun.com/foreign/saudi-princes-wife-gets-house-arrest-for-lying/45613/.

4. *United States of America v. Hana F. Al Jader,* No. 05–10085–RCL (n.d.).

5. Ibid.

6. Zoe Tabary, "Malawian Housemaid Wins U.S. Human Trafficking Case after Three Years 'in Prison,'" *Reuters* (November 28, 2016): accessed July 6, 2017, http://www.reuters.com/article/us-trafficking-usa-malawi-idUSKBN13N1SW.

7. Stephen Rex Brown, "United Nations Diplomats Treated Illiterate Maid Like Indentured Servant, Paid Her 2 Cents an Hour over 4 Years: Suit," *NY Daily News* (February 26, 2015): accessed July 6, 2017, http://www.nydailynews.com/new-york/diplomats-treated-maid-indentured-servant-suit-article-1.2129972.

CHAPTER TWELVE

Knocking at Your Door

A nation's greatness is measured by how it treats its weakest members.
—Mahatma Gandhi

As a 25-year-old server at a Waffle House in Columbus, Ohio, Johnathan Terrell Stewart was barely making ends meet. Tips were meager, and he was fed up with the fights and robberies in and around the restaurant. He aspired to something greater and desperately wanted a change.

It seemed like fate when Johnathan was assigned to serve a table of door-to-door magazine sales crewmembers. They convincingly described their business as a lucrative entrepreneurship, which allowed them to live a carefree life and travel all across the United States. By the end of their meal, Johnathan was sold. He immediately quit his job and joined their door-to-door magazine sales crew to begin his new and improved life.

Once he left, Johnathan was brainwashed every morning at a meeting and ridiculed every evening if he did not make his quota. Away from his social support, he depended on the crew for survival. They addicted him to drugs and coerced him to work long hours for little compensation through the façade of a festive lifestyle. However, the reality was that he was being exploited. Each evening, he, along with the rest of the crewmembers, turned over their hard-earned money to the manager. If he made it to the end of the year, he would have surely found that he was in a deficit, due to the money deducted for the food, transportation, cellphones, and motels that he shared with multiple crewmembers.

However, his exploitation didn't last very long. A few weeks after he left, Maryland police contacted Johnathan's grandmother. They told her that her grandson had been found dead in a motel room from a heroin overdose. According to media reports, "his body was shipped back home shirtless, in jeans and tennis shoes; all his belongings, including his wallet and cellphone, disappeared along with his crew, whose name remains unknown."[1]

Unfortunately, Johnathan's experience in door-to-door sales isn't an anomaly. Human trafficking is suspected in similar sales crews across the United States. Victims are typically juveniles or young adults who often face assault, abandonment, and other forms of serious victimization. However, they usually consent to entering the business, which makes their eventual exploitation and victimization difficult to identify.

For example, 18-year-old Kaylan Goodman left home in Bay City, Texas, under suspicious circumstances—abandoning her job as a sales clerk at the Shiny Penney, an apartment full of belongings, and her pickup truck, which was left in a vacant lot.[2] She told her family that she had joined a door-to-door magazine sales company—Lrumar Publications—which brought her to Denver, Colorado. Her parents contacted the police after her cellphone was turned off and her Facebook page was deleted. However, once found, Kaylan told the authorities that she was safe and consenting. She even claimed to be dating the crew manager, Scott Biddle. Yet, her disappearance remained suspicious.

Kaylan's sister, Lorrie, claimed that in a phone call, she was told that Kaylan was hiding with a group of approximately 19 people. Kaylan asked her sister to stop the Facebook and Twitter campaign and allegedly told her, "I can't leave. You don't understand. They won't let me go."[3]

Online complaint boards on the company Kaylan worked for—Lrumar Publications—describe encounters with despondent salespeople. "A guy came to our door who smelled terrible, looked terrible and seemed desperate!"[4] one military family described. Unhappy customers were more concerned with securing refunds for their purchases than the employment circumstances of the salespeople.

Many door-to-door sales crewmembers are recruited from lower socioeconomic environments, including runaways and homeless youth. They are promised opportunities for travel and career advancement, indoctrinated by speeches and clever videos, as well as forged romantic relationships. As in Kaylan's case, the situation doesn't cross the line into trafficking until the teen is forced, defrauded, threatened, or coerced into staying in the exploitive situation. Managers can also exploit employees into selling sex and becoming addicted to drugs. Compliance can be achieved through violence, abandonment, or resource deprivation.

These kids sometimes work 10 to 16 hours per day, six or seven days a week, while their pay is withheld, and they are left to survive on meager food stipends (e.g., $5 to $10 per day). If they don't make their quotas, they may be forced to sleep outside or be starved and beaten. If and when they ask to leave, these marginalized youths can be abandoned thousands of miles away from home with little or no money in hand.[5]

Stephanie Dobbs, who worked as a door-to-door salesperson with Young People Working, LLC, had been abandoned by her sales crew in different and unfamiliar cities 11 times over the course of three years.[6] Because she was an independent contractor, the company had no obligation to get her home. Dobbs explained that crew managers attempted to conceal abuses through festive atmospheres, with partying, drugs, and alcohol. However, the façade would dissipate over time, exposing the reality, which was that "managers can intimidate you, make you feel like you owe them, humiliate you, even beat you," Dobbs explained.[7]

One of the earliest and most widely publicized cases on the peril of traveling sales crews involved a 1999 car crash in Janesville, Wisconsin, which resulted in the death of seven crewmembers, including 18-year-old Malinda Turvey. Turvey's father, Phil Ellenbecker, subsequently worked to improve the safety of young door-to-door salespeople, resulting in the passage of Malinda's Act in March 2009.[8] The progressive Wisconsin law requires at least semimonthly payment of wages, background checks for new employees, and safety certification of the vehicles used to transport door-to-door sales workers. It also prohibits an employer from stranding employees; withholding employees' money, identification, phone, or any other personal property during the course of employment; or restricting communication between workers and their family or friends.

* * *

Traveling sales in the United States dates back to the late nineteenth century. The rise of large mass manufacturing firms, such as National Cash Register, Eastman Kodak, Coca-Cola, Westinghouse Electric, and Carnegie Steel, led to an increase in door-to-door sales.[9] The average salesman would travel alone, through planned routes of evaluated customers, while collecting sales reports and receipts. Salesmen had monthly or weekly quotas and were trained on a variety of tactics, such as how to stand or hand over a pen, when attempting to close a sale.[10]

During the early twentieth century, door-to-door salesmen began peddling goods from more mass-manufacturing firms, such as Wrigley's Chewing Gum, General Electric, Burroughs, and Pepsi-Cola.[11] Since then, traveling sales have waxed and waned with the economy. For example, after World War II, there was a spike in sales crews, which included war veterans who couldn't find employment.[12]

Although the living and working conditions on the sales crews became increasingly harsh and at times cruel, the members were often desperate for the work and, therefore, rarely reported the abuses.[13] Unlike the professional door-to-door salesmen of the late nineteen and early twentieth centuries, exploitation is more prolific in today's crews. Modern crews include mostly young people aged 17 and 24 who can end up becoming entrenched in the exploitive underground economy while facing physical and emotional abuse by managers.

Although statistics are difficult to come by, on any given day, there are tens of thousands of young people traversing the United States with traveling sales crews. Many of them working under substandard and dangerous conditions. Their compromised access to opportunities for social mobility and lack of life experience make it difficult to recognize the schemes utilized to manipulate and exploit them.

Many of these door-to-door labor trafficking cases are reminiscent of the girl I encountered selling all-purpose cleaner on my home doorstep in Montclair, Virginia. However, the unfortunate reality is that it is very difficult to identify this type of labor trafficking, and even if it is correctly identified, positive interventions are rare.

Many homeowners can't overcome their disdain enough to see that these kids and young adults could be victims in need of help. If a solicitor becomes upset when a customer doesn't want to purchase a product, seems desperate, asks for water or food, or to use a restroom, these could be red flags that this person is in an exploitive situation. However, a lack of empathy for solicitors is pervasive.

For example, even though I was proud of my community and the sense of unity and philanthropy it exuded, many of the Montclair Moms were absolutely ruthless when it came to their perceptions of solicitors, in my opinion. One homeowner in my community posted this on social media,

> I freaking loathe solicitors. I swear, not one single person knows what "No Soliciting" means, which the huge sign in my flower bed as you walk up to my door reads. I'm not an irrational person, but I swear, when I open the door, all I want to do is screech like a banshee and forcibly hold their heads in front of the sign and schooling them on the meaning of the phrase, just like one would rub a pet's nose in urine.[14]
>
> —Anonymous Montclair Mom, 2013

This type of mentality helps make solicitors an exploitable population. A solicitor's interaction with people is typically limited and focused on the product they are selling, as opposed to their treatment. Persons who would potentially intervene in their exploitation are few and far between. More often, if an annoyed neighbor who is being pestered by a solicitor calls the police, it will be to have the door-to-door salesperson removed from the neighborhood or cited for soliciting without a license. Some law enforcement agencies take the position that the "most effective way to reduce complaints about solicitors is to aggressively enforce all laws that apply to conducting business."[15]

Instead of criminalizing sales crewmembers, the public needs to recognize their potential for victimization. Police officers should receive training on how to identify the red flags of exploitation and have accessibility to resources for suspected victims. These young people include daughters, sons, brothers, sisters, mothers, and fathers. Even if the door-to-door solicitor is off-putting, they are at high risk of being labor trafficked and may need your help. It is imperative that we respond accordingly.

Notes

1. Virginia Pelley, "Human Trafficking: Mag Crew Kid at Your Door Could Be a Victim," *Aljazeera* (February 24, 2015): accessed July 6, 2017, http://america .aljazeera.com/articles/2015/2/24/human-trafficking-victim-mag-crew-kid-at -door.html.

2. Dana Hertneky, "Police: Some Door-to-Door Salespeople Forced into Human Traffic," *News on 6* (May 7, 2013): accessed July 6, 2017, http://www.newson6.com /story/22189066/police-some-door-to-door-sales-people-forced-into-human -trafficking.

3. "Kingfisher Police Locate Missing Teen," *KOCO News 5* (February 23, 2012): accessed July 6, 2017, http://www.koco.com/article/kingfisher-police-locate -missing-teen/4287474.

4. National Consumer Complaint Forum. Lrumar Publications LLC Complaint Board (n.d.): accessed July 6, 2017, https://www.complaintboard.com /lrumar-publications-llc-l10376.html.

5. "Traveling Sales Crews: The Perils of Life on the Road," National Consumers League (September 2009): accessed July 6, 2017, http://www.nclnet.org /traveling_sales_crews_the_perils_of_life_on_the_road.

6. Darlena Cunha, "Trapped into Selling Magazines Door-to-Door," *The Atlantic* (April 20, 2015): accessed July 6, 2017, https://www.theatlantic.com/business /archive/2015/04/trapped-into-selling-magazines-door-to-door/388601/.

7. Ibid.

8. "Traveling Sales Crews: The Perils of Life on the Road," National Consumers League (September 2009): accessed July 6, 2017, http://www.nclnet.org /traveling_sales_crews_the_perils_of_life_on_the_road.

9. Walter A Friedman, *Birth of a Salesman: The Transformation of Selling in America* (Cambridge, MA.: Harvard University Press, 2005).

10. Ibid.

11. Ibid.

12. "History of Traveling Sales Crews," Parent Watch, Inc. (n.d.): accessed April 22, 2017, http://www.parentwatch.org/generalinfo-history.html.

13. Ibid.

14. Montclair Moms, Facebook (2013).

15. George D. Dahl, *Patrol Officers Reference Guide to Door-to-Door Solicitors*, Louisville Metro Police Department (n.d.): accessed July 6, 2017, http://graphics8 .nytimes.com/packages/pdf/national/Louisville_Police_Guide.pdf.

CHAPTER THIRTEEN

Dark Side of Chocolate from the Côte d'Ivoire

When people eat chocolate, they are eating my flesh.
—Drissa, freed cocoa slave[1]

In preparation for my daughter's fourteenth birthday party, I went shopping at my local Target for sweets to put in the purple organza goodie bags for her guests. Luckily, because she's a Libra, there were plenty of large bags with assorted candies to choose from in advance of Halloween. At the time, a two-pound bag with 60 individual servings of M&Ms, peanut M&Ms, Twix, and Snickers cost $10.79. From the empty spaces on the shelf, I could tell that a few bags had already been bought.

Although that was the type of candy my daughter and her friends would like, I took pause in making a purchase. For some reason, my eyes were drawn to a small display at the end of the candy isle. The single shelf was filled with over 100 thin, brown-paper envelopes, embellished with twine. Although the packaging wasn't particularly eye-catching, especially for candy, its uniqueness drew my curiosity.

A white sign with green lettering was affixed to the left of the shelf. It read, "Direct trade chocolate." The small batch, bean-to-bar, chocolate manufacturer, Askinosie, had produced three types of single-origin chocolate bars, which were on display—dark milk chocolate with goat's milk, dark chocolate with crushed almonds and vanilla bean, and plain dark chocolate. The packaging stated that all their chocolate was made with beans from Mababu, Tanzania.

While I was at Target, I watched several customers select bags of the name-brand chocolates and place them in their red shopping carts; however, not a single person selected one of the Askinosie bars. They didn't even stop to give them a look. In fact, there wasn't any gap in the display to suggest that a single purchase had been made. Perhaps it was the high price tag that comes with handcrafted, direct-trade chocolate—$4.99 for one 1.7-ounce bar. Maybe the people shopping at this Target in Dumfries, Virginia, didn't understand the importance of "single origin" and "direct-trade." To many of these consumers, chocolate is chocolate. It may not have mattered to them where it came from or how it was made; they were just looking for the ideal combination of the best taste and price. If they knew why their chocolate was so cheap, would they still make the same purchase? Would they choose to value name brand and price over human life?

* * *

As a teenager, Drissa left his village in Mali to look for work in Cote d'Ivoire, Africa. Upon arriving in Korhogo, a city in the Northern Ivory Coast, he was offered a job on a cocoa plantation. "With all the money you'll make, you can buy a bicycle, clothes, or food for your family," said the recruiter. After agreeing to the payment and work conditions, Drissa went with the recruiter to begin his new job, which ultimately did not meet the terms of their agreement.[2]

Drissa was forced to work 18 hours per day alongside 17 boys, who were as young as 10 years old. Each night, he was locked into one small room with over a dozen other boys and one tin can to share as a toilet. The boys, including Drissa, were not compensated for their work, only provided with a little food and water needed to keep them alive.[3]

One night, before being locked into his room, Drissa attempted to run away, but the slaveholder caught him. He was savagely beaten, causing his skin to split, leaving large open gashes across the length of his back. He relied on maggots to clean his wounds and prevent gangrene, while returning to work.

Like most child slaves in the cocoa industry, he had never tasted chocolate but was abused and exploited for its production. Today, Drissa's wounds are scarred over with keloids; however, the mental wounds from the abuse he faced still haunt him to this day.

* * *

In June 17, 1999, the International Labor Organization (ILO) Convention 182 Concerning the Prohibition and Immediate Action for the

Elimination of the Worst Forms of Child Labor convened in Geneva. The convention defined the worst forms of child labor as:

(a) *All forms of slavery or practices similar to slavery, such as the sale and trafficking of children, debt bondage and serfdom and forced or compulsory labour, including forced or compulsory recruitment of children for use in armed conflict;*

(b) *The use, procuring, or offering of a child for prostitution, for the production of pornography or for pornographic performances;*

(c) *The use, procuring, or offering of a child for illicit activities, in particular for the production and trafficking of drugs as defined in the relevant international treaties; and*

(d) *Work which, by its nature or the circumstances in which it is carried out, is likely to harm the health, safety, or morals of children.*[4]

The conclusion of the convention was that organizations should establish or designate appropriate mechanisms to monitor the implementation of processes to eliminate the worst forms of child labor. For example, holding businesses accountable for violations through sanctions; preventing the worst forms of child labor through education, vocational training, and outreach to at-risk children; and providing assistance, rehabilitation services, and social reintegration to child labor survivors.

In response, the Chocolate Manufacturers Association passed the Protocol for the Growing and Processing of Cocoa Beans and Their Derivative Products in a Manner that Complies with ILO Convention 182 Concerning the Prohibition and Immediate Action for the Elimination of the Worst Forms of Child Labor on September 19, 2001. The agreement, colloquially referred to as Harkin-Engel[5] Protocol, was signed by the president of the Chocolate Manufacturers Association and the World Cocoa Foundation, as well as executives from eight major chocolate manufacturers: Guittard Chocolate Company, World's Finest Chocolate, Inc., Nestle Chocolate & Confections USA, Hershey Food Corporation, M&M Mars, Inc., Archer Daniels Midland Company, Blommer Chocolate Company, and Barry Callebaut AG.[6]

The protocol committed significant resources to stop the practice of child labor in the growing and processing of cocoa beans; established an advisory group to conduct an ongoing investigation into the labor practices in West Africa; founded a joint action program of research, information exchange, and action to enforce the internationally recognized standards to eliminate child labor in cocoa growing and processing; and initiated baseline-investigative surveys of child labor in West Africa to facilitate evaluation and the production of evidence on how the chocolate industry was building toward credible standards.

However, after these agreements were ratified and executives assured the world that there was no longer any child slavery used in the harvesting of cocoa, evidence continued to surface. For example, undercover investigations featured in a 2010 documentary entitled the *Dark Side of Chocolate* exposed video of children being trafficked into the Ivory Coast, as well as children carrying machetes and harvesting cocoa pods on the farms. One of the cocoa farms that was captured in the documentary with child laborers as young as 10, from the neighboring country of Burkina Faso, was allegedly part of the supply chain for Nestle. According to the documentary, the children could be purchased for less than $250 each, which included the cost of transportation and indefinite use for no additional money.[7]

Similarly, a CNN Freedom Project investigation in 2012 found a 10-year-old in Daloa, Ivory Coast, who had worked harvesting cocoa since he was seven.[8]

In 2015, *Fortune* assistant managing editor Brian O'Keefe went to West Africa and found that child labor in cocoa production had actually gone up by approximately 21 percent since the chocolate companies had taken action to combat it.

Although the new laws and agreements prohibiting child labor looked good on paper from a public relations perspective, there was still evidence to suggest that millions of children continued to be deceived, sold, stolen, and used as slaves in cocoa farms.[9] Many of these children came from poverty stricken areas in Africa where there were few opportunities for work. Yet, children were expected to make money to send home to their families, making them easily manipulated by the false promises of traffickers trying to recruit them into the Ivory Coast or Ghana. The horrific reality is that these children, who were as young as seven or eight, ended up being forced into hard manual labor for 80 to 100 hours per week while receiving no compensation and no education. They were underfed and were often viciously beaten if they tried to escape. Most were never reunited with their families again.

While Americans may not be directly enslaving these children, we are consuming the by-products of their slavery, and the companies in our country enjoy the fruits of their cheap labor—an industry worth approximately $110 billion dollars per year worldwide and $18.27 billion in the United States.[10] While some may say that the United States should have no accountability for abuses faced by children nearly 5,000 miles away, others can argue that this type of apathy is what leads to their abuse in the first place. The United States does not need to consume chocolate produced through slavery, so morally, why would we want to?

A minimum of 70 percent of the world's cacao[11] production begins in West Africa, in areas that are riddled with international labor violations, child slavery, and human trafficking. Hershey and M&M Mars, which are the two largest chocolate manufacturers in the world, control two-thirds of the chocolate market in the United States.[12] According to numerous public interest nonprofit groups, such as the Global Exchange—an international human rights organization dedicated to promoting social, economic, and environmental justice around the world—these companies are supplied with cocoa that is "almost certainly produced in part by slavery."[13] However, in their defense, large companies state that there is no way they can control labor practices of their suppliers. While they recognize that smaller chocolate companies in the United States purchase only fair-trade–certified cocoa, they claim that it would be impossible for larger manufacturers.

The average U.S. citizen eats over 11 pounds of chocolate per year, which amounts to about 120 chocolate bars.[14] While the United States' purchasing power is an influential tool in compelling corporate responsibility, it is unclear whether citizens would choose to act after learning of the severe abuse faced by children in the cocoa industry abroad. Ultimately, the disconnection between source and product may lead to the continuous exploitation of children, so that we can enjoy a cheap chocolate treat.

For Americans who do care where and how their chocolate is made, there are several public resources available to assess the likelihood of human trafficking and child slave-labor in the supply chain of their favorite candy. However, these grading scales are more focused on anti-trafficking policy adoption than on practice assessment. For example, at the time of this writing Free2work.org gave Godiva, Whitman, Russell Stover, M&Ms, Milky Way, Twix, Snickers, and many other chocolates the lowest possible grade—an "F"—for monitoring and workers' rights, though this only means that the chocolate company did not monitor their suppliers and did not ensure that workers received a living wage. It does not guarantee that trafficked labor is or isn't being used.

While Americans may not have control over how chocolate is harvested in other countries, we do have the power of the purse and can demand greater oversight and accountability from the companies we purchase from. Chocolate is not worth the price of child slavery. Instead, Americans should consider using their purchasing power to support smaller manufacturers that sell direct-trade chocolate and guarantee child slaves were not exploited.

Justice will not be served until those who are unaffected are as outraged as those who are.

— Benjamin Franklin

Notes

1. "The Bitter Truth about Chocolate," Citizens for Global Solutions (September 6, 2013): accessed July 6, 2017, http://globalsolutions.org/blog/2013/09/Bitter-Truth-About-Chocolate.

2. Anir Senyah, "The Fight Against Slavery in the New Global Economy," *The New Citizens Press* (September 6, 2013): accessed July 6, 2017, http://www.tncp.net/Articles/tabid/1800/articleType/ArticleView/articleId/1341/Default.aspx.

3. Ibid.

4. Worst Forms of Child Labour Convention, 1999 (1999): accessed July 6, 2017, http://www.ilo.org/dyn/normlex/en/f?p=NORMLEXPUB:12100:0::NO::P12100_ILO_CODE:C182.

5. Named after two legislative supporters: Senator Tom Harkin, U.S. Senate-Iowa and Congressman Eliot Engel, U.S. Congress-New York.

6. Protocol for the Growing and Processing of Cocoa Beans and Their Derivative Products in a Manner that Complies with ILO Convention 182 Concerning the Prohibition and Immediate Action for the Elimination of the Worst Forms of Child Labor. Chocolate Manufacturers Association (September 19, 2001): accessed October 9, 2016, http://www.globalexchange.org/sites/default/files/Harkin EngelProtocol.pdf.

7. Miki Mistrati and U. Roberto Romano, directors, *The Dark Side of Chocolate* (2010), written by Miki Mistrati.

8. David McKenzie and Brent Swails, "Child Slavery and Chocolate: All Too Easy to Find," (January 19, 2012): accessed July 6, 2017, http://thecnnfreedomproject.blogs.cnn.com/2012/01/19/child-slavery-and-chocolate-all-too-easy-to-find/.

9. Brian O'Keefe, "Inside Big Chocolate's Child Labor Problem," *Fortune* (March 1, 2016): accessed July 6, 2017, http://fortune.com/big-chocolate-child-labor/.

10. Cocoa-nomics. CNN Freedom Project (2014): accessed July 6, 2017, http://thecnnfreedomproject.blogs.cnn.com/2014/03/04/cocoa-nomics-watch-the-documentary-in-full/.

11. Beanlike seeds from which chocolate are made.

12. "Mars Takes a Bite out of Hershey," *NBC News, Associated Press* (October 12, 2008): accessed July 6, 2017, http://www.nbcnews.com/id/27118691/ns/business-us_business/t/mars-takes-bite-out-chocolate-giant-hershey/#.WPPrAFKZPjE.

13. John Robbins, "The Good, the Bad and the Savory," *Earth Island Journal* (2002): accessed July 6, 2017, http://www.earthisland.org/journal/index.php/eij/article/the_good_the_bad_and_the_savory/.

14. Jeanne H. Ballantine and Keith A. Roberts, *Our Social World: Condensed Version*, 3rd Edition (Los Angeles, CA: SAGE Publications, Inc., 2014).

CHAPTER FOURTEEN

Slaved in India, Retailed in America

On the night of our wedding, my husband and I created a bucket list of countries we wanted to visit; a top contender for both of us was India. However, work, school, and children delayed our travel plans for several years.

In 2009, we finally decided to begin checking destinations off our list.

After several months of research on the must-see tourist locations, we arrived in New Delhi before navigating to Jaipur, Pushkar, and Agra. We wanted to experience as much as we could in our short time there, so we paid a taxi driver to take us around the northern part of the country, traveling at night and sightseeing during the day.

Our first stop was Jaipur, the capital and largest city of Rajasthan, a state in Northern India, which is known to tourists for producing beautifully ornate handmade arts and crafts. Unbeknown to us at the time, our taxi driver received a commission for bringing us to the local businesses, where we were able to watch artisans handprint on textiles, carve precious stones, and weave elaborate carpets.

None of the products involved automated machinery. Each was being produced through beautiful and ancient processes, which required skill and careful attention to detail. I was in awe, watching these unique forms of art.

Our taxi driver first brought us to an establishment to observe woodblock printing, which is one of the earliest, simplest, and most time-consuming methods of textile design. Upon entering the small factory, we saw one of the artisans draw a length of plain linen cloth from a roll over a large table. He marked it with a piece of chalk to indicate the location for the first impression.

The teenage and young adult boys and girls who printed in front of us didn't smile or talk; they just focused on their craft, while the owner of the business attempted to sell us his products.

The artisans dipped the incised wooden blocks in ink before carefully rolling them onto the linen, yielding highly artistic results. In watching this process, it was clear that the ornate, handcrafted designs were unobtainable by any other method. The owner efficiently guided us through every step of the production process, highlighting the time and the precision needed for each piece. At the end of the one-hour tour, we were directed to make our purchases before moving on to the next crafter.

Following the textile artisans, we visited a lapidary shop where we watched gem crafters cut, facet, and polish semiprecious stones by hand using spinning plates and other weathered tools. Again, the artisans did not talk and simply focused on their technique, while the owner described the gemstone crafting process. At the end, the proprietor let me hold a handful of small, loose diamonds in his retail shop, which he literally poured out of a black, crushed velvet, drawstring bag.

Our last stop of the day was at a carpet-weaving establishment. Again, everything was done by hand. Women spun the yarn on wooden wheels alongside barefooted men, who knotted the dyed thread on the warps of large vertical looms. After each knot, they sliced the strands with a hooked knife, called a dhoori. After a row of knots was completed, the men passed a strand of weft lengthwise through the warp yarns using a weaver's shuttle. Then, each man patted everything down, compressing the strands with a wooden comb called a panja. After the carpet was completed, it was taken off of the loom and trimmed by hand with large scissors before being washed, dried, and receiving finishing touches and inspection. Again, the employees didn't speak. Whenever I asked them a question, the owner would answer and continue his spiel, attempting to sell his wares.

I felt increasingly off kilter about the employment situation in these craft shops. I was aware of the pervasive child trafficking in some of these industries, but all the employees appeared to have been of legal working age, even if they were youthful looking. None of them seemed to be forced, but I would not say that they appeared happy with their employment situation. However, that alone was not an indication of trafficking.

After having a full day of sightseeing, our taxi driver began navigating to our next city just as night fell. On the way out of town, we again passed by the crafting shops that we had visited earlier in the day. As we drove, I noticed that the factory lights were still on at the textile shop. The iridescent glow from the open door and windows illuminated the workers in a line against the building. In this back alley, I watched as the young workers were provided with what appeared to be rationed food. Each was eagerly eating, including younger children, who I didn't see during the earlier tour.

I don't know for certain if these particular workers were trafficked, but after seeing this, I began further examining labor trafficking within the textile industry in India.

* * *

India is the world's third-largest textile and garment exporter behind China and the EU.[1] In some shops, Indian garment workers are required to sew nearly 150 pieces per hour and make up for any shortfall in daily targets without overtime or face deductions from their wages, which are only around 252 rupees or $4 per day.[2] According to nonprofit watchdog groups, Indian-based factories supply dozens of international companies, including GAP, Wal-Mart, H&M,[3] American Eagle Outfitters, Tommy Hilfiger, and Children's Place.[4]

For decades, many of the textiles being exported to the United States were manufactured by young children who sometimes worked 14 hours per day, seven days per week, for around $105 per month, if they were paid at all. These youth were often locked into indentured servitude contracts, termed Sumangali, and exposed to hazardous working conditions, some while being sexually harassed or molested by their bosses.[5] Child laborers were highly sought after by textile producers because their nimble fingers are perfectly suited for the crafts, and being children, they were more easily coerced to work long hours for little pay.

News coverage on the abuses faced by Indian textile workers prompted American-based companies to amend their corporate responsibility statements and publicly denounce human trafficking in their code of conduct agreements with suppliers; however, in many cases, the abuses continued. For example, GAP and H&M were previously supplied by Bombay Rayon, which was questioned for violating labor and gender rights for locking up women workers who had asked for increased wages and better working conditions.[6] Although the American companies publicly condemned the unfair practice, they now do business with Arvind International, which also faces allegations of worker exploitation.

According to one Arvind employee, "Nothing is good. But we are staying here because we have to live, and there is no other way."[7] The female worker claimed that employees were only allowed to leave the Arvind-owned hostels for migrant workers once a week, which was usually for two hours on Sundays. She stated that before they could leave the hostel they were required to register with a security guard. She believed this was meant to ensure that the workers didn't ". . . leave for our villages after taking our salary."[8] The hostels were also reported as being overcrowded, with 220 male workers in one, three-storied building.

Each year, American businesses import over $2.2 billion worth of cotton textiles from India.[9] While we may diffuse responsibility for the unfair labor practices used to make these textiles to the Indian-based companies who are directly responsible for the abuse, our purchases are indirectly fueling the exploitation. Moreover, American-based businesses are enjoying the bulk of the profits.

However, the use of slave labor has grown to such magnitude that consuming products of human trafficking is almost unavoidable. In addition to the clothes you wear, the toys you gift your child, the flowers you send your spouse, and your new smartphone were likely all touched by the hand of a slave in at least one stage of the production process. Whether it was the raw materials, the assembly of inputs, or the final stage manufacture, someone was exploited along the way. Although there are more slaves today than at any other point in history and consuming the products of their servitude is difficult to avoid, resources such as Free2work.org and Goodguide.com provide proxies for assessing how your favorite products may relate to human trafficking.

Notes

1. Amy Kazmin, "India Takes Lesson from China to Lure Workers to Garment Industry," *Financial Times* (July 25, 2013): accessed July 6, 2017, https://www.ft.com/content/cb4ca68a-f2b7-11e2-a203-00144feabdc0.

2. Pushpa Achanta, "Women Garment Workers Organize against Inhumane Conditions in India," *Waging Nonviolence* (January 12, 2015): accessed July 6, 2017, https://wagingnonviolence.org/feature/women-garment-workers-organize-inhumane-conditions-northwest-india/.

3. PTI. "Indian Workers at Walmart, Gap Factories Face Intensive Exploitation, Abuse: Report," *The Economic Times* (June 1, 2016): accessed July 6, 2017, http://economictimes.indiatimes.com/news/politics-and-nation/indian-workers-at-walmart-gap-factories-face-intensive-exploitation-abuse-report/articleshow/52535341.cms.

4. Nicky Coninck, Martje Theuws, and Pauline Overeem, "Captured by Cotton: Exploited Dalit Girls Produce Garments in India for European and U.S.

Market." Centre for Research on Multinational Corporations (May 2011): accessed July 6, 2017, https://www.slideshare.net/HAQCRCIndia/exploited-dalit-girls-produce-garments-in-india-for-european-and-us-markets.

5. "Slavery on the High Street: Forced Labour in the Manufacture of Garments for International Brands," Anti-Slavery International (June 2012): accessed July 6, 2017, http://www.antislavery.org/wp-content/uploads/2017/01/1_slavery_on_the_high_street_june_2012_final.pdf.

6. Pushpa Achanta, "Women Garment Workers Organize against Inhumane Conditions in India," *Waging Nonviolence* (January 12, 2015): accessed July 6, 2017, https://wagingnonviolence.org/feature/women-garment-workers-organize-inhumane-conditions-northwest-india/.

7. "'Unfree and Unfair'—Young Migrant Garment Workers in Bangalore, India," India Committee of the Netherlands (January 28, 2016): accessed July 6, 2017, http://www.indianet.nl/pdf/UnfreeAndUnfair.pdf.

8. Ibid.

9. Dana Liebelson, "I Tried to See Where My T-Shirt Was Made, and the Factory Sent Thugs After Me," *Mother Jones* (November 29, 2013): accessed July 6, 2017, http://www.motherjones.com/politics/2013/11/india-garment-factories-sumangali.

CHAPTER FIFTEEN

Cheap Luxury

Lynda Dieu Phan was a prosperous Vietnamese immigrant to the United States. By the age of 38, she owned two successful nail salons in Pennsylvania. Women from around the York area would frequent her salons biweekly to transform their natural nails into vibrant colors. Relaxing in the massaging pedicure chairs, the customers paid little attention to the young technicians sitting in front of them, much less the circumstances of their employment.

The success of Phan's salons was heavily due to her employees. She would often travel back to Vietnam to visit family and recruit nail technicians to work for her. Phan would tell the families of the young women that she would pay for the immigration papers and travel to the United States in exchange for the women working in her nail salon. However, instead of going through the process legally, Phan would use fraudulent means to facilitate travel, such as fake marriages. For example, one of her victims married her brother Justin, and another married her boyfriend and father of her child, Duc Cao Nguyen.

Once in the United States, Phan coerced the women into working from 10:00 a.m. until 9:00 p.m. Monday through Saturday and 12:00 p.m. to 5:00 p.m. on Sunday. The only days that the women didn't go to work were when the mall was closed for holidays. One of the salons, Da-Vi Nails USA, was located in the Wal-Mart at West Manchester Mall, serving dozens of patrons per day. However, for years the girls never said anything to the customers despite the fact they weren't being compensated for their work. The only money they were allowed to keep was the tips received from customers; however, even part of that money was given to Phan. She told the women they needed to work for three years without compensation to repay the money for immigration, attorney fees, and housing expenses. She also threatened them with jail if they told anyone about what was happening.

In addition to their exploitation at the nail salon, Phan forced the women to live in her home where they were made to sleep on the floor, cook, and clean. Their lack of English language, identification documents, and transportation inhibited their escape, but their 24-hour compliance was largely gained through Phan's false promises.

Although Phan told the women that after working for three years their debts would be settled and they would start earning a living, this promise never came to fruition. Three years came and went, and the women still didn't receive any compensation for their work. Instead, when the victims confronted her, she retaliated by charging them each $200 per month in rent and $300 per month in utilities, in addition to other fees for travel.[1]

After one of the victims realized that despite paying an unknown amount of money in legal fees to Phan over the years, she was in the United States illegally and unpaid, she decided to escape. On June 1, 2008, she wrapped her personal belongings in a sheet and ran away at 1:30 in the morning with the help of a customer.

On December 10, 2008, Lynda Dieu Phan was indicted on criminal conspiracy to commit forced labor trafficking, as well as forced labor and marriage fraud. Over a year after her indictment, Phan pled guilty. She was only sentenced to three months in jail for her crimes plus 270 days of home arrest and one year of supervised release. She was also ordered to repay the victims $300,000 in restitution.[2]

* * *

This type of indentured servitude is common in a number of industries that import labor. Nail and hair salons, massage parlors, and karate dojos have all been linked to debt bondage and human trafficking.

In 2015, *The New York Times* published an in-depth exposé on the prolific abuse and exploitation in the nail salon industry.[3] According to the investigation, the vast majority of interviewed nail salon workers reported compensation below minimum wage, if they were paid at all. Like in the case of Lynda Dieu Phan, employees claimed to be earning no wages and subsiding on meager tips, which could be docked for minor transgressions as punishment. Some of the interviewed women, who included over 150 nail salon workers and owners, also reported verbal and physical abuse as well as humiliation.

It is difficult for prospective employees who immigrate from overseas to distinguish between legitimate businesses and human trafficking syndicates. Employees may expect to pay recruitment fees and experience a period of no pay in order to reimburse costs for immigration and travel. However, they are often deceived as to the prices and the length of time for reimbursement. In addition, these systems of debt bondage are often in violation of U.S. labor laws. If they do receive compensation, a large portion of their wages is withheld for food, housing, and transportation, as well as fines for spilling polish or dropping tools.

Employers may attempt to circumvent labor laws by misclassifying employees as subcontractors. This allows them to sidestep employment regulations regarding minimum wage, overtime, payroll taxes, and unemployment insurance. However, the U.S. Department of Labor is very clear under what conditions someone should be considered an employee.

According to the Wage-Hour Division of the U.S. Department of Labor, the Fair Labor Standards Act does not outline a single test for determining whether a worker is an employee or independent contractor. Instead, they look at the *economic reality* to assess whether the worker is dependent on the employer. If they are, they should be classified as an employee.

Economic realities include:

(1) Whether the work is an integral part of the employer's business;
(2) Whether the worker's managerial skill affects her or his opportunity for profit and loss;
(3) Permanency of the worker's relationship with the employer; and
(4) Employer control of the employment relationship.[4]

The Department of Labor cites studies that suggest between 10 to 30 percent of employers may misclassify their employees as independent contractors. This statistic is most certainly higher among nail salons that labor traffic women from overseas.

Unbeknown to many nail salon patrons, labor trafficking in the nail salon industry may occur in combination with sex trafficking and/or exposure to sex work consumerism.

For example, in 2015 I wrote a story that was published in *The Washington Post* about how I discovered that men had claimed to procure sexual services at the nail salon I formally patronized with my daughters.[5] I was floored and disgusted when I read this review, which a man posted allegedly about my former nail salon in April 2013:

> *Started with a good massage that always works out the knots. On to the legs, she always brushes and grabs the man. But this time it was a little more than the*

norm. On the flip she started with my chest than went to the upper leg with some lite bumping. That's all it took for my man to stand up to see what was going on. I didn't say anything and next thing I know she grab him and started a very nice HJ. After I blow my load, she cleaned me up with hot towel and asked if I liked it, I said yes. She smiled and said see you next time.[6]

At the time of this writing, there are 16 nail salons in California, Illinois, Texas, New York, Pennsylvania, and Washington State listed on RubMaps.com, which is an erotic massage parlor review website. There are nearly 40 additional nail salons listed on the site, but they were reported by patrons as being non-erotic or closed.

While the women working at these salons may not necessarily be providing sexual services, and if they are they may not be trafficked, the manicure customers at these establishments are most likely unaware for what these men claim to patronize these establishments. I know that I wasn't aware until my own experience. However, if you open your eyes and look past the veneer, you will begin to see how pervasive these forms of exploitation are, even in places you may patronize.

For example, nearly one year after I discovered that multiple men had claimed to receive sexual services at my former nail salon, I was patronizing a different establishment when I overheard a man at the front desk arguing about his payment. I just assumed he wasn't pleased with his services until the nail technician who was giving my 15-year-old daughter a pedicure leaned over and whispered to me, "He was getting a massage and then asked her to massage down there," the woman gestured toward her genital area as she was speaking, "so (the masseuse) walked out. Now, he doesn't want to pay for the massage because she refused to touch him there."

Again, I was incredulous. This man had allegedly attempted to solicit sexual services in a nail salon full of women at 2:00 p.m. on a Saturday afternoon. He was then emboldened enough to refuse to pay for the 45 minutes of back massage that he had received before she rebuffed his sexual proposition. With tears in her eyes, the woman explained how this happens frequently.

The particular situation was quickly and discretely resolved, and many of the other customers were none the wiser. However, this is a form of sexual harassment that these nail technicians should not have to endure, and the men who harass them should be held accountable.

Whether it is labor or sex trafficking, women and men working in the beauty service industry can be exploited in a variety of ways. There are over 17,000 nail salons in the United States, with more opening every year.[7] Given the dangers for exploitation, it is important for consumers to be vigilant and report suspected incidents of exploitation to the authorities. In addition, legislators must improve inspections and vocational safeguards to protect this potentially exploitable population.

Notes

1. *United States of America v. Lynda Dieu Phan,* No. 1:08-CR-0436-01 (U.S. District Court, Middle District of Pennsylvania, February 11, 2010).

2. Ibid.

3. Sarah Maslin Nir, "The Price of Nice Nails," *The New York Times* (May 7, 2015): accessed July 6, 2017, https://www.nytimes.com/2015/05/10/nyregion/at-nail-salons-in-nyc-manicurists-are-underpaid-and-unprotected.html?_r=0.

4. Wage and Hour Division. Fact Sheet 13: Am I an Employee?: Employment Relationship Under the Fair Labor Standards Act (FLSA). U.S. Department of Labor (May 2014): accessed July 6, 2017, https://www.dol.gov/whd/regs/compliance/whdfs13.htm.

5. Kimberly Mehlman-Orozco, "My Nail Salon May Be a Front for a Brothel," *The Washington Post* (November 20, 2015): accessed July 6, 2017, https://www.washingtonpost.com/opinions/my-nail-salon-may-be-a-front-for-a-brothel/2015/11/20/65cc15e6-84c0-11e5-8ba6-cec48b74b2a7_story.html?utm_term=.3606c57efedf.

6. *Virginia Nail Salon Anonymous Review* (April 2013): accessed July 6, 2017, http://www.RubMaps.com.

7. Sarah Maslin Nir, "The Price of Nice Nails," *The New York Times* (May 7, 2015): accessed July 6, 2017, https://www.nytimes.com/2015/05/10/nyregion/at-nail-salons-in-nyc-manicurists-are-underpaid-and-unprotected.html?_r=0.

CHAPTER SIXTEEN

Stealing Our Jobs?

Bodies in various stages of decomposition peppered the southern border of the United States. In the desert heat, the organs of the deceased putrefied, as their skin blistered and body bloated. It was a gruesome sight. Although it was infrequently discussed in the U.S. media, the undocumented migrant death tolls had heightened to about one fatality per day. While some fell victim to exposure or dehydration from the extreme heat or cold experienced during the multi-day trek, criminals murdered others.

Maria was acutely aware of these dangers, which was why she made the conscious decision to pay a smuggler to help her cross the border illegally from Mexico into the United States. She needed the assistance in navigating the perilous terrain, which included dangerous waterways, deserts, and mountains. Moreover, she didn't want to be sexually assaulted under the infamous rape trees, which were already decorated with the panties from hundreds of victims.

In preparation for her migration, Maria reached out to Jose Zavala-Acosta, a Mexican national, known for smuggling people from Mexico and Honduras into the United States. Maria was acquainted with Jose through an uncle, who had been successfully smuggled by him years earlier. She was excited and relieved when Jose agreed to serve as her guide.

After scheduling the date of departure, Jose provided Maria with a list of items to carry—an emergency thermal blanket, food, water, heat packs, hat, backpack, and comfortable shoes wrapped with cloth, to conceal her footprints. She could only take one backpack with her on the journey, so she brought merely items needed to survive, along with her identification, money, and a few family photos.

Maria did exactly what Jose said during the journey. She walked for days, and he guided her, protecting her against the elements, both natural and social. As soon as they crossed safely into the United States, he had a car waiting to pick them up, with food and water. Once in the vehicle Maria breathed a sigh of relief, thinking the danger from the illegal crossing had been successfully averted, but it was just beginning.

The car transported Maria and Jose to the end unit of a small brick strip mall in a predominately Latino community of Houston, Texas–La Potra Bar. Jose Zavala-Acosta provided the bar with free labor and cocaine, and Maria was his latest procurement.[1] The club owner, James Cabrera, paid Jose for Maria so that she would be forced to work at the nightclub as a prostitute to pay her smuggling fees and newly acquired debt.

Zavala-Acosta was sentenced to 24 months imprisonment for alien smuggling, and Cabrera committed suicide while in custody pending federal charges for human trafficking. After being released and deported, Zavala-Acosta was arrested again on February 28, 2014, for attempting to illegally enter the United States near Carrizo Springs, Texas. He was eventually convicted and sentenced to 57 months of imprisonment and a three-year term of supervised release, which was upheld on appeal in 2016.[2]

* * *

Generally, there are five different types of foreign nationals in the United States: legal immigrants, illegal immigrants, legal nonimmigrants, illegal nonimmigrants, and undocumented migrants (see Table 16.1).

According to the PEW Hispanic Center, there are approximately 11.1 million unauthorized foreign nationals residing in the United States as of 2014.[3] Demographic data suggest that around 60 percent of these unauthorized foreign nationals are undocumented migrants who crossed the border without documentation or with false documentation, and 40 percent are illegal nonimmigrants who violated their terms of entry or overstayed their visa.

Contemporary tightening of international borders has increased the difficulty of undocumented migration to the United States. To circumvent these new barriers, more undocumented migrants are relying on the services of skilled organized crime syndicates, operating as smugglers, a.k.a. coyotes, to successfully traverse the international border and its new-found security. The $5,000 to $10,000 fee charged by smugglers is often worth the price, as the risk of detection and detention is lowered, and the rate of survival increases. Although the interaction with smuggling cartels presents a new set of dangers for undocumented migrants, including a

Table 16.1   Foreign National Typology

Legal	Illegal
Immigrant: Legal *permanent* resident or green card recipient; An immigrant can eventually apply to become a naturalized U.S. citizen.	**Illegal Immigrant:** Violated the terms of entry by committing a crime of moral turpitude, becoming deportable under the Illegal Immigration Reform and Immigrant Responsibility Act (IIRIRA) of 1996.
Nonimmigrant: Legal *temporary* visitor and visa recipient; A nonimmigrant may include guest workers, tourists, students, and other short-term visitors to the United States.	**Illegal Nonimmigrant:** Violated the terms of entry by committing a crime of moral turpitude *or* overstaying a temporary visa, becoming deportable. **Undocumented Migrant:** Crossed the border by completely evading immigration checkpoints *or* entered through other fraudulent means, such as using another person's travel documentation; immediately deportable.

heightened risk of physical and sexual assault, successful illegal border crossing rarely happens without their assistance (less than 10%).

Human smuggling, while similar to human trafficking, can be distinguished because once individuals are smuggled into the destination country, they are free to leave. Foreign nationals who are trafficked are exploited upon arrival in the destination country through force, fraud, threats, or coercion into commercial sexual exploitation or indentured servitude to pay off their migratory debt.

Undocumented migrants are often targeted for human trafficking victimization because their illegal status puts them between a rock and a hard place. They are dissuaded from seeking out redress from authorities due to the fear of deportation, so they bide their time, hoping their exploitation will come to an end.

* * *

Although human smuggling is not synonymous with human trafficking, smuggled undocumented migrants are at high risk of being trafficked and stories such as Maria's are common.

For example, Cesar and Geovanni Navarrete were sentenced to 12 years each in federal prison on charges of conspiracy, holding undocumented migrant workers in involuntary servitude, and peonage on tomato farms in Florida and South Carolina.[4] According to court documents, they beat, threatened, and restrained the undocumented migrants by locking them in trucks. The men were also accused of paying the migrants minimal wages and forcing them into further debt to facilitate compliance and extend the amount of time needed to repay the smuggling fees to the Navarrete family.

Human smuggling operations that result in human trafficking often involve familial networks.

Another example is the case of the Mondragon brothers—Maximino Mondragon, Oscar Mondragon, and Victor Omar Lopez.

According to an interview with an anonymous family member,[5] their father, who was a wealthy and recognizable businessman in his local community in El Salvador, raised the brothers. He allegedly fathered more than 70 children after the traumatic loss of his first-born son. His wife at the time became frantic due to the death of their only child and the two did not have any more children. Mondragon Sr. dealt with the loss by fathering as many children as he could with different women. When the mother of one of his children would move on to a new relationship, he would take the child away, as he didn't want another man raising his offspring.

Mondragon Sr. made all his children work for him as corraleros, which meant they looked after his cows, bulls, and his hacienda. After migrating without documents to the United States, the defendants obtained legal permanent residency. Maximino and Victor both became naturalized citizens, while Oscar remained a legal permanent resident (LPR).

When the brothers first arrived in the United States, they worked construction jobs before moving to Houston where they opened their own bars, as well as smuggled and trafficked undocumented migrants.

On November 8, 2004, a confidential informant alerted Immigration and Customs Enforcement officers that a man by the name of Walter was smuggling aliens to work at his bar, called El Cuco. The man, Walter Alexander Corea, would charge undocumented migrants from El Salvador, Guatemala, and Honduras $6,000 to $8,000 each for transportation to the United States. However, after arriving, he would substantially increase the smuggling fees to facilitate debt bondage and force the young female undocumented migrants to work in his bar as prostitutes.

The Mondragon brothers served as smuggling drivers for Corea and exploited some of the trafficked women in their own bar—El Potrero de Chimino. According to the indictment, one woman who worked at the bar identified herself as "Blanca," told undercover agents that she was originally from El Salvador, and her smuggling fee was increased to $14,000 once she arrived in the United States.[6]

The Mondragon brothers used their citizenship and legal permanent residency statuses to travel back to El Salvador where they recruited new undocumented migrants to be smuggled and trafficked. They also helped keep the trafficked migrants compliant through direct and implied threats if they tried to escape. At times, the brothers would become violent.

One of their victims stated that Lopez locked her and a bar patron inside the bar overnight in an effort to force her to have sex. When she became pregnant, Maximino paid a co-defendant $300 to perform an abortion. Forced abortions happened more than once, under the direction of the Mondragon brothers. The fetuses, sometimes alive, were either thrown in the trash, buried, or dumped.[7]

On April 28, 2008, Lopez was sentenced to 109 months in federal prison,[8] Oscar Mondragon was sentenced to 180 months, and Maximino Mondragon was sentenced to 156 months, with three years post-release supervision. The three brothers were also ordered to pay a share of $1.7 million in restitution to their victims.[9]

* * *

Undocumented migrants represent a particularly exploitable population. Although the federal government offers legal visas for victims of crime (U-visa) and victims of human trafficking (T-visa), many are unaware of these programs. Moreover, they can still face deportation, despite their victim status. As such, many undocumented migrant victims of human trafficking can be exploited into compliance for fear of deportation or retaliation if they were to escape.

Immigration reform must address the endemic abuses within the legal temporary visa system, as well as bring undocumented migrants out of the shadows. Regardless of a person's foreign national status in the United States, they should feel empowered to report victimizations, exploitation, and abuse.

Notes

1. "La Potra Bar Investigation Results in Convictions and Prison Terms," FBI (January 10, 2011): accessed July 6, 2017, https://www.fbi.gov/houston/press-releases/2011/ho011011.htm.

2. *USA v. Jose Zavala-Acosta,* No. 15–50154. (April 1, 2016). U.S. Court of Appeals for the Fifth Circuit.

3. Jens Manuel Krogstad, Jeffrey S. Passel, and D'Vera Cohn, "5 facts about illegal immigration in the U.S.," Pew Research Center (November 3, 2016): accessed July 6, 2017, http://www.pewresearch.org/fact-tank/2016/11/03/5-facts-about-illegal-immigration-in-the-u-s/.

4. Steven Beardsley, "Brothers Receive 12-Year Prison Terms in Immokalee Human Slavery Case," *Naples Daily News* (December 19, 2008): accessed July 6, 2017, http://archive.naplesnews.com/news/local/brothers-receive-12-year-prison -terms-in-immokalee-human-slavery-case-ep-400544123-344259152.html.

5. Anonymous. Family History of Mondragon Brothers (December 3, 2016).

6. *United States of America v. Walter Alexander Corea, Maximino Mondragon, Victor Omar Lopez, Oscar Mondragon, Kerin Silva, Olga Mondragon, Maria Fuentes and "Comadre."* No. H-05-890M. (n.d.).

7. Harvey Rice, "Prostitution Case Alleges Smuggling, Forced Abortions," *The Houston Chronicle* (November 24, 2005): accessed July 6, 2017, http://www.chron .com/news/houston-texas/article/Prostitution-case-alleges-smuggling-forced -1915684.php.

8. "Two Men Sentenced for Human Trafficking and Alien Smuggling Charges," FBI (April 28, 2008): accessed July 6, 2017, https://www.justice.gov/archive/opa /pr/2008/April/08-crt-350.html.

9. "Houston Man Sentenced for Human Trafficking and Alien Smuggling Charges," FBI (April 27, 2009): accessed July 6, 2017, https://www.justice.gov /opa/pr/houston-man-sentenced-human-trafficking-and-alien-smuggling -charges.

PART 3

Overcoming Barriers to the Abolition of Modern Slavery

The intention of this book was to take each reader behind the headlines of human trafficking in the United States. I realize that many of you may have heard stories of pimp-controlled sex workers, exploited migrants, domestic servants, and sex trafficking of runaway and homeless youth prior to reading this. However, despite this foreknowledge, I felt that the realities discussed herein would still beggar belief and could contribute to the in-depth insight needed to catalyze more effective reform.

By now, you know that slavery is not a thing of the past and that there are more slaves today than at any other time in human history. I've explained how these crimes now touch every community in the United States, from the impoverished inner-city neighborhoods to the middle-class suburbs and alcoves of wealthy estates. Narrative accounts of real-life trafficking cases; interviews with convicted human traffickers, victims, and commercial sex consumers; as well as empirical research and details from criminal case files were shared in the hopes of exposing you to the grim realities of the well-known and more obscure forms of human trafficking and its byproducts.

However, despite these realities, this crime still plays a largely unrecognized role in our day-to-day lives. It is important to also understand that advancements in awareness and anti-trafficking resources have not changed the status quo. Victims of trafficking continue to be criminalized by law enforcement, and offenders continue to exploit and profit from new recruits.

The following section is where the rubber meets the road. The upcoming chapters will expose some of the barriers to effective anti-trafficking interventions. Unfortunately, much of the publicized efforts to combat human trafficking avoid hard decisions for cheap headlines. While some modern-day abolitionists are truly committed to the cause, many anti-trafficking advocates are more concerned with their bottom line and public accolades than the rescue and restoration of victims, much less the arrest and conviction of offenders.

Now that you are more aware of the red flags of human trafficking, the intention of the following section is to enlighten you to hollow anti-trafficking policies so that you can better advocate for social and legislative changes to end this scourge in America.

CHAPTER SEVENTEEN

Hidden in Plain Sight

I don't want you to just drop me off and forget about me like they all do.
—Human Trafficking Survivor

August 21, 2015, Springfield, Virginia

It was 2:30 on a Friday afternoon, and I was en route to a 3:00 p.m. doctor appointment. As I drove, I remember noticing the beautiful new construction to Springfield Mall. The previously dilapidated shopping complex had been completely renovated into a luxurious mecca of consumerism.

All of a sudden, I saw a white female with blonde hair thrown from a black sedan onto the sidewalk. I immediately stopped my truck, as I watched a black male exit the driver's side of the vehicle and chase after the woman, throwing luggage and belongings in her direction. The woman cowered in fear, as the man quickly returned to the car and drove off, making a U-turn at the next intersection. I followed his vehicle, while dialing 9-1-1.

"Fairfax County 9-1-1, where is your emergency?" said the operator.

"Yes, I'm at the corner of Franconia and Loisdale, and I just saw what looks like a domestic violence incident. This guy threw a woman out of his car and drove off."

I repeated the license plate number to the operator twice before the car escaped onto the highway.

"I am not sure if this is just domestic violence, but the out-of-state license plate makes me think it may be human trafficking," I said. Sex traffickers tend to move victims up and down the I-95 corridor on the East Coast.

While on the phone with the dispatch officer, I made another U-turn, returning to the victim, who was sitting on the curb of the street in front of her belongings. When she saw my white Escalade approach, she later told me that she thought I was another man coming to victimize her. Her hands cradled her tear-streamed face, apprehensively waiting to be dragged into another exploitive situation.

I pulled over in the turning lane and put on my emergency blinkers. Cars quickly passed me as I exited from the driver's side.

"Do you need help?" I asked, with the 9-1-1 operator still on the phone. "I saw what just happened to you. Are you okay?"

Surprised to hear a female's voice, she turned and looked up at me, eyes puffed and red from crying.

"Yes, um," she sniffled, trying in vain to compose herself, "I, I, just need to go to the bus station. This guy, he just left me here and I, I need to get up to my aunt in Connecticut."

"Okay, okay. I can take you, but I'm on the phone with the police. Do you need them to help, are you hurt?"

"No, no. I don't want the police to get involved. I just want to go to the bus station."

"Okay, I'll give you a ride."

I hung up the phone with the dispatcher and helped load her belongings into the trunk of my truck. Wanting to know more about the situation so that I could help, I tried to make small talk. She was suspicious and initially didn't open up to me.

"Why are you asking all these questions? Are you a cop?" she asked.

"No, I'm not a cop, but I'll tell you what I am," I paused and looked over at her for a brief moment, while I continued driving, "I'm a criminologist and an expert on human trafficking. I advocate for victims, and your situation makes me think you may be a victim."

She paused in silence and disbelief. The serendipity of someone with my expertise driving by just as she was being victimized made her decide against going to the bus station. Unsure of her next steps, she asked me to drop her off at the local mall, while I went to my doctor's appointment. She left her belongings in my truck and texted me her number so that we could meet up in one hour, giving her some time to think.

While I was in the waiting area of my doctor's office, I used my iPhone to Google her phone number. Immediately, the search displayed numerous advertisements for escort services. "Jamie Lee (Christy Candy) Stellar Reviews. Si Habla Español. Specials Available." The photos depicted the identical blonde-haired woman who was sitting on the side of the road in gray sweatpants and a stained, white tank top. It was the same woman, but the pictures masked the abuse with fishnet dresses, lace nightgowns, latex bodysuits, and matching platform heels. I was certain the man who threw her out of the car was her trafficker—her pimp.

I called one of my local anti-trafficking acquaintances, Detective Bill Woolf, and explained the situation. I knew he had numerous contacts with victim service providers, so he could possibly help deliver the resources she needed to break the trauma bond with her pimp and improve her life. I didn't know if she would talk to Detective Woolf, since he was a police officer, but he asked me to try and find out: (1) How she got hooked up with this guy, (2) his number, and (3) links to any ads soliciting her services online.

After my doctor's appointment, I returned to Target to pick up the woman. I texted her as soon as I was out in front of the mall. Once she was back in my truck, we continued talking about her victimization, and she told me that she was ready to make a change in her life. She decided that she was willing to speak with law enforcement and seek victim services. I called Detective Woolf so that we could meet up, and he could take her to an undisclosed safe house for victims.

Before taking her there, I treated her to dinner and coffee. There she told me more details about her victimizations, showing me where her first pimp shot her in the leg at point-blank range, requiring a vascular transfusion. She parted her hair to show me where her last pimp busted her skull open and explained how he used to drown her in bathtubs. *"It took him five days to dig a hole so deep that would take me five years to get out of,"* she said.

After connecting her with services, I wanted to find out more about the man who victimized her. She told me that they were down in Virginia because her pimp was on pre-trial release for another criminal case—a malicious wounding charge for crimes he committed against a different woman. After she told me, I looked up her sex trafficker's name in Virginia's General District Court Case Database. He was officially charged with Virginia Criminal Code § 18.2–51. This criminal violation is defined as, "If any person maliciously shoot, stab, cut, or wound any person or by any means cause him bodily injury, with the intent to maim, disfigure, disable, or kill, he shall, except where it is otherwise provided, be guilty of a Class 3 felony." While her trafficker was out on bond, he was required to periodically check in with the court.

Later that month he had a preliminary hearing, and I attended.

I sat behind him in the courtroom and watched as he went before the judge. The prosecutor explained that they hadn't been able to get in contact with the victim and asked for a continuance. The trafficker's defense attorney explained that it was onerous for his client to continue driving back down to Virginia from his home in New England, but the judge wasn't having it. Apparently, a condition of his pre-trial release was that he didn't leave the State of Virginia. The man's defense attorney hemmed and hawed after admitting that his client had violated the terms of his probation. The judge reminded him to stay in the state but didn't revoke his probation, despite the admitted violation.

I wanted to tell the court what else he had been doing while on pre-trial release, but I was told not to speak up. The police investigating didn't want to tip him off to the fact that law enforcement was aware of his most recent crimes, so I bit my tongue, and walked out of the courtroom after he left.

A little over one month later, his malicious wounding charge was nolle prosequi because the victim in that case failed to show up to court to testify. The prosecutors couldn't locate her to serve her with a subpoena, so he was free to go. To my knowledge, he was never charged for the crimes against the second woman either. I don't know why.

* * *

After learning about how her trafficker was able to evade punishment, I asked this woman about where he would sex traffic her. She told me that he would take her to 10th and K Streets when they would visit the DC metropolitan area. Between 4:00 a.m. and 6:00 a.m., he would have her walk "the track," which is an area known for street-level commercial sex advertisement.

I decided to go and see for myself.

While my kids and husband were at home asleep, I drove to "the track" during the fall of 2015. At that point, I had studied sex trafficking for nearly a decade, but I was still in shock by what I saw.

In plain sight, women walked the streets literally in G-strings and bikini tops, while their pimps watched from a close distance. Cars would stop and pick the women up, right in plain view of every passerby. If police drove past, they would just flash their floodlights on the women and yell at them to get off the street, if anything. However, the girls would return as soon as the cop cars left.

During one of my observations, on September 6, 2015, a man, whom I believed to be a pimp, even attempted to recruit me into the commercial sex trade, as I walked around the block documenting the social interactions.

"I am just saying you're cute, that's all," he told me through the passenger window of his vehicle.

"Oh, thank you," I replied, "What are you guys doing out here?"

"Just, a, watchin', uh, the same thing you doin'."

"So, you're here trying to help people?"

"Yeah, helping people. Maybe we should call each other, if you like helping people. We could help each other help people." I don't think he understood that I was an anti-trafficking criminologist—he thought "helping people" was a euphemism for commercial sex.

As we spoke, a woman in green platform heels, thigh-high fishnet stockings, a thong, and bikini top, walked in front of his car and approached the passenger door of a dark-colored minivan.

These types of interactions were frequent. After a woman would enter a customer's car, they would drive around the corner and park on the street, where she would perform fellatio on the driver, right there in the vehicle. Pimps instructed their exploited sex workers on how to sell themselves to customers, as well as how to avoid being stolen by other pimps, by keeping their eyes down and crossing the street if approached.

I alerted the DC metropolitan police to these illicit enterprises on one occasion. The responding officer told me that he believed all the women were consenting sex workers, and even if they were trafficked, he didn't handle those crimes—they were the responsibility of the sex trafficking vice unit.

Instead of investigating my concerns, the officer asked me where my husband was. I told him, "At home with my children, asleep." The officer further inquired why I was down in that area at that hour. I explained that I was a criminologist who specialized in sex trafficking, and I wanted to see where these girls were being sold. The officer then told me, "*Mmmm. If I was your husband, I would have you locked up in that bedroom,*" while looking me up and down.

I didn't know how to react to his statement. All I could think was if he would say something like that to me, an academic scholar, how was he interacting with these sex workers and victims of sex trafficking? What was he capable of saying to them, and how would that impact their perceptions of law enforcement, even if they were inclined to seek help?

* * *

After these experiences, I again felt so disheartened by the status of our anti-trafficking efforts in the United States.

Time after time, I followed cases where the trafficker was able to operate with impunity, rarely held accountable for their crimes or punished with slap-on-the-hand sentences, and all the while, the women, men, and children who were being victimized were met with few opportunities for improving their life prospects.

The woman whom I had rescued in 2015 told me why she didn't escape sooner: "Most people treat us like trash, and that's just the God's honest truth." After being criminalized with offenses related to her victimization and living in the commercial sex trade for years, legitimate independent living appeared unattainable to her. "Even if I'm being exploited and getting my ass beat every day, at least I have a roof over my head," she confessed.

Although I served on local human trafficking task forces and had established dozens of contacts with anti-trafficking service providers, I had a hard time finding this woman placement in a quality safe house. I received the runaround from many organizations that were receiving millions of anti-trafficking dollars. Even when I reached viable service providers, I was frustrated to learn that their waiting lists were too long, or the living conditions were dismal. Her recovery, continuity of care, and the provision of health services were all compromised by nonexistent or inadequate housing, lack of vocational training, unavailable transportation, and untrained staff.

I suppose this discovery was the worst part of the current status of human trafficking in America. Even if a victim is able to gain access to anti-trafficking services, which are far and few between, they provide nothing more than a short-term fix. Given the severe shortage of shelter beds for survivors of human trafficking, many victims are only afforded a few nights stay in an emergency shelter before needing to change to another location or homeless shelter.

Estimates on the number of human trafficking victims in the United States are hard to come by, due to the clandestine nature of the crime. Many anti-trafficking advocates will claim that there are approximately 300,000 victims of human trafficking in the United States, but these data aren't particularly reliable nor based in evidence.

However, we do know that there are less than 1,000 dedicated beds available to human trafficking survivors, which are located in only about 50 percent of states.[1] There are more beds available through other services, such as for homeless populations and survivors of domestic violence, which can also be used for human trafficking survivors, yet these services don't necessarily provide the needed trauma-informed care.

Despite the numerous resources funneled into anti-trafficking organizations, many victims return to their human trafficker due to failed or inadequate service provision.

Awareness is only the first step to combating trafficking in persons. We must provide greater accountability for the criminalization of offenders and longevity in service provision for survivors. As a society, we are getting better in being able to identify victims, but we continue to fail in protecting them.

Note

1. Jessica Reichert and Amy Sylwestrzak, National Survey of Residential Programs for Victims of Sex Trafficking. The Illinois Criminal Justice Information Authority (2013): accessed July 6, 2017, http://www.icjia.state.il.us/assets/pdf/ResearchReports/NSRHVST_101813.pdf.

CHAPTER EIGHTEEN

Disposable Kids

Theme

Despite the increase in anti-trafficking funding, policy, and resources in recent years, victims are still infrequently identified, and offenders are rarely convicted. Instead, misinformation continues to be perpetuated in the media, and legal actions demonstrate a critical knowledge gap, which can result in policies that may do more harm than good.

With regard to sex trafficking, Americans are regularly misinformed about the nature of the crime. People think they or their children are at risk of being kidnapped by sex traffickers, which is not necessarily the reality. Kids who are actually at high risk of being trafficked are often ignored and can be treated like disposable people by authorities and social service providers. Misinformation on the mechanisms of human trafficker recruitment is problematic because it can potentially divert the attention of law enforcement, the public, and the media away from actual human trafficking situations.

For example, in March 2017, there were two viral human trafficking stories that were brought to my attention within the same week. One of the stories involved kids who were at high risk of being sex trafficked, but the media initially ignored the story, and the connection to trafficking was quickly dismissed by law enforcement. The second account involved kids who were at low risk of sex trafficking, but it immediately went viral. The juxtaposition of these two anecdotes illustrates how human trafficking cases in the media can center around sensationalized misinformation, while those who are truly at risk may be overlooked, dismissed, or ignored.

Missing DC Teens

During the week of March 20, 2017, dozens of news outlets around the country published stories about the missing teenagers in Washington DC. "Missing black girls in DC spark outrage, prompt calls for federal help," read one headline.[1] "Mainstream media ignored missing DC girls because of race," read another.[2]

According to the stories, over the course of a few weeks, more than one dozen black and Latina kids were reported missing from Washington, DC, but there wasn't much media coverage until a Twitter campaign went viral and prompted a national response.[3] Social media users were furious that there wasn't more attention about these missing kids and alleged that it was because they weren't white.

The story sparked a national debate on race and victimization. However, while many private citizens were appalled that more wasn't being done, law enforcement defended that they were following established protocol, regardless of race. They also claimed that Amber Alerts™[4] were not issued because the teens appeared to have left consensually as runaways, and the claims of concerned citizens were not accurate. The police explained that the disappearances didn't span a few days or weeks but rather several months, and the number of missing kids was declining.[5] Moreover, although members of the community were concerned that sex trafficking was involved in the disappearances, DC police contended that there was no evidence to support these suspicions.

On March 28, 2017, *The Baltimore Sun* published an article I wrote about the missing teens in DC.[6] I contended these kids were still at high risk of being trafficked and urged law enforcement and concerned residents to continue actively looking for these at-risk youth. My sentiment, which was based in my anti-trafficking experience, was that labeling a child as a runaway should not be a justification to reduce efforts to recover the child, even if that was the current procedure.

IKEA Mom

Less than one week after *The Baltimore Sun* published my article, I was contacted by reporters from *Women's Health*[7] and CBS[8] to give my response to a story that had gone viral about a mom who had suspected that her kids were targeted by sex traffickers while they were shopping at IKEA. Essentially, the woman was shopping with her mother and children when she noticed a well-dressed, middle-aged man and a casually dressed, young man in his 20s. She alleged that the men were circling the area where her family was testing out couches in IKEA. The mom felt that the men were following them, so she naturally assumed they were human traffickers who were targeting her kids.

The original social media post about her alleged encounter racked up over 100,000 shares and tens of thousands of reactions from concerned parents across the United States. Countless mothers and several news sources lauded this Caucasian mother's vigilance and awareness on the "red flags" of trafficking.[9] However, I, along with many other human trafficking experts, felt that it was most likely not an instance of attempted trafficking but rather an example of a sensationalized story and widely disseminated misinformation.

Juxtaposition Between Low-Risk and High-Risk Human Trafficking Stories

Skilled human traffickers infrequently kidnap victims. They are more likely to recruit targets through ingratiation, false promises and deception, as well as faux relationships. Like most forms of violent crime, victimizations are more likely to occur between acquaintances as opposed to strangers. This allows traffickers to maintain control for longer periods of time by exploiting victims through manipulation, while evading law enforcement. The manipulation tactics used by traffickers function like an invisible tether, as opposed to a physical chain.

However, stories such as the one from the mom in IKEA are often given more credence than actual instances at high risk of human trafficking.

For example, although the authorities had quickly dismissed the likelihood of the DC missing teens being trafficked, they were the ones at greater risk despite having left consensually. In addition to concerns regarding whether the level of law enforcement intervention was affected by the race of the victims, the fact that these kids didn't receive the same level of recovery efforts as others who were kidnapped was incredibly disheartening. These kids, who runaway or face homelessness, are at elevated risk of being recruited into sex trafficking situations and/or forced to engage in survival sex. It doesn't make sense to not prioritize efforts for their recovery considering the high likelihood of becoming trafficked.

Moreover, we need to be considerate of how we disseminate information about these kids. While the story of the IKEA mom was broadcast with an accompanying photo of the Caucasian mom, well dressed and smiling, alongside her kids, some of the stories on the black and Latina missing teens in DC were circulated with accompanying photos that appeared to be mug shots. Even if a child is a runaway or engaged in delinquency, they are not disposable. They deserve the same level of service provision as any other child, especially considering their high risk of being exploited in the commercial sex industry.

While a child may do bad things, it doesn't mean she or he is a bad child. No person should be treated like a throwaway commodity. Missing children, regardless of whether they are a runaway or a victim of kidnapping, need to be recovered and provided services, including policies that address the root causes for their disappearance.

However, despite these realities on child sex trafficking, which disproportionately effects marginalized youth, the media can be unscrupulous with regards to the dissemination of misinformation. At times in my interactions with news outlets, I felt that the media would rather exploit the situation or the victim in order to sensationalize the story rather than disseminate the truth.

For example, on April 15, 2017 a reporter by the name of Tom Evans, who worked for *Express Newspapers* in the UK, contacted me for an interview. He was interested in doing a story on the 10-year anniversary of the Madeleine McCann disappearance.

Three-year-old McCann had gone missing from her family's holiday vacation apartment in Praia da Luz in Portugal on May 3, 2017. Her disappearance had not yet been solved, and Evans was interested in doing a "human trafficking angle" on the story. Specifically, he e-mailed me saying, "I think the UK's media focus will be on finding Madeleine but I want to have a closer look at human trafficking gangs."[10]

In his initial e-mail, Evans sent me nine questions, focusing on a connection between McCann's disappearance and human trafficking. Specifically, he asked:

1. *Do you believe Madeleine McCann was a victim of human trafficking? (Naturally no one can answer this with any certainty but do you feel it is a credible explanation for the disappearance?)*

2. *If she was trafficked, what would that involve? i.e. what sort of conditions would she have been put through, what would the trafficker's prime motivation be for picking up a three-year-old girl?*

3. *What regions are the most likely final destination when people are trafficked from Southern Europe? (My understanding is that North Africa, South-East Asia and the Middle East are common)*

4. *Is there an age where a girl of Madeleine's age might be deemed useless to their cause? i.e. Is there any chance whatsoever a group might let her go?*

5. *Is there a particular age-range/gender/ethnicity favoured by human traffickers?*

6. *Are there any regions or specific countries that are particularly vulnerable? (Bearing in mind I will be writing this for a primarily British audience—so holiday destinations such as Spain, Portugal, Italy, Croatia, Cyprus etc will be central)*

7. *From your work with victims of human trafficking, could you briefly explain the horrors of what it's like?*

8. *Do you see the so-called migration crisis in Europe as a potential problem? Interpol statistics seem to suggest it is on the rise?*

9. *What long-term objectives do you suggest governments should take in order to clamp down on human trafficking and do you see any progress being made on this point?*[11]

I felt that his angle would perpetuate an unlikely scenario, so I responded in part by saying:

> While I am not intimately familiar with this particular case, given my experience on the methods of human trafficker recruitment and control, I feel that it is unlikely that Madeleine McCann was a victim of human trafficking.
>
> The reality isn't like the movie Taken. Human trafficking is typically a more clandestine crime, which is able to evade detection from law enforcement by utilizing recruitment methods that facilitate complacent victims, like fraud, deception, ingratiation, and faux relationships. Experienced human traffickers rarely kidnap due to the difficulty in maintaining control of victims and staying under the radar from police scrutiny.
>
> With that being said, a local pedophile with a history of child sex tourism may be a more likely culprit in this case. This person would be a commercial sex consumer, as opposed to trafficking distributor. In my opinion, international police should consider focusing on scouring the dark web and commercial sex review sites. Many of these men share information and photographs of their crimes with other pedophiles around the world. I also would look for users who posted or commented actively prior to the crime, but not immediately after her disappearance.

However, the interview I gave was not sensational enough, so Evans took my statements out of context to create a click-bait story instead.

The headline read, "REVEALED: 'THIS is who snatched Madeleine McCann and THIS is how to find them.'"[12]

The reporter even went as far as to completely misquote me as saying, "A local paedophile with a history of child sex tourism is the most likely culprit in this case." This was something that I unequivocally did not say nor write at any time. However, it helped him entice readers.

Although Evans subsequently apologized for misquoting me, which he claimed was an accident, the damage was already done, and another theory was thrust into the equation, distracting from evidence-based explanations for McCann's disappearance.

Ultimately, behind the sensationalized headlines and polices on human trafficking crimes are the harsh realities faced by victims and lack of efficacy by law enforcement. The public needs to understand how the media can sometimes shape stories, which may not necessarily reflect the reality but are intended to draw an audience. This practice does a grave injustice to actual victims, who remain in the shadows of America.

Notes

1. Laura Jarrett, Samantha Reyes, and David Shortell, "Missing Black Girls in DC Spark Outrage, Prompt Calls for Federal Help," CNN (March 26, 2017): accessed July 6, 2017, http://www.cnn.com/2017/03/24/us/missing-black-girls-washington-dc/.

2. Sanaa Lathan, "Mainstream Media Ignored Missing DC Girls Because of Race," TMZ (March 25, 2017): accessed July 6, 2017, http://www.tmz.com/2017/03/25/sanaa-lathan-missing-black-girls-washington-dc/.

3. "Where Are They? Outrage over Perceived Increase in Missing Black, Latina Girls in DC," *USA Today* (March 24, 2017): accessed July 6, 2017, https://www.usatoday.com/story/news/nation-now/2017/03/24/where-are-they-outrage-over-missing-black-latina-girls-washington-dc-police/99573222/.

4. An alert issued through an emergency response system that includes information about a missing child.

5. "DC Missing Girls: Cops Say They're Runaways Not Crime Victims," TMZ (March 25, 2017): accessed July 6, 2017, http://www.tmz.com/2017/03/25/d-c-missing-girls-washington-d-c-runaways/.

6. Kimberly Mehlman-Orozco, "What Every Parent Should Know about Sex Trafficking," *Baltimore Sun* (March 28, 2017): accessed July 6, 2017, http://www.baltimoresun.com/news/opinion/oped/bs-ed-sex-trafficking-20170328-story.html.

7. Korin Miller, "This Mom Claims She Encountered Human Traffickers at IKEA and People Are Freaking Out: Here's What You Should Know about the Dangers of Human Trafficking," *Women's Health* (March 29, 2017): accessed July 6, 2017, http://www.womenshealthmag.com/mom/ikea-human-trafficking.

8. Jennifer Earl, "Mom's Warning about 'Human Trafficking' at IKEA Goes Viral; What You Need to Know," *CBS News* (March 30, 2017): accessed July 6, 2017, http://www.cbsnews.com/news/moms-warning-about-human-trafficking-at-ikea-goes-viral/.

9. Alex Laser, "Mom Shares Harrowing Story of Alleged Encounter with Human Traffickers at IKEA," *AOL News* (March 28, 2017): accessed July 6, 2017, https://www.aol.com/article/news/2017/03/28/human-trafficking-ikea/22014029/.

10. Tom Evans. E-mail correspondence to Dr. Mehlman-Orozco (April 16, 2017).

11. Ibid.

12. Tom Evans, "REVEALED: 'THIS Is Who Snatched Madeleine McCann and THIS Is How to Find Them,'" *Daily Star* (April 23, 2017): accessed July 6, 2017, http://www.dailystar.co.uk/news/latest-news/607636/Madeleine-McCann-Maddie-mystery-missing-disappearance-Portugal-suspect-revealed.

CHAPTER NINETEEN

Whac-a-Mole Crusade Online

Misinformation fuels the misidentification and failed service provision of human trafficking victims, which in turn contributes to the impunity of offenders. The United States is missing the mark in our anti-trafficking policies as well. Just like the news stories about human trafficking, anti-trafficking interventions are often more about public perception, as opposed to reality and efficacy.

For example, the latest anti-trafficking efforts focus on third-party liability. These interventions attempt to criminalize or hold civilly liable businesses that are used by traffickers to market and exploit their victims. One of the most well-known attacks is against a website used for commercial sex advertisements—Backpage.com.

Between 2010 to present, Backpage.com has been sued in multiple civil courts across the United States, and its executives faced criminal charges in California. Anti-trafficking advocates alleged that the website facilitated child sex trafficking. However, this publicly disseminated narrative isn't accurate and doesn't provide a complete story.

While consenting and trafficked sex workers have been advertised by third parties on the website, that was not the impetus for the creation of Backpage.com. Moreover, Backpage.com does not make sex trafficking any easier than other classified websites.

To understand how Backpage.com came to be in the crosshairs of anti-trafficking advocates, attorneys general, and legislators across the United States, it is important to first understand the history of the website and, more importantly, its predecessor–Craigslist.org.

Craigslist actually began in the mid-1990s, after a self-proclaimed nerd named Craig Newmark created a listserv of friends and acquaintances to keep them informed about events, job openings, available housing, and culture in San Francisco. They called it "Craig's list." Once the list grew to over 240 e-mail addresses, Newmark decided to post the information for public consumption on an eponymous website—Craigslist.

Shortly after Craigslist became nationally popularized in the early 2000s, Village Voice Media, led by Michael Lacey and James Larkin, created Backpage.com. At the time, Village Voice Media administrated several news outlets that relied on paid advertisements to support their journalism, and Craigslist's free platform for classified ads resulted in millions of dollars of lost revenue. The website's name, Backpage, was a nod to the back page of print newspapers, which typically contained classified advertisements. Although attorneys general were alleging that these websites were unlawfully designed for promoting commercial sex and evading law enforcement, the reality was that Craig created Craigslist to be a decent guy, while Lacey and Larkin created Backpage to support their journalism.

However, their classified websites eventually morphed into something they hadn't intended. The postings on both platforms were driven by what the community wanted, which was (in part) a market for commercial sex, so both websites accommodated with the creation of erotic services sections. Given the potential for misuse, Craig Newmark enabled users to "red flag" offensive postings, which could prompt deletion from the virtual commons. However, law enforcement took notice and requested cooperation, information, and additional oversight from the website.

In addition to the user-generated flags, the website began requiring third parties to provide working phone numbers and valid credit cards, so there could be a paper trail for law enforcement, if needed. After becoming aware of the sex trafficking that had occurred on his website, Newmark even vowed to donate all profits from the erotic section to various charities, particularly those that addressed child exploitation and human trafficking. However, it wasn't enough. Craigslist had been dubbed "the Wal-Mart of child sex trafficking,"[1] and attorneys general from across the country claimed that they were "the only player in the sex industry who is in a position to stop these ads."[2]

In 2010, Craigslist bowed under national pressure and removed the adult services section from the website, but the commercial sex advertisements didn't stop. They were simply displaced to other websites—mostly to Backpage.com. Luckily, Backpage.com also cooperated with law enforcement, and the advertisements were still used to rescue victims, prosecute offenders, protect erroneously criminalized sex trafficking survivors, track patterns in the commercial sex market, and prevent the trafficking of consenting sex workers.

They will find another way

However, following a slew of legal actions and legislative hearings, Backpage.com also shuttered the adult section of the website in early 2017. Although anti-trafficking advocates had claimed that doing so would combat the sex trafficking scourge, the advertisements were again displaced, this time to the dating section of Backpage.com.

The reality is that this crusade against Backpage.com is futile and could actually further inhibit the United States' anti-trafficking efforts. Websites such as Backpage.com are actively used by law enforcement as a catalyst to rescue victims, prosecute offenders, protect erroneously criminalized sex trafficking survivors, and prevent the trafficking of consenting sex workers.

For example, Rishi Sanwal was sentenced to over 12 years in prison for sex trafficking children after an ad he posted on Craigslist led FBI agents and Sacramento police detectives to his illicit operation. He was prosecuted for sex trafficking a 17-year-old girl, but subpoenaed documents from Craigslist indicated the possibility of a second victim. This type of case is not an anomaly. Police officers utilized the same sting tactics with Backpage.com.

In 2010, for instance, 46-year-old Troy Bonaparte was convicted of involuntary servitude, trafficking in person for forced labor services, and pandering. The sheriff's police vice unit targeted him after responding to an advertisement he posted on the escorts section of Backpage.com.

Similarly, a Backpage.com advertisement led to the arrest of Myrelle and Tyrelle Lockett for sex trafficking teenage girls at various suburban hotels. The twin brothers were eventually convicted of human trafficking for forced labor services and involuntary sexual servitude of a minor. However, the case began when sheriff's detectives responded to an online classified advertisement for commercial sex.

These websites brought the clandestine crime of child sex trafficking out of the shadows and online, where it could be identified and investigated.

On April 24, 2017, I even utilized a Backpage.com advertisement to initiate the investigation and recovery of a potentially sex trafficked woman. While finalizing research for this book, I found a review on USA-SexGuide.info from a man who claimed that a young woman in the Winston-Salem area of North Carolina was being sex trafficked. Specifically, his review about the commercial sex provider read:

> *This girl has a developmental disability and is being used by her mother.*
> *Even mongers need to draw a line somewhere. It can be argued that her disability means she doesn't really know what she is consenting to.*
> *This is not like a woman who has demons she should have known better to avoid. This is someone who is fully being abused by a parent.*[3]

After locating the woman's Backpage.com advertisement, I immediately contacted Winston-Salem law enforcement, as well as law enforcement in Thomasville, North Carolina, prompting instantaneous investigations. These advertisements alone were the catalyst. Approximately two hours after I reported the information, law enforcement called me to confirm that they had completed an undercover sting and had the woman in custody. She did appear to suffer from a developmental disability, and she admitted to engaging in commercial sex. The officer told me that their next steps were to investigate the mother for potential exploitation and connect her daughter with social service providers.

When debating the ethics of commercial sex advertisements, it is important to understand that the alternative to websites such as Backpage.com is not that the commercial sex industry would be eradicated. The only alternative to these commercial sex advertisements is that the illicit industry would be pushed further underground, on restricted access and off-shore based websites that may not cooperate with law enforcement, or on the streets.

In their symbolic crusade against Backpage.com, anti-trafficking advocates, attorneys general, and legislators are forgetting that correlation does not equal causation. Just because the plurality of sex trafficking cases involve advertisements from the website, it does not mean they are the root of the phenomenon nor the conduit. The fact of the matter is that the Internet has modernized the commercial sex industry, and while most cases brought to the attention of law enforcement may involve Backpage, this could simply be because the website is the primary resource being used by law enforcement to set up stings, and its administrators are highly cooperative with investigations (just like Craigslist).

In addition to a wealth of evidence illustrating the investigative utility of these advertisements, consensual sex workers and sex worker consumers corroborate some of the complexities with these third-party liability measures. Specifically, consenting sex workers feel that the website decreases their likelihood of being trafficked and victimized by allowing them to screen clients on their own terms.

According to one anonymous sex worker,

Closing Backpage would only be a feel-good and far-reaching attempt by law enforcement to appear effectual, but I believe focusing on one site is virtually fruitless. The possible closure would make the sex industry less safe. Online advertising with a reputable source is a valuable safety resource, which stands to be eliminated with a closure.[4]

Another sex worker explained,

Sex work is safer for everyone when they can access sites like Backpage to adver-
tise with. They depend less on third parties when they can post ads themselves.
And it's perfectly logical that if Backpage is willing to work with police to get the
perpetrators of trafficking and to save underage people from being exploited, why
on earth would you want to shut that avenue down? It's cutting off their nose to
spite their face.

Sex worker consumers also believe the criminalization of websites
such as Backpage is futile and ignores other organizations that are also
indirectly linked to activities in the commercial sex trade. For example,
on October 7, 2016, one sex work consumer stated,

Its bull crap. Arresting the CEO's of Backpage to stop sex trafficking makes
just as much sense as arresting the CEO's of Holiday Inn, Marriott, Best Western
hotels because sex workers have used their businesses. Or arresting the CEO's of
Gucci, or the CEO's of Nordstrom because escorts bought their clothes from there.
Or arresting the CEO of Boost Mobile because they use their phones. These dis-
trict attorneys have their heads up their own asses.
 This is like the war on drugs, how's that going? It's basically a shell game, if BP
is shut down, something else will popup and replace it. You would think they
would want BP around so authorities could identify the possible underage and
people forced into the business. At least you knew where most of the action was,
instead of solving the problem, this will do the opposite and make it more difficult
to track them down because now you do not know where they are![5]

There is a long history of evidence to suggest that pursuing prosecution
or civil litigation against Backpage.com will just displace the advertisements to another website.

When Craigslist.org shuttered the adult section of its classified advertisement website in 2010, the commercial sex advertisements were displaced to Backpage.com. When Backpage.com shuttered its own adult
section in early 2017, the advertisements were simply displaced to the dating section of the website.[6]

Ultimately, there are alternative forums for sex traffickers and consenting commercial sex workers to market their illicit services.

In addition to websites that specifically cater to the commercial sex
industry, such as Humaniplex.com and CityVibe.com—"Your Local Escort
Directory"—sex traffickers have been found marketing services and soliciting new recruits on social media platforms, such as Facebook[7] and Instagram,[8] and dating websites, such as OKCupid and Tinder.[9]

While anti-trafficking advocates may not care whether the advertisements are displaced to another website, it is important to understand that other websites may not be as cooperative with police investigations and subpoenaing information would be a logistical nightmare. According to one commercial sex consumer:

> *Let's say that I post here that I scooped Sally Q and paid her $40 for a BBBJ*[10] *and a got a nice CFS*[11]? *The point is—How can a post on here lead to any kind of real legal action? How would LE*[12] *tie an anonymous poster name to a real live person? You think LE is going to spend the money to get a subpoena to obtain IP addresses from this site? Oh Wait! All of the servers for this site are off shore, as are the Mods. How much extra would it cost to get the State Department and foreign GubMints involved? Are you sure that Jackson*[13] *would comply with such a request? What if the poster was using a proxy to access the site? How is that kind of cost justified for a misdemeanor crime? So in essence this is nearly like Vegas. What is said here is kinda insulated.*[14]

Jackson, the moderator of USASexGuide.info, has also made it known that his website would not be cooperative with law enforcement investigations. Moreover, he has prepared for the prospective closure of Backpage.com by creating his own classified advertisement website, specifically designed for commercial sex—USAAdultClassifieds.info. In response to the attempted criminalization of Backpage.com administrators, Jackson posted a link to his new website along with the following message, "Are you kidding? That's great news for us, we are ready. New version coming out soon. Unlike them we aren't tied to the USA."[15]

If law enforcement continues demonizing open-access forums that are used for police investigations, some of the traffic could be displaced to websites that may be more difficult to access. For example, while the media has been focused on Backpage.com, there has been no mention of websites such as AlwaysOnTheHunt.com, which requires a referral-based registration. Websites like this should be of greater concern to the public and law enforcement, considering that men on the site allegedly disregard consent, advocating for stealthing and raping passed-out women.[16]

Last, there are various forms of technology that are used by sex traffickers, consenting sex workers, and commercial sex consumers. It is not reasonable to place blame on every business that happens to become a third party to a commercial sex exchange.

For example, many international sex tourists discuss communicating with commercial sex workers using WhatsApp or Kik messenger, among other communication applications. Both messaging apps use data rather than phone time, so they are essentially free. WhatsApp also includes a translation program, which facilitates messages to non-English speakers.

At the time of this writing, WhatsApp was mentioned in 441 posts on InternationalSexGuide.info in countries around the world, including Abu Dhabi, China, India, Indonesia, Malaysia, Sri Lanka, Turkey, Spain, Dubai, Morocco, Germany, Kenya, Slovakia, Sierra Leone, Philippines, Hungary, Zambia, United Arab Emirates, and Pakistan.

In the end, there is no evidentiary nor theoretical basis for why any attorney general or legislator should rationally expect for sex trafficking or the commercial sex industry to wane from the prosecution or civil liability of Backpage.com. What is more likely is that the advertisements will continue to move elsewhere, perhaps to the Dark Web and on sites less inclined to cooperate with law enforcement, thus creating additional barriers to combat the burgeoning commercial sex industry online. Instead of attempting to criminalize Backpage.com, legislators should focus on passing policy to strengthen communication, cooperation, and data sharing with law enforcement so that we can better use these websites as tools for investigation and victim rescue.

Notes

1. Staff. "Craigslist: The 'Wal-Mart of Child Sex Trade'?" *The Week* (August 5, 2010): accessed July 6, 2017, http://theweek.com/articles/492084/craigslist-walmart-child-sex-trade.

2. William Saletan, "Pimp Mobile: Craigslist Shuts Its 'Adult' Section. Where Will Sex Ads Go Now?" *Slate* (September 7, 2010): accessed July 6, 2017, http://www.slate.com/articles/news_and_politics/frame_game/2010/09/pimp_mobile.html.

3. *Winston-Salem North, Carolina Backpage Advertiser Reviews Forum* (March 31, 2017): accessed July 6, 2017, http://www.USASexGuide.info.

4. Quotes taken from responses to Dr. Mehlman-Orozco's anonymous snowball sample survey of sex workers in 2016.

5. *Backpage Advertiser Reviews Forum* (October 7, 2016): accessed July 6, 2017, http://www.USASexGuide.info.

6. Accessed July 6, 2017, http://news.trust.org/item/20170530154532-pjag0.

7. Accessed July 6, 2017, http://www.thedailybeast.com/the-sex-trafficking-kings-of-facebook.

8. Accessed July 6, 2017, http://www.nhregister.com/general-news/20160619/sex-trafficking-moves-to-social-media-to-find-victims-and-perpetrators-connecticut-authorities-say.

9. Accessed July 6, 2017, http://wjla.com/features/7-on-your-side/7-on-your-side-investigates-pimps-recruiting-prostitutes-from-online-dating-sites.

10. Bare back blow job. See Appendix A for more information.

11. Covered full service. See Appendix A for more information.

12. Law enforcement. See Appendix A for more information.

13. The owner and moderator of the USASexGuide.info forum, who is based in Brazil.

14. *Streetwalker Reports Forum in Wilmington, Delaware* (October 7, 2016): accessed July 6, 2017, http://www.USASexGuide.info.

15. Accessed July 6, 2017, https://thecrimereport.org/2017/06/14/hunting-the -internets-worst-predators/.

16. *Bareback Beauties Forum in Los Angeles, California* (April 28, 2017): accessed July 6, 2017, http://www.USASexGiude.info.

CHAPTER TWENTY

Blaming the Hotel

In addition to online websites that are used to market services for sex trafficked victims, third-party liability litigation has also recently expanded to motels and hotels.

On March 10, 2017, media outlets from across the United States began sharing news about the lawsuit against the Roosevelt Inn motel, which was described by prosecutors as Philadelphia's "epicenter of human trafficking."[1] The lawsuit alleged that a 17-year-old girl, identified as M.B., was sold into sexual slavery for two years at the hotel, beginning in 2013, when she was only 14 years old. Center City attorney Thomas R. Kline released a statement, "This is a message to the entire motel and hotel industry that if you allow and enable trafficking of youngsters, young women, or any person on your facilities, you will be held responsible and sued for damages under the law."[2]

However, as mentioned earlier, this attempt at third-party liability may be overly targeted and assumes that business owners can distinguish human trafficking victims from consenting sex workers—something that law enforcement in the United States can't even do correctly much of the time.

While M.B. was allegedly trafficked at the Roosevelt Inn to such an extent that she hired an attorney to sue the hotel for damages, anonymous commercial sex consumers online tell a different story. There were only a handful of references to the Roosevelt Inn on USASexGuide.info, and none of the posts implicated the hotel in any way of being complicit. In fact, one user explicitly undermined the narrative told in the media. On May 29, 2009, an anonymous commercial sex consumer who went by the online handle 'JerryGarcia,' posted the following under 'Streetwalker Reports':

I was going to date this girl Terry if other options (well-reviewed GFE's[3] closer to home) fell through and at the last minute found a girl on Backpage who was up on Roosevelt Blvd at a motel. I negotiated 1 hour of promised GFE entertainment for $.5[4]—so I passed up the girl who I thought so highly of for an unknown thing. This turned out to be a mistake—I went to the motel and didn't like the scene at all (Roosevelt Inn)—the front desk stopped me from going to the room and asked too many questions. When I finally got to the room, the girl opened the door, and I was very disappointed in her looks—nothing like the ad or description—had missing teeth and didn't look 19 as had been promised—so I went in the room for 10 seconds, and then bolted.[5]

Generally, commercial sex consumers claim to receive sexual services while patronizing multiple well-known and high-end hotel chains around the world, some possibly with sex-trafficked victims. It is unreasonable to assume that administrators and staff at all of these hotels knew whether the woman was trafficked and just decided to look the other way. For example, in a review of postings on USASexGuide.info and International SexGuide.info I found the following major hotel chains mentioned numerous times (see Table 20.1).

Although some of the mentions were asking for referrals on where to stay or other generic information exchanges, some men claimed to have procured sexual services in these establishments.

For example, on November 19, 2016, one man posting in a forum about Panama City explained,

Table 20.1   Mentions of Hotel Chains in Commercial Sex Forums 2016–2017[1]

Hotel	Mentioned in USASexGuide.info	Mentioned in InternationalSexGuide.info
Marriott	73	300+
Hilton	199	300+
Best Western	46	68
Hyatt	35	300+
Radisson	10	161

[1]April 15, 2016, to April 15, 2017

> *We all know Hyatt is girl friendly. I had no problems getting ladies in, the front desk only makes a copy of their passport or ID . . . On my first day I stayed at Tower House Suites, but it was booked for the rest of my time here. They also definitely have no problems with bringing ladies. I seen many other guys bringing ladies to the Tower House and the Hyatt . . . The Marriott is well know to be girl friendly also. But I try to stay at lower price places myself."[6]*

Another man posting in the Panama City forum corroborated,

> *I'm checking out today after five days at Marriott, and it is very welcoming. When you come in with your friend, go to the bell captain where he will ask your room number and copy her passport. That's it. Up you go.*
> *First night I had colleagues here so walked up to Venato and meet Lucia, a tiny Madura Colombiana. She suggested Hotel Arcos so $5 cab and $15 room with free porn. I recommend if your not comfortable with your own place. Also recommend Lucia. Well worth $.[7]*

On July 14, 2016, a man claimed he was traveling on business and stayed at the Hilton in Budapest, Hungary the week prior. He averred the hotel was "green," meaning that it allowed sex workers up to the room. When he summoned girls from the Modern Geisha Agency to the hotel, all he needed to do was make one call to the reception, and the girls were allegedly given cards for the elevator.

According to the Modern Geisha Agency website:

> *With us, you will not only find a sex partner but a real quality companion. Our ladies are all different in meaning of appearance and personality, but there are characteristics they all share: intelligence, beauty, neatness and at last but not least: discretion.*
> *We are glad to arrange a meeting with a lady for longer time as well as having a "taste" of a fine woman for a shorter period. If you would like to get an insight of a geisha's life of the 21st century, do not hesitate to contact us![8]*

On June 1, 2016, a sex tourist claimed that he had multiple women visit his room at the Best Western Ipanema in Rio de Janeiro, Brazil. He explained to other mongers, "If you booked room for 2 people, technically your guest is the 2nd occupant. They didn't ask about the 2nd, 3rd, or 4th. I checked 1st one in, and that was that. They even called up to my room like, 'Mr. So and So, Miss BlahBlah is in reception—should I send her up?' 'Yes, please!'"[9]

Red assumes they can stop. Where is it? — where [unclear]

In addition to allowing sex workers to come up to their rooms, many sex tourists explained how the women would sell services in the hotel bars or clubs. For example, on May 27, 2016, one man claimed that women could be purchased for sex in the bar of the Radisson Blu Hotel in Riga, Latvia.

In certain areas, hotels were being reported as "red," meaning that they prohibited sex workers from going to the room with customers. However, sex worker consumers would update the reports periodically, highlighting when and if a hotel switched status and became "green."

For example, JW Marriott Marquis in Dubai was reported as being red in January 2016, but it was updated to green by November 2016. One monger claimed that he only needed to "register the girl at the front desk" before bringing her to his room for the commercial sex transaction.

On October 21, 2008, a man claimed that the Hyatt Regency in Dubai instituted a new policy against sex work following a murder that took place in the hotel. The commercial sex consumer claimed that the hotel disco was full of women who were expensive, but he couldn't take them back to his room. He explained, "I took back a pair of Moscovites,[10] but the hotel wouldn't let them up. I was really pissed, especially since I will not have any action for quite some time."[11]

While some hotels would periodically institute polices to deny room access to local women, other hotels only levied a surcharge for the extra guest. For example, on April 1, 2017, one man claimed that he stayed at the Wyndham Viva V in Puerto Plata, Dominican Republic. He claimed to have brought in one sex worker with no problem and a second sex worker for an additional $70.

Similar experiences are reported at these same hotel chains in the United States. For example, a man who claimed that he had met a "Chinese spinner through WeChat"[12] mentioned the Marriott in Hawaii on October 16, 2015. He claimed that the sex worker had a room in the Marriott, "Met her at McDonald's and went to her room and did it. Service was OK. BBBJ,[13] CFS.[14] She was tight, blew in the cover.[15] Showered and then dropped her off at a condo building in Moilili."[16] He stated that he paid $200 for the encounter.

Anti-trafficking legislation should not be designed to hold third-party businesses accountable if they are not directly involved. It is extremely difficult to identify human trafficking offenses; even police misidentify victims with frequency. As such, we shouldn't expect business owners to be able to discern the difference. Instead, legislation should facilitate partnerships and information exchange to assist police investigations. Hotels should receive training on how to identify the red flags of trafficking, and there

hotel as police

should be protocol in place on when, by law, businesses and websites are required to report. If a hotel manager fails to alert law enforcement after being explicitly informed that a minor or adult is being trafficked, that person should be prosecuted to the fullest extent of the law. However, in the absence of explicit evidence, law enforcement should work with third parties to facilitate information exchange and cooperation. Human trafficking is already a clandestine crime; we don't want to push it further underground. Instead, we must empower people who may encounter human trafficking offenses with the knowledge and resources needed to report these crimes.

Ultimately, there are a number of businesses that are likely to encounter human trafficking victims during the course of their operations. Nail and hair salons; medical, dental, and mental health service providers; retail shops; hotels; flight personnel; bank tellers; and on-demand car service or taxi drivers may encounter victims of sex trafficking. Professionals in agriculture, domestic service, construction, restaurants, and any other industries involving guest workers may encounter victims of labor trafficking. While these victims are difficult to identify, it is important for corporate executives, business owners, and day-to-day operational staff to receive training from qualified professionals on how to identify the red flags of various forms of exploitation and where to report this information. Developing industry-based protocols for identifying human trafficking could help protect consumers and businesses alike. Not only is this responsible, but it could result in the identification of victims and prosecution of offenders, while reducing the liability for truly innocent businesses who may have their operations unwittingly infiltrated by human trafficking syndicates posing as legitimate consumers.

Notes

1. Joseph A Slobodzian, "First of Kind Lawsuit Accuses N.E. Philly Hotel of Accommodating Sex Trafficking," Philly.com (2017, March 10, 2017): accessed July 6, 2017, http://www.philly.com/philly/news/crime/First-of-kind-lawsuit -accuses-NE-Phila-hotel-of-accomodating-sex-trafficking.html.

2. Ibid.

3. Girlfriend experience. See Appendix A for more information.

4. $.5 is code for $50. See Appendix A for more information.

5. *Streetwalker Reports Philadelphia Forum* (May 29, 2009): accessed July 6, 2017, http://www.USASexGuide.info.

6. *Panama City Forum.* (2016, November 19). Accessed July 6, 2017, from http://www.InternationalSexGuide.info.

7. *Panama City Forum.* (2016, November 18). vhttp://www.International SexGuide.info.

8. Modern Geisha Escort Agency in Budapest. (n.d.). Accessed July 6, 2017, from http://geisha.hu.

9. *Rio de Janeiro Forum.* (2016, June 1). Accessed July 6, 2017, from http://www.InternationalSexGuide.info.

10. Russian woman, not necessarily from Moscow.

11. *Dubai-Hotel Information Forum.* (2008, October 21). Accessed July 6, 2017, from http://www.InternationalSexGuide.info.

12. A social media application used for communication.

13. Bare back blow job. See Appendix A for more information.

14. Covered full service. See Appendix A for more information.

15. Condom. See Appendix A for more information.

16. *Escort Reports in Hawaii Forum.* (2015, October 16). Accessed July 6, 2017, from http://www.InternationalSexGuide.info.

CHAPTER TWENTY-ONE

Crimmigration and Labor Trafficking

We don't mean to come illegally or without a visa. We just care about leaving the economic crisis that we go through.
—Undocumented migrant day laborer, April 4, 2009

While interventions to combat sex trafficking in the United States are largely ineffective, anti-trafficking policies targeting labor exploitation are relatively nonexistent. Best estimates suggest that labor trafficking is more prevalent than sex trafficking; however, anti-trafficking efforts in the United States are more focused on the latter. This may be in part because victims of labor trafficking are typically noncitizens who can be denied access to justice system protections and social services.

Foreign nationals have been treated as an exploitable population in the United States for centuries. U.S. immigration policy enforcement has historically waxed and waned with the economy, in order to maximize gains and minimize losses. Unfortunately, foreign nationals, both legal and illegal, are at risk for labor and sex trafficking due to several issues with U.S. immigration policy.

First, legal immigrants, particularly guest workers on nonimmigrant visas, are susceptible to human trafficking given the power differential between employers and employees. Business owners can unilaterally change the terms of employment contracts and then threaten employees with deportation if they complain. Although the United States is typically focused on immigration reform to address undocumented migration, future policies must identify mechanisms for increasing protections for guest workers, including safeguards on their living circumstances, wages, transportation, communication, and other elements of employment.

When and if a violation occurs, temporary nonimmigrant workers should feel empowered to obtain access to judicial relief and legal assistance so that they may vindicate violations of their rights without fear of deportation. Given the prolific misrepresentation by some employers, oversight and abuse deterrence must be conducted by third parties, such as officials from the Department of Labor.

In addition, changes to the current guest worker programs could reduce the likelihood of abuse. For example, the H2-A visa program requires companies to provide farm workers with food and housing in addition to pay for work performed. Instead, legislators should consider requiring a housing allowance, so residency would not be controlled by the employer and could be selected by the guest worker.

In addition to issues with the legal guest worker program, undocumented migrants are at high risk. Although there is a wealth of evidence to suggest that undocumented migrants commit proportionately less crime than their U.S. citizen counterparts, they are actively criminalized in the United States due to their undocumented migrant status. As a result, this population can be extremely vulnerable and complacent to victimization for fear of deportation.

While some may blame the undocumented migrants for choosing to cross into the United States without documentation, the reality is that it isn't necessarily a choice. Economic push-and-pull factors remain a root cause of undocumented migration from Mexico and Central America to the United States. For many of these migrants, there is no proverbial line for them to wait in to come legally. If they want to make a better life for their family, the only option for many of these migrants is to cross without documentation into the United States.

For my master's thesis, I conducted a survey of over 100 day laborers in Northern Virginia between 2008 and 2009. I asked each of them 33 questions about crime, immigration, and human smuggling. When I inquired why they didn't come to the United States legally, their responses suggested that it wasn't a choice.

According to one respondent, "There was never an opportunity to come legally. Sometimes the situation in our country makes us come and leave our family, parents, and children."[1]

Another respondent concurred, "For people with less resources, it's much more difficult to obtain the documents to travel."[2]

"There aren't equal opportunities for just anybody. Also, you've got to be someone who is of a higher academic level," said another day laborer.[3]

Ultimately, due to their illegal immigration status, undocumented migrants are often targeted by criminals and become victims to a variety of crimes, including human trafficking, robbery, burglary, and assault. They are targeted because criminals know they are unlikely to report the victimization to the police. Unfortunately, U.S. law enforcement fall short of protecting this vulnerable population.

Although T-visas are designed to protect foreign national victims of human trafficking by granting them legal nonimmigrant status for cooperating with law enforcement, victims may not be aware of the program and can be erroneously denied the visa. In order to secure a T-visa, applicants must first certify that they are a victim of a severe form of trafficking in persons and provide evidence to support the claim. They must also submit a law enforcement agency declaration form or explain why they cannot submit it to support their claim. The applicant must demonstrate how they will suffer extreme hardship, involving unusual and severe harm, if they were deported. They must have also reported their human trafficking victimization and fully comply with requests from federal, state, and local law enforcement in the investigation and prosecution of acts of trafficking or explain why they couldn't, for example due to physical or psychological trauma.

In order to address labor trafficking in the United States, we must increase safety provisions for marginalized populations. There needs to be additional awareness campaigns informing legal and undocumented migrants about their rights and changes to current immigration policy, so that labor law violators are held accountable. Foreign national populations should have access to legal assistance to facilitate the process for obtaining T-visas or other protections post-victimization.

Although immigration is a hot topic in politics and public discourse, we often omit provisions on how to protect vulnerable foreign national populations from abuse. Regardless of citizenship status, every person deserves to be protected from being trafficked.

Notes

1. Anonymous Respondent (November 17, 2008): Undocumented Migrant Survey.

2. Anonymous Respondent (March 26, 2009): Undocumented Migrant Survey.

3. Anonymous Respondent (February 16, 2009): Undocumented Migrant Survey.

CHAPTER TWENTY-TWO

Out of the Shadows

You may choose to look the other way, but you can never say again that you did not know.

—William Wilberforce

Anti-trafficking efforts in the United States can be grouped into five pillars of focus: identifying the red flags of incidents, punishing traffickers, deterring clients, protecting victims, and preventing new crimes. However, the efforts meant to achieve these goals have been largely ineffective in combating trafficking in persons. While Americans may now be better able to identify the red flags of human trafficking than in prior years, arrests of human traffickers are infrequent and often fail to result in conviction. Clients remain undeterred. Victims are often criminalized or are otherwise marginalized instead of being protected through trauma-informed care, and there is no evidence to suggest that new crimes are being prevented. In addition, U.S. efforts lag behind our European counterparts in timing and efficacy. In order to improve U.S. anti-trafficking efforts, it is important to understand where we are falling short and why.

Identifying Red Flags

In recent years, an increasing number of people and businesses have jumped on the bandwagon to combat human trafficking by becoming more aware of the red flags and reporting suspected incidents to law enforcement or one of the growing number of (overlapping) human trafficking hotlines.[1] For example, in the United States, cosmetologists,[2] flight attendants,[3] and employees in the hospitality industry[4] are all beginning to receive training on how to recognize the red flags of sex trafficking. This is important because employees working in these industries could possibly encounter sex trafficking victims at some point in their careers; however, these efforts do not necessarily provide the evidence needed to result in convictions, and victims may not necessarily be rescued after identification.

For years, experts in human trafficking have been urging law enforcement and anti-trafficking advocates to "follow the money" and focus on financial transactions that may be linked to human trafficking.[5] Human trafficking syndicates often deal with unusually large amounts of cash, which can be laundered through financial institutions or transmitted through traceable virtual transactions.[6] Only recently have law enforcement and banks in Europe begun to heed the warnings of these experts. In 2015, the Thomson Reuters Foundation established an alliance of European Bankers, including Barclays, HSBC, Western Union, Standard Chartered, Deutsche Bank, Santander, UBS, and Commerzbank, to train bank employees on how to spot and report signs of human trafficking using a practical toolkit—including red-flag indicators and case studies.[7] Banks in the United States should follow suit so that law enforcement can build cases with evidence needed to land convictions.

Punishing Traffickers

As discussed throughout this book, human trafficking prosecutions rarely result in severe punishments. If they are ever caught, human traffickers accept plea bargains for tangentially related crimes, which end in a fractioned severity of punishment.

Punishments are important because they can serve as a specific and general deterrent. Theoretically, punishments that are certain, swift, and severe would be more likely to result in prospective offenders making the rational choice not to commit a crime.

This is perhaps the reason why more organized crime syndicates are choosing to sell people over illegal guns and drugs. The risks are low because traffickers are less likely to be caught by law enforcement, and they are often able to successfully argue that their victims were consenting participants in their own exploitation. As such, if they are ever caught, many are able to secure favorable plea bargains. Also, while these criminal enterprises can sell an illicit commodity such as guns or drugs only once, they can sell a human being over and over.

To facilitate successful punishment and accountability, law enforcement should explore innovative methods for investigation such as utilizing online forums and advertisements for commercial sex as a catalyst for investigation and partnering with legitimate businesses that may encounter human trafficking victims or offenders, such as banks.

In addition, prosecutors should continue relying on expert witnesses to bridge the credibility gap of victims, as well as educate judges and jurors on the realities of human trafficking recruitment and control. On the other hand, defense attorneys can utilize expert witness testimony to protect human trafficking survivors from being erroneously criminalized.

Given the often-blurred line between consent and coercion, legislators should consider changing the law so that victims cannot sanction their labor or sexual exploitation. The element of perceived "consent" significantly contributes to the credibility gap experienced by victims in the courtroom. If a pimp is sexually exploiting a woman or a labor trafficker is holding an undocumented migrant in indentured servitude, he or she should be held accountable for trafficking, regardless of whether the victim appeared to be consenting. Changing the law so that consent is no longer an affirmative defense could assist in securing more convictions against human traffickers who exploit people for sex or labor.

Deterring Clients

Clients are also undeterred because the punishments aren't particularly severe, and the likelihood of being caught is perceived as being relatively low. If asked about sex trafficking, most of these men will say that they abhor the practice and insist they seek consenting prostitutes. However, they often, perhaps unwittingly, obtain services from women who may be forced, defrauded, or coerced into the commercial sex industry.

"John," for example, is a white, master's degree–educated man in his 40s who lived in the DC metropolitan area when I interviewed him in 2016. He claimed to have patronized Star Foot Spa and Sun Foot Spa, two Maryland businesses that were implicated in sex trafficking.[8] According to "John,"

> At a lot of the massage parlors, the workers are treated poorly because they have to work about 12 hours a day, seven days a week. Occasionally, they get a day off, but overall, they are exploited. I've learned this from building up a rapport with some of them. And then I felt a little guilty for supporting the demand side of it.

Or take "James," another DC native I interviewed. He claimed to have a master's degree and a Juris Doctorate, doing HIV policy work for a DC area nonprofit organization. Although he hadn't patronized any sex worker locally, he admitted to engaging in sex tourism. On one trip, he claimed to have purchased sexual relations with two Latina women in a western European city. In retrospect, he believed the women had been sex trafficked. "They were living together in a tiny, dingy room. There was a Sterno can that they used to cook. Laundry they had done in the sink was hanging everywhere. There was a mattress. It might have had a box spring, but I don't think there was a bed frame. They removed their clothes and told me how sexy I am and all of that," he recounted, "In the moment, I was able to convince myself that they were into it, and they did a good job selling that, too."

In their normal day-to-day lives, these men are probably considered productive members of society and (for the most part) law abiding. However, they admittedly patronized sex workers, who they later believed were trafficked. Although it can be challenging to determine who is truly consenting, being a wealthy professional who did not intend to procure services from a trafficked victim should not absolve sex slave consumers of criminal or moral liability.

Although some men may not care whether a sex worker is trafficked or consenting, some commercial sex consumers have indicated a desire to help the women whom they believe may be trafficked, but don't know how. For example, on August 3, 2014, one sex tourist in Bhubaneswar, India said:

> We gave the money and the girl came. We went to the Girl, which turned out to be very bad. I tried to talk to the fish, and felt very sorry for her. She was very depressed. I believe she is on forced prostitution. She kept asking me to take her away somewhere far and was crying. She said her boss beats her. Now I felt very guilty.
>
> We left the place without doing anything. After all how can I do this to anyone? . . . I wish I could do something for her.[9]

I have interviewed multiple commercial sex consumers and sex tourists who similarly claim that they would report suspected incidents of trafficking if they weren't at risk of being criminalized themselves. As such, law enforcement should consider decriminalizing commercial sex consumers who bring forward information leading to the arrest of a human trafficker or the rescue of a victim. Combating sex trafficking is a herculean task, and our efforts can benefit from the inside information that can be provided by morally inclined commercial sex consumers.

Protecting Victims

Criminalizing victims of human trafficking has been denounced by federal and state legislation across the United States and internationally, yet it still happens more than we would expect. Human trafficking survivors are frequently misidentified, erroneously criminalized, denied services, and sometimes even deported.

There are a number of campaigns to better inform law enforcement and service providers to correct this type of flawed treatment. In addition, an increasing number of states are passing vacatur statues to retroactively address these errors once the victim is correctly identified. These laws provide post-conviction relief for survivors of human trafficking by completely erasing criminal convictions related to their victimization.

In addition to denied service provision and erroneous criminalization, some victims are taken advantage of by the organizations, family members, and others, who are meant to protect them. Some refer to these third parties that benefit off and exploit human trafficking survivors as "victim pimps" or as engaging in "traffixploitation." This phenomenon was termed "secondary exploitation" by human trafficking survivor and scholar, Claudia Cojocaru.[10]

In my interviews with human trafficking survivors, one woman explained, "It's like they're swinging a baseball bat and stop halfway. We need more help if they truly want us to succeed." She went on to describe how the assistance she received from one organization was discontinued as soon as she completed a victim statement for donors. Although she wasn't yet fully restored and reintegrated into society, they used her information as a human trafficking survivor success story to help their organization secure additional funding, before sending her on her way.

Organizations being funded to provide services to human trafficking survivors must employ staff who are adequately trained in trauma-informed care. Moreover, there should be mechanisms in place to assess the efficacy and the outcomes of their services. At present, although there is an increasing amount of resources to help victims, there is little accountability to ensure that it is being responsibly appropriated.

Preventing New Crimes

Ultimately, new crimes are not being prevented because U.S. anti-trafficking interventions are not based in evidence. I have witnessed first-hand how human trafficking grant recipients and task forces can be recalcitrant to third-party evaluation.

For example, on December 6, 2013, I attended a meeting of the Northern Virginia Human Trafficking Task Force. After the task forced opened the meeting up for questions, I asked,

Many service providers produce descriptive statistics or frequencies in 'research reports' as evidence of intervention 'success.' However, a report by the Campbell

Collaboration, which is the leading producer of evidence-based research in the field of criminology, found that there is not one rigorous evaluation on the effectiveness of human trafficking interventions in the world. Are you planning to establish quasi-experimental or experimental research methods to actually empirically evaluate the efficacy of your interventions?

I asked this question because I was exceptionally committed to making sure that victims were receiving the funding appropriated toward their assistance. Moreover, I was acutely aware of the lack of research on the efficacy of prevention and intervention strategies in reducing sexual exploitation.[11] The study I cited to the task force evaluated anti-trafficking interventions from around the world, including raising awareness, providing education and employment to changing the legislation, prosecuting perpetrators, and empowering victims. The authors concluded that the existing research evaluations were mostly of poor quality, so the effectiveness was still relatively unknown.

To that effect, I wanted to make sure our local efforts were (as much as possible) based in evidence and provided the greatest assistance to the most victims.

In response to my question, the Virginia assistant attorney general and anti-trafficking coordinator at the time told me that, "academic research does not plug into the goals of the task force." She went on to say that researchers were not welcome to participate in their task force meetings.

I remember how jaded I again felt after hearing this. It seemed like the organizations receiving funding to combat trafficking didn't care whether their efforts worked. I felt that they only cared how it looked to their donors and the public. After all, for organizations truly committed to reducing the incidence of human trafficking, why wouldn't external evaluation be welcomed?

Human trafficking is a crime because people value money over human life. The same should not be true about the organizations and the collaborations charged with protecting survivors, prosecuting offenders, and preventing new crimes.

Evidence-Based Interventions

To better combat human trafficking, it is important for law enforcement to utilize innovative tactics to catalyze more investigations and improve their capacity for deterrence. This concept is founded in routine activities theory, which postulates that crime occurs when three things converge in time and space: (1) a motivated offender, (2) a suitable target, and (3) lack of a capable guardian. This theory is currently used to support hot-spot policing strategies, which deploy law enforcement to areas with high concentrates of crime in order to prevent new offenses. Research suggests that crime significantly decreases when law enforcement is deployed to crime hot spots.

In addition, laws must empower victims and others who may encounter human trafficking to come forward and alert authorities, without fear of criminalization. Many victims are exploitable because they are in some way marginalized and fear the legal consequences for reporting their victimization. Both legal and undocumented migrants may fear deportation, which is a real threat despite T-visa provisions. Sex-trafficked women fear being criminalized as prostitutes or for crimes related to their victimization. In addition, commercial sex consumers fear being criminalized for solicitation of prostitution and, therefore, may not report red flags of sex trafficking, even if they were so inclined. Although legalizing the commercial sex industry is not the answer, considering that it provides a protective veneer for illicit enterprises to flourish, Amnesty International[12] and others agree that decriminalization of sex workers and commercial sex consumers could empower these populations to report victimizations, including sex trafficking.

Simultaneously, U.S. legislators should continue efforts to address the socioeconomic factors that contribute to the motivation of offenders and targeting of victims. The majority of victims are targeted and exploited because human traffickers prey and manipulate their needs. For people coming from lower socioeconomic areas, these needs may be physiological (e.g., food, water, and shelter) or related to their safety. For those trafficked from middle- or upper-class communities, these needs may be related to feelings of love and belonging, self-esteem, or self-actualization. Anti-trafficking efforts should consider programs that screen at-risk populations (foreign nationals and minors) for unmet needs and provide social services to fill identified gaps. For example, see the sample screening tool for juveniles in Appendix F.

In the end, combating the human trafficking scourge is our collective responsibility. For years, this crime has been hidden in plain sight in small towns and big cities across America, but not anymore. Anti-trafficking advocates are more equipped than ever before with the knowledge needed to identify the red flags of human trafficking. Now we need to start bridging the gap between law and policy to make sure that victims are protected and offenders are held accountable. We must discontinue scapegoat politics and avoiding the hard decisions, so that we can start building the evidence base needed to ensure our resources are being used efficiently and effectively.

Human beings should never be treated as a means to an end. Each individual, no matter their nationality, needs, or socioeconomic status, should be treated as an end in themselves.

Notes

1. Human trafficking hotlines can be a waste of resources in many areas. Most simply connect callers with local law enforcement, similar to dialing a non-emergency police line, and provide information on local human trafficking service providers, which is also publicly available through a simple Google search. These services can be duplicative, with multiple county, state, and national hotlines providing the same assistance. As such, the appropriated funding, which can be hundreds of thousands of dollars, may be better spent on housing or vocational services for survivors.

2. Jennifer Jordan, "Hair Salons Join in the Fight against Human Trafficking," Fox 8 Cleveland (October 11, 2016): accessed July 6, 2017, http://fox8.com /2016/10/11/hair-salons-join-in-the-fight-against-human-trafficking/.

3. Jacey Fortin, "Flight Attendants Fight Human Trafficking with Eyes in the Sky," *The New York Times* (February 7, 2017): accessed July 6, 2017, https://www .nytimes.com/2017/02/07/us/flight-attendants-human-trafficking.html.

4. Cheril Lee, "Hotels Trained to Spot Human Trafficking," KIOS-FM Omaha Public Radio (May 8, 2017): accessed July 6, 2017, http://kios.org/post/hotels -trained-spot-human-trafficking.

5. Louise Shelley, *Human Trafficking: A Global Perspective* (Cambridge, MA University Press, 2010).

6. Andrew Prozes "How Banks Can Help Stop Human Trafficking," *American Banker* (July 17, 2015): Accessed July 6, 2017, https://www.americanbanker.com /opinion/how-banks-can-help-stop-human-trafficking.

7. Ed Upright, "Bank Staff Will 'Red-Flag' Trafficking Suspects with Powerful New Tool," Thomson Reuters Foundation (May 2, 2017): accessed July 6, 2017, http://news.trust.org/item/20170502164958-vpaxd/.

8. Sophia Barnes, "Maryland Spa Owner Charged with Human Trafficking," NBC Washington (April 1, 2016): accessed July 6, 2017, http://www.nbcwashington .com/news/local/Maryland-Man-Charged-for-Human-Trafficking-374327191 .html.

9. *Other Areas-Bhubaneswar Forum* (August 3, 2014): accessed July 6, 2017, http://www.InternationalSexGuide.info.

10. Accessed July 6, 2017, http://www.antitraffickingreview.org/index.php /atrjournal/article/view/198/187.

11. Peter van der Laan, Monika Smit, Inge Busschers, and Pauline Aarten, "Cross-Border Trafficking in Human Beings: Prevention and Intervention Strategies for

Reducing Sexual Exploitation," Campbell Collaboration (2011): accessed July 6, 2017, https://www.campbellcollaboration.org/library/trafficking-strategies-for -reducing-sexual-exploitation.html.

12. Amnesty International Publishes Policy and Research on Protection of Sex Workers' Rights, Amnesty International (May 26, 2016): accessed July 6, 2017, https://www.amnesty.org/en/latest/news/2016/05/amnesty-international -publishes-policy-and-research-on-protection-of-sex-workers-rights/.

Acknowledgments

Words cannot express the sincere gratitude that I feel for my family. Beyond all others, they have been my inspiration and support throughout my scholarship and career.

To my beautiful and kindhearted daughter, Destiny—all of my passion for social justice begins with you. My path in life was arduous at times, but you were my first inspiration for success and made me want to make the world a better place. Everything I have and everything I have become is because of you. Thank you. I love you more than you will ever know.

For my mother, Belinda, you have sacrificed so much to be there for me when I needed you. For every barrier that I thought was insurmountable, you taught me to persevere. Once, you told me, "When you get through this fire you're in, you will be forged like steel." You were right, and thank you. You showed me the meaning of unconditional love and how to be selfless. Every day I aspire to follow in your footsteps. I just hope I can measure up.

My littlest ones—Mia, Rio, and Nicolas—you are the reason why I smiled through every adversity that I faced. Each of you, with your own special personality and talents, brought and continue to bring such incredible joy to my life. I don't think you will ever know how important this was for me, especially given my difficult and disheartening area of research. I can't wait to see who you become and the greatness you will bring to this world. I love you very much, and I am so thankful to be your mom.

And to my husband, Luis. I couldn't have chosen a better man to be the father of my children. You are amazing, and I feel privileged to have you as my partner. We have faced our own challenges, but your support has never wavered. Words cannot express how much I care for you and how thankful I am for everything you do for our family.

I am also exceptionally grateful for everyone who read early drafts of my proposal and book and supported my writing in various ways. You know who you are. Thank you!

In particular, I would like to express my sincere gratitude to my dear friend and talented attorney, Jessie Mahn; my neighbor and sister in Soroptimism, Kati Mangrio; my family, Brett and Barry Mehlman and Michael Weinstein; my former student and current colleague, Terri Hines; my fellow author Brian Stolarz; and superstar attorney Mac VerStandig.

I would like to also thank Dr. Louise Shelley and Lisa Johnson-Firth, J.D. for opening my eyes to the scourge of human trafficking in the United States, as well as my graduate school mentors Dr. James Willis, Dr. Cynthia Lum, and Dr. Jon Gould for encouraging my scholarship throughout the years.

To the ladies of Soroptimist International of Woodbridge, thank you for being so philanthropic and altruistic in your work to combat human trafficking and help marginalized girls around the world. You have encouraged me since the day I met you. As a token of my appreciation, I would like to donate 50 percent of my proceeds from this book to your organization for a discretionary scholarship for human trafficking survivors. I am confident that you will use the funding wisely and help those in great need.

For the kids who have participated and graduated from the TEAM SummerQuest program with the Manassas City Police Department, I know you have experienced some things in your life that are difficult to cope with. In fact, some of you have lived through things that would be challenging for someone twice your age to handle, but you have persevered. I know it may be hard to have this type of foresight as teenagers, but think of your future and where you want to be when you grow up. You have control over your destiny and are resilient. I, for one, believe in you, and as a symbol of my confidence, I would like to donate a portion of my proceeds from this book to a scholarship for TEAM SummerQuest graduates. Trust in yourself! Especially you, M.

I owe a very special debt of gratitude to my literary agents Ronald Goldfarb and Gerrie Sturman. You believed in me and continue to champion my work. Because of you and your advocacy, this book was connected with an extremely talented editor, Hilary Claggett from Praeger. Thank you so much for everything you do and all of your support. Words cannot express how truly appreciative I am to know both of you.

Last, but certainly not least, to all of the human trafficking survivors I have met and worked with over the years. Your strength and resiliency continue to hearten me. Thank you for never giving up. As I am sure I have told you before, "When God pushes you to the edge, trust Him fully, because only two things can happen. Either He will catch you if you fall, or He will teach you how to fly."[1]

I say that because I truly believe that you are unconquerable and will overcome the difficult adversities you face. I have never met anyone stronger, and I will always be there for you, unconditionally, should you need me.

To all of the other human trafficking victims and survivors who may come across this book—please know that you too are resilient. When you feel like you can't find a way out of your situation, and you will experience that feeling, please read this poem and know that you are not alone, and you are Invictus.

> Out of the night that covers me,
> Black as the Pit from pole to pole,
> I thank whatever gods may be
> For my unconquerable soul.
>
> In the fell clutch of circumstance
> I have not winced nor cried aloud.
> Under the bludgeonings of chance
> My head is bloody, but unbowed.
>
> Beyond this place of wrath and tears
> Looms but the Horror of the shade,
> And yet the menace of the years
> Finds, and shall find, me unafraid.
>
> It matters not how strait the gate,
> How charged with punishments the scroll,
> I am the master of my fate,
> I am the captain of my soul.
>
> —*Invictus* by William Ernest Henley, 1875

Note

1. Quote from unknown author.

Appendix A: Sex Work and Sex Trafficking Argot[1]

Money

.2=$20. Synonym: **Jackson.**

.4=$40.

.6=$60.

.8=$80.

$=$100. Synonyms: **One rose, Benjamin,** or **Bennie.**

$$=$200. Synonym: **Two roses.**

$$$=$300. Synonym: **Three roses.**

$$$.5=$350.

Donation, *noun.* Payment to a sexual service provider. Synonyms: **Sugar, doe, help, roses,** or **tips.**

PU, *verb.* **Pay up,** act of paying a sexual service provider.

Proprietor Typologies

AMP, *noun.* **A**sian **m**assage **p**arlor providing sexual services under the guise of offering massages.

Bottom, *noun.* Female victim of a sex trafficker who has been indoctrinated enough to facilitate the recruitment, control, and exploitation of other sex workers despite being exploited herself. When and if the Bottom also significantly benefits from the financial exploitation of other victims, she may be considered a sex trafficker by law enforcement. Synonym: **Bottom bitch.**

Cuidandero, *noun.* Latino pimp. Synonym: **Cuidador.**

Madame, *noun.* Female manager of an outcall, call girl agency.

Mamasan, *noun.* Female manager of an Asian massage parlor. Synonym: **Mama.**

Papasan, *noun.* Male manager of an Asian massage parlor.

Pimp, *noun.* A man who provides protection and arranges clients for sex workers in exchange for a portion of the proceeds from the commercial sex exchange. When and if the pimp utilizes force, fraud, coercion, threats, or deception for the purpose of exploitation or pimps a juvenile, he is also considered a sex trafficker. The majority of pimps engage in mental manipulation and financial exploitation, making them sex traffickers. Synonym: **Daddy.**

Sex Worker/Sex Trafficked Victim Descriptions

Babyback, *noun.* Young, petite, attractive Asian female sex worker.

Call girl, *noun.* Outcall commercial sex worker.

Independent, *noun.* A commercial sex worker who is self-employed. Synonyms: **Indie** or **freelance.** An independent commercial sex worker who escaped a pimp is called a **rogue** or a **renegade.**

Lolita, *noun.* A commercial sexually exploited minor. The term is a derivative of the 1955 novel *Lolita*, by Vladimir Nabokov, about an adult who becomes sexually involved with his 12-year-old stepdaughter, whom he nicknames Lolita.

Lot lizard, *noun.* A derogatory term for a commercial sex worker who advertises at truck stops.

Snowie, *noun.* A Caucasian commercial sex worker. Synonyms: **Snow bunny** or **snowflake.**

Spinner, *noun.* A very petite and thin female sex provider.

Stable, *noun.* Multiple commercial sex workers controlled by the same pimp.

Streetwalker, *noun.* A commercial sex worker who advertises services on the street. Synonyms: **SW, working girl, WG,** or **lady of the night.**

The help, *noun.* A commercial sex worker. Synonym: **Provider** or **pro** (i.e., **prostitute**).

Treintera, *noun.* A commercial sex worker who is sold to Latino men at construction or day-laborer sites. Consumers are charged $30, which is *treinta* in Spanish, in exchange for 15 minutes or ejaculation, whichever comes first. Synonym: **Treintona.**

Commercial Sex Consumers

AA, *adjective*. African American. Many Caucasian commercial sex workers frequently turn down African American male consumers, posting "No AA Men" in advertisements.

Chronophile, *noun*. A person with an age-based sexual attraction.

Hobbyist, *noun*. A man who patronizes sex workers. Synonyms: **Monger, John**, or **trick**.

Lurker, *noun*. Someone who reads about the experiences of others in procuring commercial sex services in online forums, but does not post about his or her own experiences.

Nepiophile, *noun*. A person with an attraction to infants and toddlers under the age of three.

Pedo, *noun*. Pedophile, a man sexually attracted to children under the age of 12.

Sexual Services

Bareback, *noun*. Commercial sex act without a condom. Synonym: **BB**.

BBBJ, *noun*. Bare back blow job, fellatio without a condom.

BBFS, *noun*. Bare back full service, copulation without a condom.

Bothing, *verb*. When a man performs cunnilingus on a woman, while the woman provides fellatio to the man simultaneously. Synonym: **69**.

CBJ, *noun*. Covered blow job, fellatio with a condom.

CDS, *noun*, Covered doggy style, sexual intercourse where one partner is penetrated from behind by the other, while utilizing a condom.

CFS, *noun*. Covered full service, sexual intercourse between a sex worker and a patron, with a condom.

CIM, *noun*. Cum in mouth, fellatio that results in ejaculation into the sex worker's oral cavity.

CIP, *noun*. Cum in pussy, copulation that results in ejaculation into the sex worker's vagina.

CMISH, *noun*. Covered missionary sexual intercourse position, with the male lying on top of the female and penetrating while wearing a condom.

COB, *noun*. Cum on breasts, ejaculation onto the sex worker's chest.

Completo, *noun*. Commercial sex services including anal sodomy.

Cover, *noun*. Condom. Synonyms: **Glove, raincoat, umbrella, beret, hat**, or **Jimmy**.

DATY, *noun*. Dining at the Y. Cunnilingis, with the female's legs spread in the shape of the letter 'Y'.

DFE, *noun.* Dead fish experience: Coitus with a commercial sex worker who just lies there during the act, without much response. Synonym: **Starfish** (i.e., lying in the shape of a starfish in bed).

DFK, *noun.* Deep French kiss.

DT, *noun.* Deep throat, referring to fellatio into the throat.

Facial, *noun.* Ejaculating on sexual provider's face. Synonyms: **COF**, or **cum on face**, and **pearl necklace**.

FIV, *verb.* Finger in vagina, digital penetration.

4-hand massage, *noun.* $40 in exchange for an erotic hand massage.

FS, *noun.* Full service or full sex (i.e., copulation).

GFE, *noun.* Girlfriend experience. Commercial sex companionship that mimics a conventional relationship, in addition to sexual services.

Greek, *noun.* Anal intercourse. Synonym: **Mediterranean**.

HE, *noun.* Happy ending, erotic hand massage. Synonym: **HJ** (i.e., hand job).

Mish, *noun.* Missionary sexual intercourse position, with the male lying on top of the female.

Nooner, *noun.* Patronizing a sex worker during lunch hour, which is popular with married men.

NOVA, *noun.* Sexual service provider is limited to erotic hand massages, no oral, vaginal, or anal intercourse.

Nuru massage, *noun.* An erotic massage technique in which a nude masseuse covers his/her body with oil and then rubs against the client's nude body.

P4P, *noun.* Pay for play or pay for pussy, referring to the exchange of money for sexual services.

Quickie, *noun.* Short-term sexual encounter, usual less than 30 minutes.

R&T, *noun.* Rub and tug (massage followed by a hand job).

Russian, *noun.* Sexual service involving rubbing the patron's penis between the sex worker's breasts.

Stealthing, *verb.* Removing a condom mid-coitus, without the sex worker's knowledge, and continuing the sexual act without the sex worker's consent for unprotected sex.

TS, *noun.* Table shower.

Vitamin V, *noun.* Viagra. Prescription drug used to treat erectile dysfunction and enhance sexual performance stamina.

With, *noun.* Sexual service with a condom.

Without, *noun.* Sexual service without a condom. Synonyms: **Raw**, **uncovered**, or **sunny** (i.e., no "raincoat").

Law Enforcement

Ellie, *noun.* Law enforcement. Synonyms: **LE, LEO**, or **Uncle**.

Advertisement and Review Services

AFF, *noun.* AdultFriendFinder.com: A social network website used to arrange casual sex.

AOTH, *noun.* AlwaysOnTheHunt.com: A website used by commercial sex consumers to share information about and review commercial sex providers in the United States. Known for the lack of moderation and questionable ethics in commercial sex exchanges.

BP, *noun.* Backpage.com: An online classified advertisement website where advertisements for commercial sex can also be found.

CL, *noun.* Craigslist.org: An online classified advertisement website where advertisements for commercial sex can also be found.

CV, *noun.* CityVibe.com: An online commercial sex advertisement website, known as your local escort directory for escorts, escort videos, BDSM, massage, and more.

ECCIE, *noun.* ECCIE.net: An escort client community information exchange website, containing information on escort cams, girlfriend experience commercial sex exchanges, and consumer-reviewed escorts.

EROS, *noun.* Eros.com: A website described as "The Ultimate Guide to Escorts and Erotic Entertainment." Named after the Greek god of sexual attraction.

HX, *noun.* Humaniplex.com: An online website where advertisements for commercial sex can be found.

P411, *noun.* Preferred411.com: A screening service used to connect commercial sex consumers with "upscale adult companionship."

RM, *noun.* RubMaps.com: A website that is described as the Internet's #1 massage parlor review site, offering high quality honest Asian massage parlor reviews, written by real users. The website's tagline is "Where fantasy meets reality."

SA, *noun.* SeekingArrangement.com: A website used by financially secure men, including commercial sex consumers and others, for dating young and attractive women or obtaining a mistress.

TER, *noun.* TheEroticReview.com: The largest erotic entertainer review website in the world, including 120,000 adult entertainers reviewed by over 1,000,000 consumers. Described as the "Zagat guide of the adult entertainment industry."

Track, *noun*. A location where commercial sex workers are advertised on the street. Synonyms, **the ho stroll** or **stroll**. A **kiddie stroll** is a location were juvenile commercial sex workers are advertised on the street.

USASG, *noun*. USASexGuide.info: A website used by commercial sex consumers to share information about and review commercial sex providers in the United States. **InternationalSexGuide.info** (ISG) is the international equivalent.

Locations for Exchange of Services

Casa de citas, *noun*. Spanish phrase for a brothel.

FKK, *noun*. Technically stands for *Freikörperkultur,* which is Germany's nudist movement or culture. However, sex tourists use the acronym to refer to German brothels.

GF, *adjective*. **G**irl friendly or **g**uest friendly. Typically used to describe a high-end hotel that does not prohibit sex workers from spending the night. Synonym: **Green**.

In-call, *noun*. Any location where the commercial sex consumer travels to the commercial provider for services, such as the sex worker's place of residence or hotel room.

Notel, *noun*. No tell. Typically used to describe a low-end hotel, where commercial sex services can be exchanged in secrecy.

Outcall, *noun*. Any location where the commercial sex worker travels to the consumer for services, such as the hobbyist or monger's place of residence or hotel room. Synonyms: **TOS** or **t**ake **o**ut **s**ervice.

Red, *adjective*. Used to describe a high-end hotel that prohibits sex workers from spending the night or entering the room of the commercial sex consumer.

Soapland, *noun*. Japanese brothel. Synonyms: **Soap house** or **Mizu shōbai**.

Telly, *noun*. Hotel.

Two-call system, *noun*. The commercial sex consumer will call twice for in-call commercial sex providers: first, to set up an appointment time and obtain general directions to the in-call location, and second, to obtain specific information on which room or apartment the sexual services will be provided. This is a tactic to evade law enforcement.

Other

Bitcoin, *noun*. Cryptocurrency and electronic payment system, which automatically launders money used in virtual transactions.

Cheese pizza, *noun*. Child pornography. Synonym: **CP**.

Choosing up, *verb.* Transfer of a commercial sex worker between pimps. Synonym: **Trading up**.

Crowns, *noun.* Symbols revered by pimps and tattooed on sex workers to mark them as property.

Dark Web, *noun.* Underground Internet, which requires specific software or configurations to access websites, such as **TOR**.

Diamonds, *noun.* Symbols revered in commercial sex subculture and lifestyle.

420, *noun.* Marijuana use is acceptable during the commercial sex exchange.

HHR, *noun.* A half-hour's worth of services with a commercial sex worker. Synonym: **HH**.

HR, *noun.* An hour's worth of services with a commercial sex worker.

Out of pocket, *adjective.* A term used by a pimp to describe a commercial sex worker who has become disobedient by failing to turn over money, defying orders, talking back, or trying to escape.

Pastebin, *noun.* A storage site used to catalog **Dark Web** sites and .Onion dark website links.

The game, *noun.* How pimps or pimp-controlled commercial sex workers refer to the commercial sex trade. Synonym: **The life**.

The hobby, *noun.* How commercial sex consumers refer to the commercial sex trade.

TOR, *noun.* **T**he **O**nion **R**outer, free software used to anonymously browse the Internet and Dark Web. Provides users with a fake IP address and bounces information across relays around the world to make it difficult to trace. Allows users to create hidden websites through .Onion links.

Trap house, *noun.* A residence used to sell drugs, as well as prostitute in certain areas.

Trap phone, *noun.* A prepaid cell phone that is used by human traffickers, as well as drug dealers and others engaging in illicit transactions, because it is untraceable and can be disconnected at any time.

Turned out, *adjective.* A commercial sex worker who has been indoctrinated into the commercial sex industry through a combination of mental manipulation, coercion, deception, and periodic physical force. Synonym: **Seasoned**.

VPN, *noun.* **V**irtual **p**rivacy **n**etwork, which allows users to access publicly shared information on the Internet through a private network, encrypting their IP address similarly to TOR.

Note

1. Definitions for terminology and abbreviations were obtained from a variety of commercial sex advertisement and review websites, including USASexGuide.info, InternationalSexGuide.info, RubMaps.com, Craigslist.org, and Backpage.com.

Appendix B: Sample Human Trafficking Expert Witness Testimony Outline

I. Qualifying the expert witness

   a. Employment

   b. Education

   c. Training

   d. Specialized Experiences

      i. For example: Task forces; peer reviewer; publications; teaching; research with human trafficking victims and offenders; and prior expert witness testimony.

II. Respond to opposing counsel challenges and ask court to admit expert

III. Bridging the victim credibility gap

   a. Rape trauma syndrome (RTS): Counterintuitive behaviors; discrepant accounts; promiscuity and sexual dysfunction; failed or delayed reporting; and desensitization to violence.

   b. Child sexual abuse accommodation syndrome (CSAAS): Secrecy; helplessness; delayed or unconvincing disclosure; retraction; entrapment and accommodation.

IV. Bridging the knowledge gap on human trafficking crimes and offenders

   a. Trauma bonding: The complex emotional relationship that often exists between human traffickers and their victims.

   b. Control and obedience are maintained through a combination of emotional manipulation, feigned affection, physical and emotional abuse, and common goals.

    c.   Consequences for victims:

        i.   Attachment to the trafficker or the perpetrator of the trauma, which serves as a coping mechanism.

        ii.   Distrust of law enforcement, family, and others.

        iii. Failure to report victimization or delayed reporting, as well as omissions, errors, and discrepant accounts.

        iv. Misidentification by law enforcement and service providers.

            Consequences: Revictimization; erroneous criminalization; creates a credibility gap for victims; impedes the prosecution of offenders; and facilitates the control of victims by offenders.

V.   Case-specific examples

    a.   For example: Is the "bottom girl" or "bottom bitch" a sex trafficking co-conspirator?

        i.   In my opinion, no. They are victims with long-term trauma bonding with their offender. However, they can be implemental in trafficking new victims. The likelihood of them returning to an exploitive situation post law enforcement intervention is very high. They may engage in human trafficking actions, but I wouldn't consider them a human trafficker, per se.

Appendix C: Gathering Data from Human Trafficking Survivors

In building a human trafficking case, it is important for investigators and service providers to pay attention to elements of *coercion, deception*, and *fraud*. Often, persons unfamiliar with human trafficking crimes will ask straightforward questions that are focused predominantly on physical *force* and abuse. This approach may explain why so many victims are misidentified and erroneously criminalized.

To break the trauma bond between victims and offenders, it is important to approach each human trafficking survivor mindfully—never threaten criminal action in response to recalcitrance to cooperation. Instead, attempt to build trust with the victim by giving her or him a *voice* and treating her or him with *dignity and respect*, while being *neutral* and *trustworthy* in your interactions.

Although the following questions may seem to collect banal information in a repetitive manner, the information gathered through these inquiries may provide an important foundation of understanding and evidence in the long run.

Human trafficking victims are manipulated into concealing information and being distrusting of persons who may be inclined to help them. As such, the repetitiveness of these questions is designed to uncover response inconsistencies, which may be a red flag given the context.

In addition, the questions can be used to uncover a victim's lack of agency, specifically focusing on whether they are having their housing, finances, transportation, communication, or food regulated or controlled by their employer, as well as whether they are doing something they did not intend or are not comfortable with due to debt-bondage, deception, fraud, or coercion.

For example:
Foreign Nationals:

1. How did you travel to the United States?
    a. If traveled with a visa, ask: What type of visa did you travel with?
        i. Ask: Who, if anyone, sponsored your visa?
            1. If sponsored, ask: How much did they charge you for the visa?
                a. Ask: Do you still owe any money for your visa?
                b. Ask: How have you been able to pay off this visa debt?
2. How old were you when you came to the United States?
3. What year did you come to the United States?
4. Where (at what port of entry) did you enter the United States?
5. Have you returned to your home country since your arrival?
    a. If no, ask: Why not?
6. What states in the United States have you visited?
7. In what states in the United States have you worked/lived?
8. Where did you work when you *first* came to the United States? Is this what you thought you would be doing?
    a. How much money did you earn per hour?
    b. How much money did you take home per day?
9. Have you ever gambled?
    a. If yes, ask: How much gambling debt have you accrued?
        i. Ask: How have you been able to pay off your gambling debt?
        ii. Ask: Do you currently owe any money for gambling?
10. Do you have physical possession of your travel documentation (i.e., passport or visa)?

Foreign and Domestic:

1. Housing
    a. Where do you usually sleep?
    b. Who do you live with?
    c. Who do you pay rent to?
    d. How much do you pay for rent?
    e. Have you ever been homeless?
    f. Do you ever worry about your living situation?
    g. How many places have you lived over the last year?

     h. How many places have you lived over the last five years?

     i. Do you know where you will be living in six months?

     j. Do you feel safe at home?

2. Finances

     a. Where do you currently work?

          i. How much money do you earn per hour?

          ii. How much money do you take home per day?

          iii. How much money do you earn per week?

          iv. How much money do you take home per month?

          v. How many hours do you work per day?

          vi. How many days per week do you work?

          vii. Do you owe your boss any money?

          viii. What do you do in your free time?

3. Employment

     a. What were your last five places of employment (name, address, phone, and industry)?

     b. Do you feel that you are protected from harm at work?

     c. If you wanted to, could you quit your job?

          i. If no, ask: Why not?

4. Transportation

     a. Do you own a car?

          i. If no, ask: What is your primary means of transportation?

     b. Do you have a driver's license?

     c. Whom do you rely on for transportation?

     d. Have you ever paid your employer for transportation?

     e. Have you ever been stranded without transportation?

          i. If yes, ask: Could you tell me about what happened?

5. Food

     a. Have you ever paid your employer for food?

     b. Have you ever skipped meals because you didn't have enough money for food or didn't earn enough money?

     c. Have you had the size of your meals reduced because you didn't earn enough money?

6. Communication

     a. How do you communicate with your friends and how often?

     b. How do you communicate with your family and how often?

    c.   How much do you pay for your cell phone bill per month?

    d.   Have you ever had your ability to communicate with friends or family restricted?

Appendix D: Sample Sex Tourist Timeline—Dirk

Date	Location
?/?/2006	Tbilisi, Georgia
2/1/2006	Chişinău, Moldova
?/?/2007	Bishkek, Kyrgyzstan
?/?/2007	Almaty, Tajikistan
?/?/2007	Dushanbe, Tajikistan
12/20/2007	Chişinău, Moldova
2/14/2008	Koh Samui, Thailand
9/11/2008	Tashkent, Uzbekistan
9/25/2008	Ashgabat, Turkmenistan
10/03/2008	Geylang, Singapore
10/19/2008	Dubai, United Arab Emirates
12/14/2008	Macau, China
12/17/2008	Hong Kong, China
1/1/2009	Moscow, Russia
3/20/2009	Odessa, Ukraine
7/17/2009	Kuala Lumpur, Malaysia
7/31/2009	Bucharest, Romania
8/9/2009	Chişinău, Moldova
12/02/2009	Kabul, Afghanistan

(continued)

Date	Location
6/11/2010	Johannesburg, South Africa
7/17/2010	Addis Ababa, Ethiopia
11/21/2010	Cartagena, Colombia
?/?/2010	Medellin, Colombia
?/?/2010	Bogota, Colombia
?/?/2010	Panama City, Panama
?/?/2010	Lima, Peru
?/?/2010	Havana, Cuba
12/11/2010	Manila, Philippines

Appendix E: Additional Quotes from Mongers

I have travelled to 30 countries on 5 continents and mongered in most of them, and I have never gotten beaten up, robbed, or jailed while mongering. I have been mongering for over 30 years, and the only STD I ever got was the clap from a supposed girlfriend. Wrap the sausage, and you won't get anything unless you choose to eat pussy, and that is just a risk I choose to take, similar to riding my motorcycle and drinking booze. All forms of work are exploitation of the working class by the rentier class, so why should prostitution be free of exploitation? Perhaps when the revolution comes and we achieve a fair distribution of wealth prostitution will die out, but I highly doubt it.[1]

—Sex Tourist, April 12, 2004

Once a girl has made some quick cash selling her pussy; it's a slippery slope and becomes second nature to hit the street or put an ad on BP. I think many of the girls who at one time would resort to hooking are now using sugar daddy sites instead, e.g., Seekingar- rangement.[2] *Allows them the ability to delude themselves they aren't hookers. Not a bad place to look if you really want to adopt a ho or have a live-in sex slave. Lots of college girls and single moms.*[3]

—Commercial Sex Consumer, Ft. Myers, Florida, November 22, 2012

I've had 2 toddlers asleep in the next bed while I partied with mom. So what! They didn't wake up, so no problem. I would have preferred them not being there, but they were, and I had seen their mom many times before, and I wasn't about to leave.[4]

—Commercial Sex Consumer, Orlando, Florida, December 8, 2012

If you want to go for P4P than I would recommend Havana Cafe in Greenbelt 5. The finest looking girls I have ever seen. I took one for 5 days and made her bleed every day because she was so small. Helped her turn 21 (I was 36) while I was there. But paid about $100/ day for 4 days, and all associated meals/drinks. She was expensive but so worth the price to have a small 20/21-year-old girl, small perky tits, and would let me relax with her 4–5 times per day. Paid the cleaning dude $50 at the end of my stay to ensure he stayed quiet (was business trip).[5]

—Sex Tourist in Philippines, January 4, 2015

There are no "porn actresses" in Thailand, at least not officially since porn is actually banned in the Kingdom. So I'm not too certain that these "Thai" (porn) videos are indeed Thai, either filmed in Thailand or employing Thai actresses . . . From the few videos I watched in the Creampie Asian or Asia Street Meat series, I found the actresses not looking very happy, almost coerced or doing these things against their will. Some even had this weird look, as if drugged or otherwise incapacitated. These movies all had a sense of despair. Like "unless I do this, I'll be dead of hunger tomorrow, if not earlier."[6]

—Sex Tourist in Thailand, December 11, 2016

US antiprostitution laws have never eradicated prostitution. They only create an underground society where girls and women are trafficked, exploited, and abused by criminal elements. They also keep local law enforcement busy busting and abusing the girls instead of preventing or investigating real crimes. Just read the case of Oakland PD, whose entire police force was raping teenage prostitutes. Meanwhile many fine men and women in dire needs for sex have to break the laws and have their lives ruined for good. There have to be ways to accommodate conflicting needs in civilized society. Like marijuana, perhaps it's time to start petitions to change the laws to allow recreational or even medicinal sex. Hehe. Perhaps the Donald would understand everyone's primal needs for sex, just like air, water, food, and find creative ways to satisfy those needs to keep society in balance.[7]

—Commercial Sex Consumer, December 19, 2016

None of these girls are Nurses, Teachers, or Librarians and all get accustomed to using guys for what they want, particularly girls that have hit bottom and bouncing around the streets, living house to house, virtually homeless due to their drug habit. Some end up having drug dealer boyfriends, some are abused both physically and emotionally.[8]

—Commercial Sex Consumer, Youngstown, Ohio, February 11, 2017

It took a lot of work to find very tight pussy girls, and you cannot fuck them on the first date, but the 3rd date, bingo. It was worth it. I spent a lot of time trying to find these hidden gems with financial problems though the Internet. No, I do not feel sorry for them, I am happy Armenia's economy is crap. Fucking a girl next door with a Gymnast-type toned body with an extremely tight pussy is worth 1,000 high class hookers in Dubai, honest. Sometimes I have to pinch myself and say, "Am I dreaming?" But my dick says no you are not dreaming.[9]

—Sex Tourist in Armenia, March 4, 2017

Most these girls are addicts, that's the nature of the type of people looking for "quick cash." Even if they don't look it. Black, white or whatever. It could be pills, crack, heroin, *etc. That mixed chick called 'Star' is a good example. As hot as she is, a lot of guys have reported how the quality of service has rapidly declined. Now everyday her little kitty is leaking in cum, and when she started, she did everything covered I heard. Damn shame too because I wanted some of her, she my type, but I try to stay away from obvious junkies. Besides they could rob you, etc.*[10]

—Commercial Sex Consumer, Atlanta, Georgia, April 8, 2017

Anyone seen Italy around? Last time I saw her was about a month ago. Said the brothers raped her behind the tracks. I dropped her off behind that Kwick Mart south of Atlantic off Dixie and at least 10 young brothers quickly surrounded her. One of these days someone is going to get sick of seeing these young, pretty white girls getting used up by street hoods. Maybe LE or other. Anyways, nice girl, all fucked up and getting used and abused.[11]

—Commercial Sex Consumer, Pompano Beach, Florida, April 15, 2017

Notes

1. *The Morality of Prostitution* (April 12, 2004): http://www.International SexGuide.info.

2. Website for women seeking "sugar daddies." http://www.seekingarrangement .com.

3. *Ft. Myers Forum* (November 22, 2012): http://www.USASexGuide.info.

4. *Orlando Forum* (December 8, 2012): http://www.USASexGuide.info.

5. *Makati City Forum in Philippines* (January 4, 2015): http://www.International SexGuide.info.

6. *General Reports Forum in Thailand* (December 11, 2016): http://www.Inter nationalSexGuide.info.

7. *Streetwalker Reports* (December 19, 2016): http://www.International SexGuide.info.

8. Backpage Advertiser Reviews, Youngstown, Ohio (February 4, 2017): http://www.USASexGuide.info.

9. *General Info Forum in Armenia* (March 4, 2017): http://www.International SexGuide.info.

10. *BBBJ and BBFS Forum in Atlanta* (April 8, 2017): http://www.USASexGuide .info.

11. *Pompano Beach Florida Forum* (April 15, 2017): http://www.USASexGuide .info.

Appendix F: Sample Tool to Identify Youth at High Risk of Being Trafficked

The questions here can be incorporated into middle and high school health curriculums, as well as employed by counselors or direct service providers. To reduce the likelihood of social desirability bias, the questionnaire should not have any reference to human trafficking. Rather, administrators should independently use the interpretation guide below (not presented to the student) to assess whether a student may be at risk or high risk of being trafficked.

Students should be instructed to circle the number that corresponds with their degree of agreement or disagreement with each statement. Alternatively, these questions could be adapted and read aloud in one-on-one environments.

Please emphasize that there are no right or wrong answers in completing this form, and discuss the level of confidentiality you are capable of providing to the student respondents. Given the sensitive nature of some questions, please utilize this assessment at the sole risk of the implementing administrator. Consider having counselors, experienced with trauma-informed care, on stand-by.

Questionnaire

Please circle the number that corresponds with your degree of agreement or disagreement with each statement. There are no right or wrong answers in completing this form. If some of the questions seem too personal, you can skip them.

Part A

1. I never skip meals or reduce the size of my meals because there wasn't enough money for food.

Strongly Agree	Agree	Disagree	Strongly Disagree
0	1	2	3

2. I always have enough clean clothing to wear.

Strongly Agree	Agree	Disagree	Strongly Disagree
0	1	2	3

3. I never worry about my living situation.

Strongly Agree	Agree	Disagree	Strongly Disagree
0	1	2	3

4. I always have "a roof over my head."

Strongly Agree	Agree	Disagree	Strongly Disagree
0	1	2	3

5. My family doesn't move around a lot.

Strongly Agree	Agree	Disagree	Strongly Disagree
0	1	2	3

6. I know where I'll be living in six months.

Strongly Agree	Agree	Disagree	Strongly Disagree
0	1	2	3

Part B

1. I feel safe and secure at school.

Strongly Agree	Agree	Disagree	Strongly Disagree
0	1	2	3

2. I feel safe and secure at home.

Strongly Agree	Agree	Disagree	Strongly Disagree
0	1	2	3

3. I feel that my parents adequately protect me from harm.

Strongly Agree	Agree	Disagree	Strongly Disagree
0	1	2	3

4. I feel that the school adequately protects me from harm.

Strongly Agree	Agree	Disagree	Strongly Disagree
0	1	2	3

5. My life generally has routine and structure.

Strongly Agree	Agree	Disagree	Strongly Disagree
0	1	2	3

6. I have never experienced a long period of overwhelming chaos.

Strongly Agree	Agree	Disagree	Strongly Disagree
0	1	2	3

Part C

1. My family loves me.

Strongly Agree	Agree	Disagree	Strongly Disagree
0	1	2	3

2. I have good relationships with my friends.

Strongly Agree	Agree	Disagree	Strongly Disagree
0	1	2	3

3. **My parents accept me for who I am.**

Strongly Agree	Agree	Disagree	Strongly Disagree
0	1	2	3

4. **My friends like me for who I am.**

Strongly Agree	Agree	Disagree	Strongly Disagree
0	1	2	3

Part D

1. **I am successful in life, and my parents recognize me for being so.**

Strongly Agree	Agree	Disagree	Strongly Disagree
0	1	2	3

2. **I am successful in school, and my teachers recognize me for being so.**

Strongly Agree	Agree	Disagree	Strongly Disagree
0	1	2	3

3. **I'm satisfied with the responsibility that I have in life.**

Strongly Agree	Agree	Disagree	Strongly Disagree
0	1	2	3

4. **I'm satisfied with the role that I have in school.**

Strongly Agree	Agree	Disagree	Strongly Disagree
0	1	2	3

5. **I'm satisfied with my status in life.**

Strongly Agree	Agree	Disagree	Strongly Disagree
0	1	2	3

6. I'm satisfied with my reputation in school.

Strongly Agree	Agree	Disagree	Strongly Disagree
0	1	2	3

7. I have high self-esteem.

Strongly Agree	Agree	Disagree	Strongly Disagree
0	1	2	3

Interpretation Guide

For Professional Use Only

Each unsatisfied need may be a deficiency motivator, making the juvenile at risk to a trafficker who is capable of filling the void in his/her life.

Part A: Physiological Needs

Respondents who score 12–18 may be at high risk of being trafficked through the provision of food/clothing/shelter.

Respondents who score 6–11 may be at risk of being trafficked through the provision of food/clothing/shelter.

Respondents who score 0–5 may be at low risk of being trafficked through the provision of food/clothing/shelter.

Part B: Safety Needs

Respondents who score 12–18 may be at high risk of being trafficked through the provision of safety.

Respondents who score 6–11 may be at risk of being trafficked through the provision of safety.

Respondents who score 0–5 may be at low risk of being trafficked through the provision of safety.

Part C: Love/Belonging Needs

Respondents who score 8–12 may be at high risk of being trafficked through the provision of love/belonging.

Respondents who score 4–7 may be at risk of being trafficked through the provision of love/belonging.

Respondents who score 0–3 may be at low risk of being trafficked through the provision of love/belonging.

Part D: Esteem Needs

Respondents who score 14–21 may be at high risk of being trafficked through improved self-esteem.

Respondents who score 7–13 may be at risk of being trafficked through improved self-esteem.

Respondents who score 0–6 may be at low risk of being trafficked through improved self-esteem.

Index

Afghanistan, 57, 66–70, 107, 108, 223
  Bagram Air Base, 66
  Kabul, 66, 67, 70, 223
  Shanghai Restaurant, 67
  Wazir Akbar Khan, 67
Africa, 68, 107, 109, 110, 136–139, 174, 224
Alaska, 12, 13
Alcohol, 6, 53, 55, 59, 72, 79, 86, 87, 109, 131
Al-Jader, Hana, 123–127
Almodovar, Norma Jean, xviii
Al-Saud, Prince Mohammad, i, ii, 111, 123
Amaya, Rances Ulices, 71–91
Anti-trafficking organizations, xvii, 26, 46, 48, 49, 111, 120, 122, 126, 206
  Action Pour Les Enfants, 46
  Coalition to Abolish Slavery and Trafficking (CAST), 123
  Global Centurion, 111
  Michigan Law Center, xvii, 126
  Polaris Project, 26, 120, 122
  Soroptimist International, 206
  Terre des Hommes, 48, 49
Argentina, 58
Arif, Michael, 75

Armenia, 226, 227
At-risk populations, xi, 5–15, 18, 44, 46, 51, 57, 71, 79, 108, 119, 130, 161, 168, 172–174, 220, 226
  Homeless, xi, 44, 46, 71, 79, 130, 161, 168, 173, 220, 226
  Immigrants. *See* Foreign nationals
  Indigent, 18, 51, 57, 108, 119, 161
  Runaways, xi, 5–15, 130, 161, 172–174
Austria, 58
Azerbaijan, 67
  Baku, 67

Balizan, Arthur, 18
Bars, 53, 56, 65, 156, 158
  El Cuco, 158
  El Potrero de Chimino, 158
  Karaoke bar, 44
  La Potra Bar, 156
  Liberty Restaurant, 65
  Malibu Club, 65
  Monroe Club, 65
  TopGun, 56
  Tu Candela, 53
Beer garden, 44
Biddle, Scott, 130
Bitcoin, 214

Bolkovac, Kathryn, 64
Bonaparte, Troy, 179
Bongino, Joe, 53
Bonkoungou, Leopold, 126
Bosnia, 63–65, 69
    Dubrave, 63
    Tuzla, 63
Brannon, David, 39
Brazil, 52, 53, 187
    Rio de Janiero, 187
Brothels, 2, 52, 53, 57
    Alien Cat House, 2
    Centaurus, 52, 53
    L'uomo, 52
    Monte Carlo, 52
    Paritosh Den, 57
Brownback, Sam, 38
Bulgaria, 58, 59, 108
    Sofia, 108
Burkina Faso, 126, 138
Bush, George W., 46, 66

Cabrera, James, 156
California, 8, 9, 12, 17, 18, 25, 88, 89,
    152, 177, 178
    Hollywood, 2
    Los Angeles, 88
    San Francisco, 17, 18, 25, 178
Callebaut, Barry, 137
Call girls, 187, 210
    Modern Geisha Agency, 187
Cambodia, 44, 46–48, 110
    Phnom Penh, 44, 46, 47
Canada, 18
Child sex tourism, 43–48
Child Sexual Abuse Accommodation
    Syndrome (CSAAS), 13, 217
China, 24, 54, 67, 68, 145, 183, 223
    Hong Kong, 223
    Macau, 223
Chocolate, 135–141
    Askinosie, 135, 136
    Blommer Chocolate Company,
    137

Chocolate Manufacturers
    Association, 137
    Godiva, 139
    Guittard Chocolate Company, 137
    Hershey Food Corporation, 137,
    139
    M&M Mars, 137, 139
    Milky Way, 139
    Nestle Chocolate & Confections
    USA, 137, 138
    Russell Stover, 139
    Snickers, 135, 139
    Twix, 135, 139
    Whitman, 139
    World Cocoa Foundation, 137
    World's Finest Chocolate, Inc.,
    137
Christian, 11, 38
Citizenship, 34, 120, 159, 193
Clark, Michael Lewis, 46–47
Clinton, Hillary, 109, 119, 120
Cocoa. *See* Chocolate
Cojocaru, Claudia, 199
Colombia, 53, 107, 109, 187, 224
    Bogotá, 107, 224
    Cartagena, 53, 107, 109, 224
    Medellin, 107, 224
Colorado, 130
    Denver, 130
Commercial sex code
    AMP, 25, 209
    BBBJ, 55, 58, 68, 108, 109, 182,
    188, 211, 227
    BBFS, 55, 211, 227
    Bottom, 14, 162, 209, 218
    BP, 181, 213, 225
    CBJ, 211
    CFS, 182, 211
    CL, 213
    DATY, 211
    DFE, 212
    GFE, 67, 186, 212
    LE, 182, 213, 227
    NOVA, 25, 212

P4P, 105, 212, 225
Track, 7, 12, 166, 214
Vitamin V. *See* Viagra
Commercial sex consumers, 10, 12,
    24, 25, 40, 51, 52, 55, 56, 66,
    103–111, 179, 187, 188, 197, 211,
    214, 255–227
    Hobbyist, 24, 40, 51, 55, 109, 211,
        214
    John, 24, 25, 197, 211
    Lurker, 211
    Monger, 24, 51, 52, 56, 66, 103–111,
        179, 187, 188, 211, 214, 225–227
    Trick, 10, 12, 211
Comstock, Barbara, 29
Connecticut, 164
Consequences of trafficking
    victimization, 8, 9, 36, 45, 55,
        64, 106, 129, 130, 131, 136, 138,
        158, 159, 165, 168, 198, 225, 226
    Death, 36, 45
    Disease, 9, 45, 55, 225
    Drug addiction, 9, 45, 129, 130, 226
    Physical trauma, 45, 64, 106, 131,
        136, 138, 158, 165, 168, 198
    Psychological trauma, 45, 55
    Social ostracism, 45, 106, 107
    Unwanted pregnancy, 8, 45, 54, 55,
        159
Coonan, Terry, 120
Corea, Walter Alexander, 158
Cornejo, Alonso Bruno, 72, 73, 75, 78
Correctional facilities, 12, 36, 45, 47,
    71, 73, 96, 97, 100, 157
    Federal prison, 12, 45, 47, 71, 73,
        96, 97, 157
    Loretto Federal Correctional
        Institution, 100
    Snohomish County Jail, 36
Corruption, 44, 45, 47
Crimes, xii, xv, 7, 8, 12, 13, 18–23,
    27, 34, 35, 43–45, 55, 58, 64, 71,
    72, 80, 83, 87, 95, 96, 98, 106,
    107, 113, 118, 125, 130, 150,

    152, 155, 157, 163, 165, 166,
        179, 193, 217, 227
    Aiding and abetting, 19, 23
    Assault, 34, 35, 43, 130, 155, 157,
        193
    Battery, 43, 83, 87
    Conspiracy, 18–23, 71, 118, 150, 157
    Domestic violence, 34, 58, 163
    Failure to file tax returns, 22
    Failure to supply information, 20
    Fondling, 43
    Forced labor, 125, 150, 179
    Gang participation, 80
    Harassment, xii, 152
    Harboring aliens, 18, 19
    Intent to engage in sexual act with
        a minor, 45
    Involuntary servitude, xv, 96, 113,
        157, 179
    Making and subscribing false tax
        return, 22
    Malicious wounding, 80, 165, 166
    Molestation, 44
    Money laundering, 96
    Pandering, 179
    Perverted practices, 43
    Prostitution, 8, 18, 27
    Racketeering, 20–22, 98
    Rape, 7, 8, 12, 13, 43, 44, 55, 64, 72,
        83, 87, 95, 106, 107, 118, 217, 227
    Tax evasion, 22
CSAAS. *See* Child Sexual Abuse
    Accommodation Syndrome
    (CSAAS)
Cuba, 107, 224
    Havana, 224
Czech Republic, 58, 67

Dating websites/applications, 39, 130,
    179, 181, 213
    Backpage, 39, 130, 179
    OKCupid, 181
    Seeking Arrangement, 213
    Tinder, 181

Decriminalization, 60, 61, 198, 201
Department of Homeland Security, 26, 31, 44
Department of Justice, 27, 29, 118
Department of Labor, 151, 192
Department of State, 65, 69, 120, 182
Dominican Republic, 188
    Puerto Plata, 188
Drugs, 6, 7, 72, 76, 84, 87, 109, 129, 156, 212, 215, 226
    Cocaine, 109, 156
    Coricidin, 84
    Crack, 87, 226
    Heroin, 129, 226
    Marijuana, 7, 72, 76, 109, 215
    Triple C. *See* Coricidin
    Viagra, 109, 212
Duarte, Eric, 73, 83, 87

Ellenbecker, Phil, 131
El Salvador, 73, 75, 83, 88, 89, 158, 159
England, 39
Estrada, Johnny, 80
Ethiopia, 37, 38, 107, 224
    Addis Ababa, 37, 224
Evans, Tom, 174, 175
Expert witness, 14, 197, 217, 218

Fast food restaurants, 75, 117
    Burger King, 117
    Chipotle, 117
    McDonald's, 75, 117
    Subway, 117
    Taco Bell, 117
FBI. *See* Federal Bureau of Investigation (FBI)
Federal Bureau of Investigation (FBI), 17, 18, 26, 71, 97, 179
Florida, 13, 25, 40, 100, 117–120, 158, 225, 227
    Alachua County, 118
    Ft. Myers, 225
    Immokalee, 117
    Miami, 40

Orlando, 225
Pompano Beach, 227
Foreign nationals, 88, 118–120, 149, 155, 157, 159, 191–193, 197
    Illegal immigrant, 157
    Illegal nonimmigrant, 157
    Immigrant, 149, 157
    Nonimmigrant, 118–120, 157, 191–193
    Refugee, 88
    Temporary protected status, 88
    Undocumented migrant, 155, 157, 159, 191–193, 197

Georgia, 108, 223, 227
    Atlanta, 227
    Tbilisi, 223
Germany, 58–61, 67, 183, 214
    FKK, 58–61, 214
Gross, Susan Lee, 2, 27, 28
Guatemala, 158

Haiti, 118
Harris, Kamala, 9
Hawaii, 13, 115, 116, 117, 119, 188
    Maui, 115
Herrara, Henry, 83
Honduras, 155, 158
Hotels/Motels, xi, 1, 6, 7, 12, 13, 38, 53, 56, 61, 64, 68, 72, 75–77, 79, 80, 87, 94, 108–110, 129, 179, 181, 185–190, 214
    Best Western, 181, 186, 187
    Budget Inn, 79
    Hilton, 186, 187
    Holiday Inn, 68, 181
    Hotel Caribe, 53
    Hyatt, 186–188
    Marriott, 181, 186–188
    Quarry Inn, 79
    Radisson, 186, 188
    Roosevelt Inn, 185, 186
    Stratford Motel, 79
    Super 8, xi, 80
    Wyndham, 188

Hungary, 58, 187
  Budapest, 187
Huntington, Arthur, 53

ICE. *See* Immigration and Customs
    Enforcement (ICE)
IKEA mom, 172, 173
Illinois, 12, 99
  Chicago, 12, 99
Immigration and Customs
    Enforcement (ICE), 26, 27, 44,
    46, 95, 124, 158
India, 56–58, 104, 117, 143–146, 183,
    198
  Agra, 143
  Bhubaneswar, 198
  Calcutta, 56
  Jaipur, 143
  Mumbai, 57
  New Delhi, 143
  Pushkar, 143
  Rajasthan, 143
Indonesia, 54, 56, 124, 183
  Bandung, 56
  Jakarta, 56
  Yogyakarta, 56
Internal Revenue Service, 27
International Labor Organization,
    136
International marriage brokerage
    firm, 37
Iraq, 58, 64–66, 105, 106, 125
  Baghdad, 64, 66, 106
Israel, 117
Italy, xvi, 174
  Palermo, xvi
Ivory Coast, 136, 138
  Daloa, 138
  Korhogo, 136

Jackman, Tom, 27
Japan, 24, 54, 68, 214
  Tokyo, 68
  Yokohama, 68
Johnston, Ben, 63, 64

Kambalame, Jane Ngineriwa, 125,
    126
Kansas, 38
Kazakova, Ekaterina, 33
Kenya, 183
Kim, Sung Yong, 18, 19
King, Indle, 33–37
Kline, Thomas R., 185
Kosovo, 65, 69, 106, 108
  Ferazi, 65
  Prishtina, 65
Kuwait, 64
Kyrgyzstan, 34, 35, 66, 108, 223
  Bishkek, 66, 108, 223
  Manas Air Base, 108

Lacey, Michael, 178
Larkin, James, 178
Larson, Daniel, 35, 36
Latvia, 188
  Riga, 188
Laude, Jennifer, 68
Laws, xvi, 15, 19, 20, 23, 37, 38,
    41, 44–46, 89, 126, 131, 151,
    157
  Anti-Mail Order Spouse Act, 41
  Californians Against Sexual
    Exploitation Act (CASE Act), 15
  Fair Labor Standards Act, 151
  Illegal Immigration Reform and
    Immigrant Responsibility Act
    (IIRIRA), 89, 157
  International Marriage Broker
    Regulation Act of 2005, 37, 41
  Malinda's Act, 131
  Mann Act, 19, 20, 23
  Palermo Protocol, xvi
  Protect Act, 44–46
  Protocol to Prevent, Suppress, and
    Punish Trafficking in Persons,
    Especially Women and Children,
    Supplementing the United
    Nations Convention Against
    Transnational Organized Crime.
    See Palermo Protocol

Laws (*cont.*)
    Republic Act No 6955, 41
    Trafficking Victims Protection Act
        (TVPA), 41, 126
    Victims of Trafficking and Violence
        Protection Act, 38
Legal cases, 8, 9, 17–23, 43–46, 47,
    71–88, 149, 150, 155, 156, 158,
    159, 123–125
    In re: Aarica S., 8, 9
    United States of America v. Hana F.
        Al Jader, 123–125
    United States of America v. Lynda
        Dieu Phan, 149, 150
    United States of America v. Michael
        Lewis Clark, 46, 47
    United States of America v. Walter
        Alexander Corea et al., 158, 159
    United States v. Rances Ulices Amaya,
        71–88
    United States v. Richard Arthur
        Schmidt, 43–45
    United States v. Yang et al., 17–23
    USA v. Jose Zavala-Acosta, 155, 156,
        159
Legalization of prostitution, 59, 60
    Replacement effect, 59
    Scale effect, 59
Lithuania, 58
Lockett, Myrelle, 179
Lockett, Tyrelle, 179

MacBride, Neil H., 27
Macedonia, 65, 108
Mail-order brides, 33–41
    Casket girls, 39
    Jamestown brides, 39
    King's daughters, 39
Malaysia, 104, 183, 223
    Kuala Lumpur, 104, 223
Mali, 136
Malls, 17, 36, 149, 36
    Alderwood Mall, 36
    Springfield Mall, 163

Westfield San Francisco Centre
    Mall, 17
West Manchester Mall, 149
Mamasan, 25, 56, 210
Maryland, 25, 43, 44, 48, 54, 119,
    126, 129, 197
    Baltimore, 44
    Queen Anne's County, 43
    Talbot County, 43
Massachusetts, 124
    Boston, 13, 25
Massage parlors, 2, 17–23, 25–29,
    197, 209, 210, 213
    Asian Massage Parlor, 25, 26, 209,
        210, 213
    Bada Spa, 27, 28
    King's Massage, 17–23
    Peach Therapy, 2, 26–29
    Star Foot Spa, 197
    Sun Foot Spa, 197
    Sun Therapy, 29
McCann, Madeleine, 174, 175
McIntire, Billie Joe, xviii
Media, 27, 138, 150, 172, 174
    CBS, 172
    CNN, 138
    Express Newspapers, 174
    Pall Mall Gazette, xix
    The Baltimore Sun, 172
    The New York Times, 150
    The Washington Post, 27
    Women's Health, 172
Mentzel, Jerry, 38
Method of human trafficking
    recruitment and control, xv–xvii,
        1, 2, 7, 9–11, 13, 18, 25, 37, 39,
        51, 53, 54, 57, 60, 64, 76, 83, 94,
        95, 99, 101, 102, 106, 113,
        115–120, 124–126, 130, 137,
        138, 150, 151, 157–159, 173, 175,
        191, 197, 201, 210, 215, 219, 220
    Abduction, xvi, 2, 6, 73, 83, 106,
        171, 173–175
    Blackmail, 7

Coercion, xv, xvii, 1, 10, 11, 39, 54, 60, 113, 157, 197, 210, 215, 219

Debt bondage, xv, xvii, 18, 94, 113, 116, 117, 119, 126, 137, 150, 151, 158

Deception, xv, xvi, 10, 11, 37, 39, 51, 60, 99, 113, 126, 138, 151, 210, 215, 219

Faux relationship, 173, 175

Force, xv, xvii, 1, 9–11, 13, 57, 60, 76, 102, 113, 157–159, 210, 215, 219

Fraud, xv, xvii, 1, 39, 60, 63, 113, 125, 150, 157, 175, 210, 219

Gambling, 25, 220

Threat, 2, 39, 53, 94, 95, 101, 102, 115, 116, 118, 120, 124, 126, 130, 150, 157–159, 191, 201, 210, 219

Trauma bonding, 11, 13, 14, 102, 165, 218, 219

Mexico, 89, 155, 192

Michigan, 94, 96, 99

Detroit, 94, 96, 99

Minnesota, 25

Misconceptions, 1–2, 171–176

Missing DC teens, 172

Moldova, 58, 59, 64, 107, 108, 110, 223

Chişinău, 108, 223

Nostalgia, 110

Montclair Moms, x, 132, 134

Morocco, 38, 67, 183

Tangiers, 38

MS-13 gang cliques, 73, 74, 80, 83, 84

Charlotte Locos de Salvatrucha, 80

Guanacos Little Cycos Salvatrucha, 73, 80

Guanacos Locotes, 73, 74

Parke Vista Locotes Salvatrucha, 73, 83

Pelones Locotes de Salvatrucha, 80

Virginia Locotes Salvatruchos, 73, 84

MS-13 gang members, 71–87

Blue, 71–74, 76–78, 82, 83, 86

Casper, 73–87

Crítico, 75, 81, 84, 86

Cucia, 83

Cuervo, 74

Humilde, 83

Lígrimas, 80

Little Crimen, 73, 79

Looney. *See* Lunático

Lunático, 73, 87

Maldito, 73, 83, 84, 87

Murder. *See* Blue

Profeta, 83

Romero, 83

Scooby. *See* Little Crimen

Sleepy, 81

Sniper, 84, 86

Nah, Wu Sang, 18, 19

Nail salon, 149–153, 189

National Human Trafficking Resource Center, xii, 120

Naval Criminal Investigative Service, 27

Needs, xi, xii, 2, 5, 6, 8, 11–13, 18, 37, 41, 44, 80, 95, 99, 101, 102, 113, 115–118, 129, 131, 132, 136, 137, 145, 150, 151, 155, 156, 168, 178, 192, 193, 201, 202, 205, 219–221, 226, 230, 233, 234

Belonging, 102, 201, 234

Esteem, 2, 102, 201, 233, 234

Food, 2, 5, 6, 8, 44, 95, 101, 113, 115–118, 129, 131, 132, 145, 151, 155, 156, 192, 201, 219, 221, 226, 230, 234

Love, 2, 11, 12, 37, 41, 99, 102, 201, 205, 234

Safety, 101, 102, 131, 137, 193, 201, 234

Self-actualization, 201

Needs (*cont.*)
    Shelter, xi, xii, 13, 18, 80, 102,
        115–117, 150, 151, 168, 178,
        192, 202, 219, 220
    Water, 117, 132, 136, 156, 201, 226
Neeson, Liam, 1
Nepal, 117
Netherlands, 54, 67
    Amsterdam, 54
Nevada, 2, 12, 13, 97, 182
    Las Vegas, 2, 12, 13, 97, 182
Newmark, Craig, 177, 178
New York, 5, 7, 13, 25–27, 30, 49, 70,
        79, 80, 100, 124, 126, 152
    Brooklyn, 5
    Long Island, 79
Nguyen, Duc Cao, 149
Nigeria, 58
North Carolina, xi, 179, 180
    Thomasville, 180
    Winston-Salem, 179, 180

Obama, Barack, 53
Office of Justice Programs, 29
Office of Juvenile Justice and
    Delinquency Prevention
    (OJJDP), 8
Ohio, 33, 129, 226
    Columbus, 129
    Youngstown, 226
OJJDP. *See* Office of Juvenile Justice and
    Delinquency Prevention (OJJDP)
O'Keefe, Brian, 138
Operation Gilded Cage, 17, 23
Ouedraogo, Lucile Bonkoungou, 126

Pakistan, 104, 183
Panama, 107, 186, 187, 189, 224
    Panama City, 186, 187, 224
Parreira, Christina, 2
Pedophiles, 43, 45–47, 175, 211
    Chronophiles, 45, 211
    Hebephiles, 45
    Infantophiles, 45
    Nepiophiles, 45, 211

Pemberton, Joseph Scott, 68
Pennsylvania, 33, 100, 149, 152, 185
    Philadelphia, 33, 185
    York, 149
Peonage, xv, 113, 157
Perez, Hermes Salazar, 73, 74
Peru, 78, 224
    Lima, 224
Phan, Lynda Dieu, 149, 150
Philippines, 25, 43, 44, 47–49, 51, 54,
        68, 183, 224, 226
    Angeles City, 44
    Boracay, 44
    Makati City, 226
    Manila, 25, 51, 224
    Olongapo, 44, 68
    Puerto Galera, 44
    Surigao, 44
Phillips, Gary, 46
Pimp, ii, xviii, 2, 5, 8–12, 55, 56, 59,
        74, 75, 108, 161, 165–167, 183,
        197, 199, 210, 215
Pimp typologies, 10
Poland, 58
Prague, 58
Probation/parole conditions, 45
Puerto Rico, 54
Punishment, 8, 12, 18–22, 25, 28, 37,
        43, 45, 47, 68, 71–73, 87, 96, 97,
        100, 125, 157, 159, 179
    Electric monitor, 21
    Fee, 18–22, 87
    Fine, 19, 21, 22, 125
    Forfeiture, 25, 28
    Home detention, 20
    Incarceration, 8, 12, 28, 37, 43, 45,
        47, 68, 71–73, 87, 96, 97, 100,
        157, 159, 179
    Restitution, 20, 22, 87, 96, 126,
        150, 159

Quotations
    Commercial sex consumers, 51, 52,
        54, 55, 57–59, 65–68, 105–107,
        109, 111

Convicted human traffickers, 5, 11–13, 88, 93, 99–101
Human trafficking survivors, 165
Sex workers, 180, 181

Race, xi, xv, 5, 12, 24–27, 30, 43, 66, 80, 88, 89, 104, 107, 108, 156, 163, 172–174, 197, 209–211, 213, 226, 227
   Asian, 24–27, 30, 66, 209–211, 213, 226
   Black, xi, 5, 12, 88, 104, 172, 173, 211, 226
   Hispanic, 80, 89, 156, 210
   Middle Eastern or North African, 107, 108, 174
   White, xv, 43, 108, 163, 172, 173, 197, 210, 211, 226, 227
Rape trauma syndrome (RTS), 13, 217
Restraining order, 37
Retail clothing, 145, 181
   American Eagle Outfitters, 145
   Bombay Rayon, 145
   GAP, 145
   H&M, 145
   Nordstrom, 181
   Wal-Mart, 145
Revictimization, xvi, 218
Reyes, William, 73, 79
Rivas, Alexander, 73, 84, 85
Romania, 58, 59, 63, 107, 223
   Bucharest, 223
Routine Activities Theory, 200
RTS. *See* Rape trauma syndrome (RTS)
Runaway, xi, 6, 8, 12, 75, 130, 172–174
Russia, 35, 36, 57, 63, 106, 109, 190, 223
   Moscow, 35, 36, 106, 190, 223
   Volgograd, 57
Ryan, Kevin, 17, 18

Sanwal, Rishi, 179
Saudi Arabia, 123, 124
   Riyadh, 124

Schlozman, Brad, 17
Schmidt, Richard Arthur, 43–45
Secondary exploitation, 199
Secret Service (U.S.), 53, 54
Serbia, 58, 63
Sex offender registry, x
Sex tourism, 43–60
Shelter, 2, 8, 38, 71, 81, 101, 168, 201, 234
   Emergency shelter, 168
   Homeless shelter, 168
   Runaway shelter, 8
   Women's shelter, 38
Sierra Leone, 183
Singapore, 68, 104, 223
   Geylang, 104, 223
Sivan, Troye, 30
Slavery, xv, xvii, 18, 71, 72, 103, 119, 123, 126, 127, 137–139, 161, 185
Slovakia, 67, 183
Smugglers, 156
Smuggling fee, 18, 158
Social media, ix, x, 130, 172, 181–183
   Facebook, ix, x, 130, 181
   Instagram, 181
   Twitter, 130, 172
Solicitation crews, ix–xiii, 129–133
   Begging, xii
   Cleaning products, xi-xiii
   Magazine subscriptions, xii, 129, 130
   Trinkets, xii
South Africa, 58, 107, 109, 100, 224
   Johannesburg, 109, 224
   Sandton, 109
South Korea, 2, 18, 27, 65, 68
   Pusan, 68
Soviet Union, 97, 104, 108
Spain, 58, 67, 174, 183
Sri Lanka, 183
Street sex trafficking, 7, 12, 166, 214
   Track, 7, 12, 166, 214
Suicide, 38, 95, 96, 156

Tabak, Morris, 18
Tajikistan, 223
  Almaty, 223
  Dushanbe, 223
Tanzania, 58, 135
  Mababu, 135
Task force, xv, 25, 26, 27, 29, 199, 200
Terwilliger, Zachary, 74
Texas, 12, 13, 130, 152, 156, 158
  Bay City, 130
  Carrizo Springs, 156
  Houston, 13, 156, 158
Thailand, 24, 46, 54, 61, 68, 104, 107,
    108, 110, 115–117, 223, 226
  Bangkok, 46, 54, 108
  Koh Samui, 223
Trump, Donald J., 120
Turkey, 183
Turkmenistan, 109, 223
  Ashgabat, 109, 223
Turvey, Malinda, 131
Types of trafficking
  Agricultural labor trafficking,
    115–122
  Domestic juvenile sex trafficking,
    6–16
  Domestic servitude, 123–128
  Erotic massage parlors, 17–32
  Gang controlled sex trafficking,
    71–92
  Labor trafficking in bars and clubs,
    93–102, 155–160
  Labor trafficking in beauty
    industry, 149–154
  Mail order brides, 33–42
  Solicitation crews, 129–134

Ukraine, 58, 64, 93, 97–100, 223
  Odessa, 223
United Arab Emirates, 58, 67, 106,
    183, 188, 190, 223, 226
  Abu Dhabi, 58, 183
  Dubai, 58, 67, 106, 183, 188, 190,
    223, 226

United Nations, xvi, xix, 45, 69
  Convention Against Transnational
    Organized Crime, xvi
  International Children's Emergency
    Fund, 45
  UNICEF, 45, 49
Universities
  George Mason University, x
  University of Nevada, Las Vegas, 2
  University of Washington, 35
Undercover sting, 48, 179, 180
U.S. Department of Labor, 151, 192
U.S. military, 45, 56, 63–66, 68, 69,
    104, 105, 108
  Air Force, 63
  Army, 45, 63, 64
  Contractor, 64–66, 69, 104, 105,
    108
  DynCorp, 63–65
  Marines, 68
  Navy, 68
  Uniform Code of Military Justice,
    66
  Veteran, 56, 63
Uzbekistan, 58, 107, 108, 223
  Tashkent, 108, 223

Vietnam, 44, 149
Village Voice Media, 178
Virginia, ix–xi, 2, 24, 26–29, 31, 32,
    64, 71, 72–76, 78–80, 83, 84,
    89–91, 93, 94, 100, 132, 133,
    136, 153, 163, 165, 166, 192,
    199, 200, 206
  Alexandria, 71, 74, 89
  Annandale, 2, 26, 31
  Arlington, 83
  Dulles, 93
  Dumfries, 136
  Fairfax, 75, 81, 163
  Falls Church, 79
  Manassas, 80, 206
  Montclair, ix, x, 132, 134
  Prince William County, 80

Reston, 64
Springfield, 163
Tidewater, 25
Virginia Beach, 93, 94, 100
Woodbridge, 206
Visas, 2, 38, 39, 65, 88, 93, 116, 117, 119, 120, 122–126, 156, 157, 159, 191–193, 201, 220

Washington, 34, 36, 117, 152
Seattle, 34
Tulalip Indian Reservation, 36
Washington, D.C., ix, 1, 7, 72, 89, 172
Websites, xviii, 23, 27, 29, 30, 32, 38, 54, 60, 61, 67–70, 112, 152, 153, 177–186, 189, 190, 202, 213–215
AdultFriendFinder.com, 213
AdultSearch.com, 23
AlwaysOnTheHunt.com, 213
Backpage.com, xviii, 27, 29, 30, 177–183, 186, 213, 215
BP. *See* Backpage.com
CityVibe.com, 181, 213
CL. *See* Craigslist.org
Craigslist.org, xviii, 177–181, 183, 213

ECCIE.net, 213
Eros.com, 213
Free2Work.org, 139, 146
GoodGuide.com, 146
Humaniplex.com, 181, 213
InternationalSexGuide.info, 54, 60, 61, 67–70, 112, 183, 186, 189, 190, 202, 214, 215
Preferred411.com, 213
RoseBrides.com, 38
RubMaps.com, xviii, 23, 29, 32, 152, 153, 213, 215
SeekingArrangement.com, 213
TheEroticReview.com, 213
USASexGuide.info, xviii, 23, 28, 31, 32, 41, 42, 61, 70, 183–186, 189, 214, 215
White slaves, xv
Wisconsin, 131
Janesville, 131
Wolf, Frank, 28, 29
Woolf, Bill, 165

Yang, Young Joon, 18, 19

Zambia, 183
Zavala-Acosta, Jose, 155, 156, 159

About the Author

Kimberly Mehlman-Orozco holds a PhD in criminology, law and society from George Mason University, with an expertise in human trafficking. She currently serves as a human trafficking expert witness for criminal and civil cases across the United States, and she is the founding partner of America's leading human trafficking consulting firm, Mahn, Mehlman & Associates, LLC. Her writing has been featured in *Thomson Reuters Foundation*, *Forbes*, *The Washington Post*, *The Baltimore Sun*, *The Houston Chronicle*, *The Crime Report*, *The Hill*, and *The Diplomatic Courier*, among other publications.